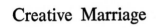

Creative Marriage

Books and Monographs by Albert Ellis

AN INTRODUCTION TO THE PRINCIPLES OF
SCIENTIFIC PSYCHOANALYSIS
(*Journal Press, 1950*)

THE FOLKLORE OF SEX
(*Charles Boni, 1951; Grove Press, 1961*)

SEX, SOCIETY AND THE INDIVIDUAL (with
A. P. PILLAY)
(*International Journal of Sexology, 1953*)

SEX LIFE OF THE AMERICAN WOMAN AND THE
KINSEY REPORT
(*Greenberg: Publisher, 1954*)

THE AMERICAN SEXUAL TRAGEDY
(*Twayne: Publisher, 1954; Lyle Stuart, 1959*)

NEW APPROACHES TO PSYCHOTHERAPY TECHNIQUES
(*Journal of Clinical Psychology, 1955*)

THE PSYCHOLOGY OF SEX OFFENDERS
(with RALPH BRANCALE)
(*Charles C. Thomas, 1956*)

HOW TO LIVE WITH A NEUROTIC
(*Crown: Publisher, 1957*)

SEX WITHOUT GUILT
(*Lyle Stuart, 1958; Hillman Books, 1959*)

WHAT IS PSYCHOTHERAPY?
(*American Academy of Psychotherapists, 1959*)

THE PLACE OF VALUES IN THE PRACTICE
OF PSYCHOTHERAPY
(*American Academy of Psychotherapists, 1959*)

THE ART AND SCIENCE OF LOVE
(*Lyle Stuart, 1960*)

ENCYCLOPEDIA OF SEXUAL BEHAVIOR (with
ALBERT ABARBANEL)
(*Hawthorn Books, 1961*)

Books by Robert A. Harper

MARRIAGE
(*Appleton-Century-Crofts, 1949*)

PROBLEMS OF AMERICAN SOCIETY
(with JOHN F. CUBER and WILLIAM F. KENKEL)
(*Henry Holt, 1956*)

PSYCHOANALYSIS AND PSYCHOTHERAPY: 36 SYSTEMS
(*Prentice-Hall, 1959*)

A GUIDE TO RATIONAL LIVING (with ALBERT ELLIS)
(*Prentice-Hall, 1961*)

Creative Marriage

by Albert Ellis, Ph. D.
and Robert A. Harper, Ph. D.

LYLE STUART • NEW YORK

Creative Marriage

Third Printing, October, 1969

Library of Congress Catalog Card Number 60-11426

Queries regarding rights and permissions
should be addressed to
Lyle Stuart
239 Park Avenue South
New York, N.Y. 10003

Edited by Eileen Brand
Published by Lyle Stuart

Manufactured in the United States of America

Table of Contents

Note

Since this book is in every sense a collaborative effort and its ideas have been reviewed and agreed upon by both authors, the pronoun *we* is used in the discussion of these ideas. The psychotherapy and marriage counseling cases used for illustrative purposes, however, have been seen by each of the authors separately in his New York or Washington practice. The pronoun *I* is therefore used in the exposition of these cases.

The names used in the case histories are fictitious, of course.

Introduction

This is a self-help book on marriage and, by its very nature, it will be an object of suspicion to many of our professional colleagues. Psychologists, psychiatrists, social workers, marriage counselors, and others who devote themselves to helping people deal more effectively with their life problems tend to view critically any book which includes "solutions" to some of these problems.

We do not claim to have easy answers to marriage difficulties which, when patly self-applied, will render our readers forever happy. But we nonetheless contend, as a result of years of experience counseling with married and about-to-be-married couples, that many individuals can considerably improve their marital situations by being helped to look directly and rationally at themselves and their mates and to take appropriate actions in the light of such a look.

Assistance to ailing engagements or marriages is usually most effective when troubled individuals go for individual counseling or group psychotherapy. Many of the individuals and couples with whom the authors have worked, however, have said that they also wanted a book that discusses some of the concerns that are taken up in marriage counseling and psychotherapy sessions. It is for these persons, and many others like them who have had some professional help with their marital problems, that we offer this book as an adjunct to the more personalized assistance they have received. We also hope that other relatively self-reliant and undisturbed people who, for one reason or another, have never received personal counseling or therapy will be able to find some help in the material we have included in this book.

Since there is already an abundance of handbooks on marriage, some readers may question the desirability of a newcomer. We feel that we have produced something different. Unlike the usual marriage books, this one skips the commonplaces of budgets, dating, wedding and honeymoon plans, and community participation. We consider such matters worthwhile, but not entirely pertinent to the central issues to be discussed.

The main concerns of marriage in our society—concerns that usually get little or no attention in the standard marriage text—are personal upsets, irrational prejudices, and the inability of individuals to communicate effectively with each other. These upsets, prejudices, and communication difficulties tend to be particularly crucial in love-sex relationships. Hence, we devote the major portion of this book to the sex and love aspects of marriage. Children, in-laws, and divorce are also aspects of family life which are often badly handled and are particularly in need of some direct and rational light. On these kinds of topics, therefore, we place the major emphases in the chapters that are to follow.

We have done our best to make this book different from the usual marriage handbooks, not only in the topics it emphasizes but in the way they are treated. Both authors, in their frequent appearances before such societies as the American Association of Marriage Counselors, the American Academy of Psychotherapists, the National Council on Family Relations, and the American Psychological Association, have acquired reputations for squarely and unhypocritically facing sex-love issues. We do not intend to jeopardize our reputations by any circumlocutions in these pages.

What is said in this book derives from no armchair speculation. We have both had a great deal of experience as marriage and family educators and, more particularly, as psychotherapists and marriage counselors. Our combined experience in treating people with moderate and deep-seated premarital and marital problems is, we can say without any false modesty, rich, varied, and extensive. It is this congealed experience which, we hope, will be found helpful in the following pages.

Albert Ellis,
New York City
Robert A. Harper,
Washington, D. C.

1

Modern Marriage: Hotbed of Neurosis

Most couples who enter marriage today expect two main things from their relationship: regular sex satisfaction and the enjoyments of secure and intimate companionship and love. They normally get neither. Why?

Take the case of the sexually frustrated vocational counselor who came to see me recently. "I know a great deal about problems of marriage," he said at the start of his first session. "In fact, even though I mainly deal with people's vocational difficulties, I am always getting into their married lives, too. You know—people don't come to work on time, or keep losing jobs, and that sort of thing because their wives keep them up all night quarreling or things like that. You know how it is."

"Yes," I said. "And just as your vocational counseling takes you into marital areas, so does my marriage counseling take me, frequently, into people's job and business problems."

"I can well imagine that it does. Anyway, the thing's damned aggravating! Here it's my business, you know, and I do it practically all the time, patching up my clients' squabblings with their wives and that sort of thing, and, well damn it all, I can't do a thing with my own wife. Not a thing!"

"You mean——?"

"I mean sexually. Yes, that's what I mean: sexually! Not a thing."

"She doesn't satisfy you that way?"

"Satisfy me? Oh, no; that's not the problem at all. I'm satisfied, all right. Too satisfied, in fact! But she—never. Day and night she keeps after me. This morning, for instance. Wouldn't let me out to get to work. Held me up until I almost missed the train. Hugging and kissing and pressing up against me. God, like a cat in heat! Constantly. Never satisfied. And I was always reasonably good at sex. Still am, I think. Not that *she* thinks so!"

This thirty-five-year-old husband then went on to state that his thirty-year-old wife nagged him considerably, neglected their three children, made great financial demands on him, and was most unreasonable in many other ways. Once he had begun his tirade against his wife, he could not be stopped; and he even kept ignoring most of my questions and comments as he self-righteously assailed his wife in one outburst after another. I finally managed to get in a few words edgewise:

"But *do* you ever satisfy your wife sexually?"

"Well, frankly, I'm so disgusted, these days, by her inordinate demands that I hardly have the heart to do it at all."

"But how about previously, when you first married? Did you satisfy her then?"

"I tried to. But it was always impossible. As I said, I'm really not bad at sex. Had a reputation, in fact, before I married. But

14

she's really something! I can do it, well, say twice a week. But she wants it every night. Or more! What can you do about a thing like that?"

"Don't you know?"

"Satisfy her, you mean, in other ways? Without having . . . well, without——"

"Yes, apparently you do know. Without having actual intercourse. You know perfectly well, apparently, that you can satisfy a woman, whether you yourself are sexually interested or not, without having penile-vaginal coitus. So even if your wife wants sex relations more than you desire them, you can still satisfy her thoroughly."

"Oh, yes. I realize that. I read your books, *Sex Without Guilt* and *The Art and Science of Love*. I have even recommended them to some of my clients who have sex problems."

"What's the trouble, then? Why *don't* you satisfy your wife sexually, if that is what, according to your own story, is upsetting her so much? Why can't you spend five or ten minutes, every night in the week if necessary, giving her an orgasm— or three or four of them, if that is what she thinks she needs?"

"Well—uh—look. It's—You see, it's like this—"

And this husband went on, in beautifully evasive language, to explain that he didn't *feel* like satisfying his wife when she was acting the way she was; that her non-sexual demands also disgusted him and made him sexually unresponsive; that she didn't *really* seem to love him, even though she wanted him sexually all the time; and so on. It was quite clear, after he had been talking for a few more minutes, that sex, really, was *not* his main marital problem.

What actually bothered him, as I then started to show him, was his own thoroughly *unrealistic expectations* of marriage. He expected, merely because he *was* married, that his wife would be completely loving, exactly attuned to him sexually, financially undemanding, a wonderful mother, a devoted daughter-in-law to his mother, a thoroughly well-adjusted per-

15

son in her own right, etc. When, because of her all-too-human (and quite expectable) fallibility, his wife did not measure up to this highly idealized picture that he thought she *should* attain, my client immediately started to go on a little sit-down strike of his own. He kept telling himself that his wife did not *deserve* to be satisfied sexually; and thereby appreciably helped to make matters between them immeasurably worse.

"Granting," I said, "that your wife may have all the deficiencies that you have been listing during the last half hour, is there anything that *you* are doing to help her overcome them?"

"Like what?"

"Like satisfying her sexually, for example, so that she'll have an incentive to try to please you in other ways. Like being unusually nice and calm when she is nagging you. Like asking her tactfully and encouragingly to try to be a little nicer to your mother. Like helping her with the children when she is having a difficult time handling them. Do you ever do any things like these to try to better her situation and yours?"

"But look at what she is doing to *me!*"

"Yes, but isn't that exactly the same sentence that she's saying to herself many times a day: 'Look at what he's doing to *me*'?"

"I guess you're right. I suppose she is."

"And, anyway, do two wrongs make a right?"

"No; I know they don't."

"You 'know' it; but you don't seem to act on that knowledge. Your real problem, as I said before, is your *own* unrealistic expectations. Because you think that your wife *ought to be* different from the way she is—when you really mean that *you would like it better* or that *it would be preferable* if she were—you keep beating her over the head when she fails to live up to your idealized views. She then resentfully goes into a dive and makes even more sexual and other demands on you—thus causing your expectations to be that much more unrealistic and, in fact, unrealizable as long as you continue to employ your self-defeating and wife-defeating tactics."

"You suggest, then, that I force myself to be nice to my wife and thereby try to get her to lessen her sex demands on me?"

"Yes, but not *just* that. I suggest, even more importantly, that you change your *own* attitudes toward your wife and what you think *ought to be* expected of her. Then, instead of having to try to force yourself, against the grain as it were, to be nice to her, you will easily and almost automatically treat her better. If you, because of *your* changed attitudes, no longer think of her as a bitch who is depriving you of your 'just' and 'natural' husbandly due, but as a woman who is perhaps doing her best, under very difficult and sexually-deprived circumstances, to come to terms with you and the children, then you will *want* to be nice to her. For both her sake and your own. Then you will *want* to satisfy her sexually. With that kind of an attitude well established on your part, it will be very difficult *not* to have a much better marriage than you and your wife are now having."

It would be nice if I could say that, after this first-session presentation of what seemed to be some of the real problems of his marriage, my client immediately went home and started acting much differently toward his wife. He didn't; and several more marriage counseling sessions, as well as several with his wife, were required before he was able to start changing his attitudes and his marital behavior. Eventually, however, he did stop pitying himself and made a real attempt to satisfy his wife sexually, and their marriage noticeably improved.

The point to be emphasized here is that there are two expectations with which most people today go into marriage—the hope for regular sex satisfaction and the enjoyments of secure and intimate companionship and love. These two goals are not only intimately related to each other but to the *general* personality patterns and life expectations of the married partners. People go into marriage (or premarital affairs) with a basic set of assumptions, beliefs, attitudes, or philosophies of living. If their basic assumptions are objective, open-minded, and rational, their behavior, both in and out of marriage, will likewise tend to be reasonable and undisturbed. If, as is alas! usually the case in our society, either (or both) marriage partner's basic beliefs are prejudiced, unrealistic, and illogical, his or her marital behavior will also tend to be unreasonable and disturbed.

But this is only the beginning. Since marriage is that kind of relationship where two people ceaselessly intercommunicate and interact, if one of them behaves erratically or negatively, his or her behavior will have some significant effects on the actions and feelings of the other. In most instances, the other partner will react by behaving equally or more erratically or negatively. Then, of course, the first badly behaving partner in turn will be re-affected by the thoughts and doings of the first partner, and so on, in an endless vicious circle.

Premarital emotional disturbance, in other words, almost invariably leads to marital disturbance, which then leads to still further disturbance. By the time the mutual negativism of the partners has reverberated against each other several times, the fact that either or both partners were *originally* irrational or neurotic is quite lost from sight. Each becomes convinced that it is the other, or the marriage, which is causing the enormous upset that now exists.

My vocational counselor client, for example, was quite convinced, when he first came to see me, that he had been a perfectly normal, well-adjusted individual prior to his marriage. He was certain that only his wife's inordinate sexual and other demands had caused him to become tense, disgusted, and unhappy. When I finally was able to convince him that it was his *own* attitudes *toward* his wife's demands, rather than those demands themselves, that were causing his unhappiness, and that he had had similar unrealistic attitudes before he ever met his wife, he was much more willing to work toward changing these attitudes as well as to improve his marriage.

This same client, of course, freely admitted that his wife had been a very disturbed individual before their marriage— even though, at that time, he had not realized how disturbed she was. But, as I again showed him, he did not in any manner *accept* his wife's disturbance, or consider it a characteristic *to be worked on*. Instead, as is usually the case with individuals who are intimately associated with neurotics in our society, he incessantly *blamed* his wife for *being* neurotic; and thereby, of course, helped to make her more self-blaming and even more neurotic. When he was able to look into his own heart and stop blaming his wife, he enabled her to relieve considerable of her negative pressure on herself, and thereby to become less disturbed.

Most people in our culture, then, *enter* engagement and marriage with their full share of irrational ideas and neurotic behavior. They are relatively *blind* to both their own and their mate's disturbances. When they finally see these neurotic manifestations, they stubbornly refuse to *accept* them. Instead, they *blame* the other for being trouble and *pity themselves* for having to live with such a troubled person. They thus help intensify both their own and their partner's original neuroses; and the net result is a marriage that is a veritable hotbed of emotional upsets. Talk of the halt trying to lead the blind! Or the blaming trying to lead the blamed.

Only by having a fairly detailed view of some of the how's and why's of individual and societal disturbances today is one likely to be well prepared for the experience of felicitously entering and lovingly sustaining a good marital relationship. We turn in the next chapter to a consideration of some of these major how's and why's.

2

Factors Causing Marital Disturbance

What are some of the main factors causing frequent marital disturbance in our society?

First, the whole of modern social life, of which marriage is an integral part, is today in such a state of rapid change and complex confusion that many personal goals and desires tend to be swept away in the general cultural storm. Since every couple and every marriage are part of the large society in which we live, and since this society is notoriously in a state of severe turmoil, it would be strange indeed to find that most people today were living in a state of effortless marital bliss.

Most of us are aware that modern social conditions produce many dramatic problems, such as war, crime, delinquency, overpopulation, urban and suburban monotony, poverty, and racial strife. But we less often realize that much of the deep-seated unhappiness and the neurotic symptoms of the "average" man and woman of our civilization are insidious but still statistically "normal" tolls of our wayward modes of living. In an ideal society, it may be possible to have thoroughly unneurotic individuals and couples; but ours is hardly that ideal.

As both of the authors of this book frequently stress to their clients and patients: "Do your best, by all means, to understand the society in which you live, and to make suitable allowances for its flaws and idiocies in raising your children in it. But let's have no illusions: since you live in an imperfect culture, you are bound, to some degree, to have imperfect selves and imperfect offspring. No matter how sane and intelligent may be your own modes of child-raising, your children will suffer from other less sane and intelligent influences: from contacts with their friends, their teachers, books, movies, TV shows, etc. Tough! But these are the facts and you must, to some degree, accept them—or else become a hermit. Make all the allowances you will for your culture; but you still can't completely escape it. Sick people are in large degree—though not completely—a product of a sick society. Be forewarned."

A second reason why marriages or the people in them tend to be so emotionally warped today is because people tend to use them as dumping grounds for problems acquired in other aspects of their lives. Not only do most husbands and wives inflict difficulties on each other which they acquired originally in their parental homes, but they also tend to project daily confusions, conflicts, and frustrations which originate from their non-marital relationships. Most men, for example, meet with various problems at their work. There they are not free to express openly aggressive feelings which they engender in themselves by not realistically accepting work frustrations. So they often bring these feelings home and express them against their wives.

21

Similarly, most wives have grievances of their own in relation to careers which they may have away from home or to the demanding routines of homemaking and care of their children. They fail to see realistically, temporarily accept, and then planfully do something effective about the frustrations of their careers or their homes. Instead they irrelevantly bring these frustrations—or the negative emotions which they allow to surround them—into the relatively relaxed, intimate, personalized relationship with their husbands. The dumping of such extraneous problems into the marriage breeds still more problems. These, still again, are not squarely faced and tackled but are "resolved" by self- and marriage-destroying outbursts of temper and hostility.

A third main reason for widespread upset in marital relationships is the fact that our customs concerning both courtship and marriage are, to a considerable extent, distinctly conducive to the growth of illogical, inflexible, self-defeating thoughts and actions. Although our society is now a little less Puritanical in its outlook toward sex than it was in earlier periods, the sexual side of courtship and marriage is still clouded with considerable super-romanticism and antisexualism.

Love, especially what is vaguely referred to as "true love," is represented as somehow entirely separate from the "baser" sex impulses and is supposed to follow various ethereal and unrealistic channels as described in our movies, television scripts, magazine stories, and other sources of romantic beliefs.

As Dr. Karen Horney, among others, frequently pointed out, *should's, supposed to's, ought's,* and *must's* are the inevitable equipment of disturbed individuals. The neurotic particularly believes that (a) he himself *should* act in a perfectionistic, wholly moralistic way and that (b) everyone else also *should* behave in this idealistic manner. From the first of these unrealistic beliefs he acquires anxiety, guilt, and self-doubt; and from the second, suspiciousness, hostility, and self-righteousness. He then, of course, carries these unrealistic *should's* into

22

his premarital and his marital relationships. He ends up, as is only to be expected, loathing himself and his mate.

During courtship, irrational expectations may never come up against a serious showdown. It is relatively easy to hide from reality in the high romantic grass of young unmarried love. But, comes the marriage, and truth will out. This man or this woman to whom you are married cannot possibly measure up to your unrealistic expectations. And your mate is bound to meet with similar frustrations of his or her expectations of you. While it is possible for you both to learn to face the realities of married life, or to restructure your expectations so that they conform to reality, the evidence is overwhelming that a majority of present-day married couples do not actually do this. They respond to reality in illogical, inflexible, self-defeating ways; in short, they develop or perpetuate their own neuroses.

Which brings us, once again, to the very core of most serious marital disturbances: the emotional disturbance of the married partners. A simple definition of neurosis is the one stated in one of our previous books, *How to Live With a Neurotic*: stupid behavior by non-stupid people. Neurotic behavior consists of self-defeating thoughts and actions. It is the process of rendering oneself unhappy in a situation where all the necessary attributes actually exist and could be realized. But the neurotic individual shortsightedly does *not* take advantage of his own intelligence and planning ability; on the contrary, he sabotages his own ends.

In no set of human relationships are neurotic patterns more observable and more pernicious than in marriage and family life. For not only do married neurotics execrably influence each other and make themselves two or three times as unhappy as they need be, but they also pass on their patterns of disturbance to their children—who, in turn, later marry, raise their own families, and thus perpetuate similar self-defeating modes of living.

23

As we noted previously, human disturbance almost always results from the individual's mistaken, unrealistic, or illogical beliefs, or philosophies. Since the symptoms of his disturbance —for example, his fears, guilts, and depressions—take on what is generally called an "emotional" tone, and since they usually lead to physical feelings and consequences—such as feelings of nausea or pain and symptoms of high blood pressure, ulcers, or migraine headaches—it is easy to forget, or to fail to see in the first place, that these disturbed "emotions" are actually the result of early-ingrained and later self-repeated and sustained ideas or attitudes. But they are.

Human beings, for the most part, talk to themselves in simple declarative sentences. And when these sentences are rational and logical—when the individual tells himself something like, "Jones doesn't like me; that's too bad; now let's see what I can calmly do to get him to like me better."—his "emotions" are appropriate and undisordered. But when he tells himself irrational and illogical sentences—such as, "Jones doesn't like me; it's absolutely terrible and awful that he doesn't like me; I can't stand his not liking me; and this proves that Jones is a blackguard."—his "emotions" are inappropriate, negative, and self-defeating.

If, in other words, an individual is theoretically capable of acting in a non-self-defeating way, and he actually defeats himself and brings needless anxiety and hostility into his relationships with himself and others, he must be thinking unclearly, illogically. He must have some unrealistic value system which blocks his potential of thinking, feeling, and acting in a reasonable manner. If a person is to be helped to think clearly and do away with his unrealistic value system, he must be shown (a) that he is irrational, (b) exactly how he is repeating nonsensical ideas to himself, (c) where and how he originally learned to do this kind of illogical thinking (or was indoctrinated with silly ideas), (d) that there is a good possibility of his becoming rational, (e) exactly how he can attack his illogical ideas and

24

replace them with more realistic ones, and (f) how he can finally build generalized rational philosophies of living, so that he will ultimately automatically think, for the most part, in sane and undefeating ways.

This process of showing a disturbed individual exactly how he has learned and is now himself sustaining nonsensical ideas, which (consciously or unconsciously) lie behind and keep sustaining his "emotional" disturbances or his neurotic symptoms, is called rational psychotherapy. In their professional writings, the authors of this book have developed the theory and practice of rational therapy and are continually working to perfect it.

As applied to marital problems, rational analysis largely consists of showing each spouse that his or her disturbed behavior (in or out of marriage) arises from underlying unrealistic beliefs or philosophies. The client is then shown what these beliefs are and how they are producing individual and marital upsets. Thirdly, he or she is given some understanding of how the irrational value system originally arose and how it is being (wittingly or unwittingly) sustained and reinforced. Finally, the counselee is helped to replace his or her self-defeating ideas and attitudes with more rational and more effective philosophies. This change in the value system of the client is achieved not only by discussion in the counseling situation but by his being induced to think for himself when he is outside the session and by fear-removing and hostility-dispelling actions that he is induced to take under the therapist's guidance.

In this book we are trying to help people with problem marriages to undergo a similar process. Although we obviously cannot listen to their particular problems and thereby discover the special set of irrational beliefs that are causing their neurotic interactions with their mates; fortunately this is not absolutely necessary (even though it is highly desirable). This is because there are actually only a limited number of patterns of self-defeating marital behavior. In outlining and unraveling some of these main patterns, we shall almost inevitably uncover at least some of those which exist in any individual instance.

Take, for instance, a case which one of us presented at a symposium on Neurotic Interaction in Marriage, which was sponsored by the Counseling Division of the American Psychological Association, and on which both authors of this book were panelists.

A husband and wife who had been married for seven years came for marriage counseling because the wife was terribly disturbed about the husband's alleged affairs with other women and the husband was "fed up" with his wife's complaints and general unhappiness and thought it was useless going on. It was quickly evident that the wife was a neurotic individual who believed that she had to be greatly loved and protected; hated herself thoroughly for her incompetency; severely blamed everyone, especially her husband, for not loving her unstintingly; and felt that all her unhappiness was caused by her husband's lack of affection.

The husband, at the same time, was a moderately disturbed individual who believed that his wife should be blamed for her mistakes, particularly the mistake of unjustly thinking he was having affairs with other women. He also believed that it was unfair for his wife to criticize and sexually frustrate him when he was doing the best he could, under difficult circumstances, to help her.

In this case, the somewhat unorthodox procedure of seeing both husband and wife together at all counseling sessions was employed. I often find this method to be time-saving, in that the main difficulties between the mates are quickly arrived at. I have observed, too, that the witnessing of one mate's emotional reeducation by the other spouse may serve as a model and incentive for the second spouse's philosophic reorientation. The husband-wife-therapist group, in this sense, becomes something of a small-scale attempt at group therapy.

26

Because the husband, in this case, was less seriously disturbed than the wife, his illogical assumptions were first brought to his attention and worked upon. He was shown that, in general, blame is an irrational feeling because it does neither the blamer nor his victim any good; and that, in particular, although many of his complaints about his wife's unrealistic jealousy and other disturbances might well have been justified, his criticizing her for this kind of behavior could only serve to make her worse rather than better—thus bringing more of the same kind of behavior down on his head.

The husband was also shown that his assumption that his wife *should* not berate or sexually frustrate him was erroneous; since why *should* not disturbed individuals act in precisely this kind of manner? He was led to see that, even though his wife's actions were mistaken, two wrongs do not make a right—and his reaction to her behavior was equally mistaken. For, instead of getting the results he wanted, he was only helping make things worse. If he really wished to help his wife—as he kept saying that he did—then he had better, for the present, *expect* her to act badly, stop inciting himself to fury when she did so, and spend at least several weeks returning her anger and discontent with kindness and acceptance. Thereby he would give her leeway to tackle her own disturbances.

The husband, albeit with some backsliding at times, soon began to respond to this realistic approach to his wife's problems; and, in the meantime, her irrational assumptions were tackled by the counselor. She was shown how and why she originally acquired her dire need to be loved and protected— mainly because her mother had not given her the love she required (or thought she required) as a child—and how necessarily self-defeating it was for her, as an adult, to continue to reinfect herself with this nonsensical belief. Her general philosophy of blaming herself and others was ruthlessly revealed to her and forthrightly attacked. She, like her husband, was shown just how such a philosophy is bound to alienate others, rather

27

than win their approval or get them to do things in a different and presumably better manner.

Finally, the wife's notion that her unhappiness was caused by her husband's lack of affection was particularly brought to conscious awareness and exposed to the merciless light of rationality. She was shown, over and over again, how her unhappiness could come only from within, from her own attitudes toward external events such as her husband's lack of love, and that it could be expunged only by her facing her own part in creating it.

As the husband in this case started accepting his wife's neurosis more philosophically, she herself was more easily able to see, just because he was not goading and blaming her, that she was the creator of her own jealousies, self-hatred, and childish dependency. She began to observe in detail the sentences she kept telling herself to make herself unhappy.

On one occasion, when the counselor was explaining to the husband how he kept goading his wife to admit she was wrong, and how the husband ostensibly kept trying to help his wife think straight but actually kept showing how superior he was to her, the wife interrupted to say:

"Yes, and I can see that I do exactly the same thing, too. I go out of my way to find things wrong with him, or to accuse him of going with other women, because I really feel that I'm so stupid and worthless and I want to drag him down even below me." This, in the light of her previous defensiveness about her jealousies, was real progress.

After a total of twenty-three joint sessions of counseling, the fate of the marriage of this couple was no longer in doubt and they decided to go ahead with having a child, which they had previously avoided because of their mutual uncertainties. They also solved several other major problems which were not necessarily related to their marriage but which had previously proved serious obstacles to happy, unanxious living.

This is a fairly typical example of how a couple with a severe marital problem may be treated by a rational therapeutic approach to marriage counseling. It indicates some of the main irrational beliefs—such as the belief that one must be loved for oneself, no matter how badly one acts toward one's mate —which keep constantly cropping up to make people, and especially married couples, disturbed.

There are many other similar irrational beliefs, but most of them can be placed under ten or twelve major headings. As far as neurotic interaction in marriage is concerned, as a matter of fact, the basic unrealistic philosophies which upset people can fairly adequately be listed under five major headings:

1. *The dire need for love.* One of the major irrational assumptions that many persons in our society acquire is the notion that it is a dire necessity for an adult human being to be approved or loved by almost everyone for almost everything he does; that what others think of one is more important than gaining one's own self-respect; and that it is better to depend on others than on oneself. Applied to marriage, this means that the illogical and neurotic individual firmly believes that, no matter how he behaves, his mate, just because she *is* his mate, *should* love him; that if she doesn't respect him, life is a horror; and that her main role as a wife is to help, aid, succor him, rather than to be an individual in her own right.

When *both* marriage partners believe this nonsense—believe that they *must* be loved, respected, and catered to by the other —they are not only asking for what is rarely accorded an individual in this grimly realistic world, but are asking for unmitigated devotion from another individual who, precisely because he demands this kind of devotion himself, is the *least* likely candidate to give it. Under such circumstances, a major marital disaster is almost certain to occur.

The idea that one has to be thoroughly loved, admired, and liked by others, particularly by one's mate, is particularly beaten into almost all our heads in this society. Thus, we continually place an emphasis on the importance of getting consistently and unusually favorable responses from our associates and of feeling that one is somehow a failure, or worthless, whenever such responses are not forthcoming.

Actually, there are a great many other interesting and satisfying goals in life and in marriage than receiving affection. And it is difficult, if not impossible, to have intimate interaction with anyone over a period of time, especially in a domestic relationship such as marriage, without having your interests and desires interfere to some extent with the interests and desires of your mate; and vice versa. If, therefore, the fulfillment of a major pleasure is blocked by your spouse, however legitimately, it is idealistic nonsense to believe that you will love, admire, and like her wholeheartedly during the very moment that she frustrates you.

If you pretend that you ineffably love your marriage partner at the very moment when she is blocking your heartfelt desires, you are most likely to build up considerable resentment toward her. Even if you are not conscious of this resentment, it will probably come out indirectly, and perhaps all the more destructively, in other situations. If, however, you do not keep up this kind of pretense, then your spouse, if she is typically in the throes of the I-must-at-all-costs-at-all-times-be-adored philosophy of our culture, will almost certainly feel (that is, tell herself) that it is terrible that you have not given her your unconditional and permanent love, admiration, and acceptance. Either way, then, as a result of your mate's (or your own) holding this love-is-a-necessity policy, you are likely to sabotage whatever real feelings of love may originally exist in your marriage.

This over-emphasis in our culture on being loved is a prime example of how realistic *desires* can be easily and insidiously translated into neurotic *needs*. To some extent, young children *need* to be loved—that is, they require a certain amount of love and esteem, help and support, from the persons around them if they are to survive well physically and develop sufficient

30

self-love, self-esteem, and self-confidence to become healthy and effective personalities. But, however necessary being loved may be for children (and there is some experimental evidence to indicate that even this may be exaggerated as a need after the child has passed the stage of early infancy), there is no evidence whatever that being loved or approved is absolutely necessary for adults. It is pleasant, nice, desirable for adults to be loved; but it is most questionable that it is really essential.

When one *believes,* however, that it *is* essential for one's happiness to be greatly loved, this very belief *makes* being loved a requisite for stability and happiness. Or, stated differently, when one *defines* one's well-being in terms of being accepted and approved by others, one makes it necessary, by that very definition, to be so accepted and approved. And when, in reality, one is *not* suitably loved, one will definitely, under these definitional circumstances, be miserable. Curiously enough, whenever this misery occurs, there is a tendency for most human beings to forget completely that it has been wholly caused *not* by the lack of love they receive but by their own *definition* of the "necessity" of their receiving this love.

The translation of the perfectly legitimate desire to be loved by one's mate into the idiotic and quite illegitimate so-called *need* to be adored by him or her is probably the most fundamental irrationality of millions of married individuals. This single unrealistic notion accounts for the highest percentage of serious neurotic interactions in marriage.

2. *Perfectionism in achievement.* A second major irrational belief which most disturbed people in our culture seem to hold is that a human being should or must be perfectly competent, adequate, talented, and intelligent in all possible respects and is utterly worthless if he or she is incompetent in any way. When married, these disturbed individuals tend to feel that, as mates, and particularly as sex partners, they should be utterly successful and achieving. The wife therefore berates herself because she is not a perfect housewife, mother, and

bedmate; and the husband flays himself because he is not an unexcelled provider and sex athlete.

From this point on, things inevitably go from bad to worse. Becoming depressed because of their supposed inadequacies, both husband and wife may compulsively strive for perfection and almost kill themselves trying to keep up with what they consider their "normal" responsibilities.

Thus, the husband may try to have coitus with his wife every night, when he obviously is capable of doing so only once or twice a week. Or the wife may try to keep the house spotlessly clean at all times, even though she has two or three young children constantly helping to mess it up. Not only do such compulsive strivings foredoom themselves to failure; but, in addition, they tend to make the compulsively perfectionist mate abhor sex relations, housecleaning, or other aspects of marriage, and finally abhor marriage or the marital partner.

The other side of the coin of perfectionist strivings is equally dismal. Seeing that they cannot possibly attain the unrealistic marital goals that they set themselves, spouses frequently give up the battle completely, run out of the field, and actually *make themselves* into poor lovers or housemates. Thus, the husband who is perfectly capable of coitus twice a week, but not daily, may become so disgusted with himself for his "failure" that he eventually ceases all attempts at sex relations with his wife. Or the wife who cannot keep her home absolutely spotless, may give up and become slatternly, or a devoted clubwoman who is never at home, or even an adulteress who thereby stays away from her housewifely responsibilities.

3. *A philosophy of blame and punishment.* A third irrational assumption of most disturbed individuals is that one should severely blame oneself and others for mistakes and wrong-doings; and that punishing oneself or others for errors will help prevent future mistakes.

Actually, blame or hostility toward oneself almost invariably

32

serves to distract one from the real issue—"Now that I have made this mistake, how can I manage *not* to make it again?" —and to induce one destructively to focus on the false issue— "Now that I have made this mistake, how can I keep punishing myself and atoning for my great sin?" And blaming others carries one miles away from the practical problem—"Now that Smith has behaved badly toward me, how can I understand why he behaves in that manner and try to help him behave better in the future?"—and diverts one to the vicious circle of hostility—"Now that Smith has behaved badly toward me, how can I behave even worse toward him, so that he will hate me all the more and then behave still worse toward me?"

The married individual who blames others naturally tends to get upset by the mate's errors and stupidities, spends considerable time and energy trying to reform the spouse, and vainly tries to "help" a spouse by sharply pointing out the error of his or her ways. The expectable result is that the mate endeavors to act quite the same way, and brilliantly succeeds.

Because, as we previously have seen, emotionally disturbed human beings already have the tendency to blame themselves too much for their imperfections; because even healthy men and women tend to resist doing the so-called right thing when they are roundly criticized for doing the so-called wrong one; and because criticized humans tend to focus compulsively on their wrongdoings rather than calmly facing the problem of how they may *change* their behavior—for many reasons such as these, one partner's blaming another for the other's imperfections usually does immense harm.

Even counselors—who quite obviously are on their client's side—rarely can get away with blaming an individual. And spouses—who were often wed in the first place mainly because the bride or groom felt that he or she would *not* be criticized by this spouse—can virtually never do anything but the gravest harm to their relationships by criticizing their mates. But

33

negative criticism is precisely what most disturbed individuals, by their basically false philosophies of living, are driven to make.

Married couples with self-blaming tendencies, moreover, ceaselessly continue to seek out their own "horrible" imperfections and to castigate and punish themselves mercilessly for their misdeeds. In so doing, they become irritable, depressed, and sometimes a victim of complete inertia. Naturally, under these circumstances, they rarely make good companions, bedmates, or parents. Their mates then tend to become equally distressed, and often blaming or self-blaming in their turn; and separation, divorce, or a continuing mock marriage impends.

4. *Catastrophizing frustrations.* A fourth idiotic assumption which underlies and causes emotional distress is the notion that it is terrible, horrible, and catastrophic when things are not the way one would like them to be; that others *should* make things easier for one, help conquer life's difficulties; and that one should not have to put off present pleasures for future gains. This is a typically childish philosophy of life; and when it is held by adults—which (look around you!) it obviously often is—it can only lead to disappointment, disillusionment, and hostility toward others and toward fate for *not* giving one the easy living one thinks is one's due.

In their marriages, individuals who consciously or unconsciously espouse this I-cannot-stand-frustration system of values invariably get into serious difficulties. For marriage, of course, *is* an exceptionally frustrating situation in many instances, involving considerable boredom, sacrifice, pleasure postponement, doing what one's mate wants to do, and so on. Children may be delightful members of a family in many instances; but child marriages, especially when the participants are technically adults, are generally disastrous. Childish mates bitterly resent their marriages and their spouses on numberless occasions; and, sooner or later, they clearly show this resentment. Then, often feeling that *they* are not loved or that they are being frustrated in *their* desires, the spouses of these childish wives and husbands get in a few or a few hundred counter-licks themselves, and the battle is again on. The ultimate result is invariably a hellish marriage—or a divorce.

5. *The belief that emotion is uncontrollable.* A fifth and final irrational belief which we shall consider here—since this is not primarily a book on neurosis itself but on irrationality in marriage—is the mythical supposition that most human unhappiness is externally caused or is forced on one by outside people and events and that one has virtually no control over one's emotions and cannot help feeling badly on many occasions. Actually, most human unhappiness is *self*-caused and results from invalid assumptions, and internalized sentences stemming from these assumptions, such as some of the beliefs which we have just been examining.

Once a married person is convinced, however, that his own unhappiness is externally caused, he inevitably blames his mate for his own misery; and, once again, he is in a marital stew. For the mate, especially if she is herself not too mature, will contend (a) that she does *not* cause his unhappiness; and (b) that he, instead, causes hers. Of such silly beliefs, again, is the stuff of separation made.

It is our staunch contention, then, that emotionally disturbed individuals possess, almost by definition one might say, a set of basic postulates which are distinctly unrealistic, biased, and illogical. Consequently, such individuals will find it almost impossible to be happy in an utterly realistic, everyday, down-to-earth relationship such as modern marriage usually is. Moreover, being unhappy, these easily upset mates will inevitably jump on their partners—who, if reasonably well adjusted, will tend to become fed up with the relationship and to want to escape from it; and, if somewhat neurotic themselves, will return their spouses' resentful sallies in kind, thus leading to neurotic interaction in marriage.

It should be stressed at this point that, no matter how irrational the beliefs of one spouse may be, it takes two disturbable people to make for true neurotic interaction in marriage. Suppose, for example, that a husband believes he must be completely loved by his wife, no matter how he behaves toward her. Suppose he also irrationally believes that he must be competent in all respects; that he should blame others, especially his wife, for errors and mistakes; that he must never be frustrated; and that all his unhappiness is caused by his wife's behavior and other outside events rather than by his own thinking and doing.

If the spouse of this severely disturbed husband had no similar illogical beliefs of her own, she would quickly see that her husband was disturbed, would not take his hostility toward herself with any resentment, and would either accept him the way he was, or would calmly try to see that he got professional help, or would quietly conclude that she did not want to remain married to such a disturbed individual and would divorce him. She would *not,* however, neurotically react to her husband herself, thus causing a mighty conflagration where there need only be a nasty, but still limited, flame.

Unfortunately, most disturbed husbands in our culture do not have completely sane wives, and most neurotic wives have equally irrational husbands. Therefore, instead of one mate's helping the other to overcome his or her difficulties, aggravation of these difficulties is the more usual procedure. The fact remains, however, and should never be lost from sight, that it is *not* the nagging, irresponsible, or depressed behavior of one marital partner that really causes the disturbance and negativism of the other partner. Rather, it is the *attitude* of the second partner *toward* the first—as well as, just as importantly, his attitude toward *himself.* If either one of two mates were truly rational and non-disturbed, this would not automatically lead to marital bliss in every instance; but it would definitely help prevent most of the extreme difficulties which are today so prevalent in marriage.

36

3

Other Causes of Marital Disturbance

Personal turmoil, as we have been showing, is probably the main cause of marital failure in our society. But marriages fail for other reasons, too—some of which we shall now examine. There are always background differences between husbands and wives. Some of these are inescapable; but these differences may establish a groundwork for future marital difficulties. One such difference is the disparity between the ways we socialize males and females in our society.

Although differences in boy and girl upbringings are today somewhat less than in earlier times, they are still sufficient to encourage members of one sex to avoid and distrust the other. Girls, for example, come to resent boys because the latter are given certain degrees of freedom of action not commonly granted to the former and because boys are frequently induced to develop personality traits that girls have been led to believe are "not nice."

By the same token, boys tend to become tense in our civilization because more is expected of them in the way of achievement—including sex achievement—and they unrealistically react to life's frustrations. Since some of the achievements demanded of them, such as their being expected to succeed sufficiently in business or professional life to be able to support a family, are closely connected with boy-girl relationships, they eventually may come to resent females, and conceive of them as unduly pressure-bearing.

Again, girls manifest interests and attitudes that boys have been led to believe are undesirable ("sissified"), thus inducing the male to be relatively incompatible with the female. Girls also have certain special privileges—such as the privilege of being able to insult a boy without being punched in the nose for so doing. Males, under these circumstances, frequently come to be bored with or resentful toward young females.

As boys and girls move through adolescence into young adulthood, the cultural differences between them are often even more pronounced. Males are encouraged to "lay" everything in skirts; females, to save their "honor," at the very least, for the one boy whom they greatly love. Men are taught to center their interests on sports, poker, business success; women, on clothes, esthetic pursuits, homemaking. It is small wonder, under such circumstances, that males and females, even though they are romantically in love with each other, have so much lack of real understanding and such high degrees of underlying hostility in regard to one another.

To add to the sex differences that are distinctly promoted in our culture, we have the normal human differences that exist between any two individuals. Varying opinions and habits of two persons may spring, first, from their differing heredities and, second, from any number of conditioning factors in their early and later environments. These would include the kinds of families, schools, religious groups, neighborhoods, and parts of the country in which they were raised. It is consequently inconceivable that two members of modern, complex society will have exactly the same attitudes toward money, clothes, religion, occupation, politics, recreation, education, children, food, the state of the nation and the world, and so forth.

Differences occur; and some differences, even when petty (proper degree of browning of toast; what to do about used razor blades, broken slip straps, leaky faucets, a hole in a sock; how soon after a meal dishes should be washed and by whom), may lead to conflict. Actually, it is not the differences themselves which cause dissension, but the undemocratic attitude which is generally taken toward such differences. But this undemocratic attitude, too, is as much a product of social upbringing as it is of individual preference.

As a case in point, take the marriage of Marjorie and Bob Hunta. After a pleasant evening at the theater, Marjorie said to her husband, "Where do you think we should go for a late supper?"

After thinking a moment, Bob replied: "How about that new Polynesian place over on Broadway? Why don't we try that?"

"What!" was Marjorie's quick retort, "How can you even think of a place like that? All that horribly greased-up goo that they serve in those places? Only a savage would eat that kind of stuff!"

Bob, who hardly looked upon himself as a savage, was noticeably hurt. They ended up by eating in a place that neither of them liked; and instead of the satisfying sex relations which both of them had looked forward to earlier in the evening, they managed to be tired enough not to have even the mildest petting when they got home.

The point of this story is not that Marjorie and Bob are both incorrigible neurotics who cannot take strong differences of opinion expressed by the other, but that they both have been thoroughly indoctrinated, by their parents and their general culture, with the notion that *we* members of a "normal" in-group, who enjoy (or abhor) Polynesian cooking (or jazz, or crossword puzzles, or sexy novels, or what you will), are fine, intelligent, sensible human beings, while *you* members of an "abnormal" (that is, different) out-group, who have distinctly other tastes are ignoble, vulgar, senseless fools. Although both Marjorie and Bob are good Americans, who theoretically believe in democracy, freedom, and the spirit of live and let live, they actually are fascistic, thoroughly undemocratic persons who simply cannot, or at least will not, tolerate the fact of widespread human differences. Either they insist (unconsciously, if not with full awareness) that their own views and preferences are utterly "right" and "good" and that other people's opinions and desires are "wrong" and "bad"; or, with a little more liberality, they admit that others may not be "wrong," in any absolutistic sense, but still insist that these others are "foolish" or "inferior" for holding these "stupid" opinions and desires.

Marjorie and Bob, in other words, intolerantly *despise* and *loathe* those who dare to challenge their own "superiority" by being radically different from them. Their entire lives, as citizens of this culture and the various sub-groups (families, schools, neighborhoods, churches, etc.) which they have identified themselves with in the culture, have taught them to look down upon those who disagree essentially with them. Consequently, even though they love each other and have a reasonably good marriage, they keep despising and loathing each other when their basic differences come to the fore. Their marital partnership, of course, severely (though not fatally) suffers in the process.

A similar, and sometimes equally pernicious, cause of marital failure is what might be called *real* incompatibility of interests or of temperament. John and Helen, by way of illustration, are unusually tolerant and well-adjusted individuals, and either one of them could normally get along rather well in most marriages they might make. But John is a hi-fi devotee who enjoys nothing better than to stay home virtually every evening with his expensive equipment turned on full blast; and Helen can take or (preferably) leave deafening operatic broadcasts or records. Helen, moreover, is a very social-minded individual who delights in visiting others and having them visit her. John loves Helen, his work, and his hi-fi programs, but can easily do without the rest of the world.

Here we have a case of what might be called true incompatibility of interest. John and Helen are sometimes quite happy with each other—when they are eating together, going on an occasional camping trip by themselves, or having sex relations. Most of the time, however, their vital interests clash. Can their basic incompatibilities be somehow worked out so that they each get what they want out of life without infringing too much on the desires of the other? Perhaps. But perhaps, too, these interests would be much better fulfilled if they got a divorce and each found another reasonably tolerant and well-adjusted mate who just happened to have more compatible preferences.

Another source of disagreement and dissent between many husbands and wives is sex. This has at least two major aspects, the physiological and the psychological, either or both of which may be disruptive of marriage. On the physiological side, it is folly to deny that many wives and husbands have enormous differences in their sex desires and capacities. Where one mate may thoroughly desire and enjoy sex relations only once a month or so the other may literally be a once- or twice-a-nighter; and perfect adjustment under such circumstances is not going to be easy to attain, although later in this book we shall give some pointers on how it may be approximated.

On the psychological side, males and females in our culture are normally raised with quite different sex goals. In addition, they may have individual conditionings and experiences which

41

make them sexually diverse. As we noted before, males may be raised with the notion that the more promiscuous they are, the better; and girls, with the reverse idea. At the same time, a particular male may be reared, largely by his mother, to think that sex, in or out of marriage, is nasty and low; while a particular female may be raised to believe that premarital and/or marital sex relations constitute the most glorious aspect of life. If this particular fellow and girl marry, sexual problems are almost certain to follow.

In general, again, our society specifically trains both males and females to view each other with a goodly degree of sexual distrust and suspicion. We encourage both sexes to be friendly and warm to others; but not *too* friendly, not *too* warm—especially to members of the other sex. This is because of the widespread belief we seem to hold that to encourage young people to feel considerable warmth and love toward members of the other sex would lead to sexual degeneracy and the loss of all desirable sex ideals. Instead, therefore, we traditionally foster suspiciousness, caution, standoffishness, and even hostility in early male-female relationships; and these early-inspired attitudes very often remain the basic attitudinal equipment with which men and women later approach their marital sexual relationships. Disaster frequently ensues.

Still another important source of failure in marriage—and if our list seems to be growing unduly impressive and oppressive, it is merely because we are reporting instead of avoiding grim realities—is ignorance about the nature of the marriage relationship itself. Many people do not even have the most elementary preparation for the demands that marriage will make of them; and it is cavalierly assumed that they will automatically know how to adapt themselves to this most important partnership of their lives. This lack of proper preparation for marriage is really quite amazing; since we scarcely expect a person to know how to drive a car, to dance well, to strum a guitar, or to hit a golf ball without definite instruction. Surely there is no

42

reason to consider modern marriage less filled with dangers and pitfalls than far less stressful occupations and pastimes such as these.

Yet our traditions make little or no allowance for marital instruction; and, additionally, accord infinitesimal tolerance to the marital novice. Thus, newlyweds often fail to tolerate their own or their mate's initial lack of skills in sex, love, and marital affairs. Each spouse usually expects the other to have all the answers in regard to his or her side of the relationship and is distinctly critical when he or she does not. Even worse, each spouse often pretends to himself and his mate that he knows what he is doing, when this is obviously not true, and is intensely defensive of even positive suggestions in regard to his possible mistakes and shortcomings.

A twenty-five-year-old newlywed was able to admit to a marriage counselor that he really had had very little sex experience before marriage, and that he hardly knew what the different parts of his wife's genitalia were, let alone what to do about stimulating them adequately. Previously, however, when his wife had suggested that perhaps he did not know as much as he might in this respect, and that maybe he should read a book on the subject, he had defensively resisted her suggestion and had insisted that he knew all there was to know about sex. This client's wife, when she first discovered that her husband knew little about sex, was rather negative about his ignorance and her suggestion to read the sex book was given in a nasty, supercritical way. Here, then, we have an instance of both the wife and the husband being intolerant of the husband's lack of knowledge. Their actions, consequently, did little to help him overcome this lack.

We could continue, almost indefinitely, expounding some of the reasons why modern marriage tends to be so difficult and often disruptive. Since, however, the main purpose of this book is to outline some possibilities of tackling these disruptive tendencies, we shall discontinue our gruesome and rueful depictions at this point and go on to more constructive potentialities of marriage. Not all of marrying or staying married is beyond our control, even though much of it, as we have been showing, is parentally and socially determined. There definitely are practical ways of lowering the risk of marital failure. What ways? Let us turn to some of them in the next chapter.

4

Gauging Marital Compatibility

One of the worst ways to succeed at anything is to be petrified lest one fail. Or—what amounts to the same thing—to rage against oneself if, perchance, one does fail. For success at almost any complex task—and Heaven knows that the relationship of marriage is both sufficiently complex and task-ful—involves wholehearted concentration, or focusing, on the problem to be solved. And fear of failure, or blaming oneself in the eventuality of one's failing, means that one must focus on the possibility of *not* solving a problem, instead of on the problem itself.

Although it may seem so obvious as not to require stating, marriage is a *relationship*—and a difficult and demanding relationship at that. Two individuals, however fine and capable they may be, do not necessarily *relate* well, even in such relatively simple partnerships as those involved in playing tennis or co-captaining a charity drive. They normally have to *learn* to relate satisfactorily with each other; have to *work at* building their relationship; have to *focus* on getting along well together. This is particularly true of a marital partnership, which is uniquely intimate, involves huge amounts of time spent in each other's company, and supposedly lasts for the greater part of a lifetime.

If, however, people strongly feel or believe that they *should* or *must* succeed at marriage they are usually or often going to be so concerned about the possibility of *not* succeeding that they will do far more worrying and catastrophizing about this dire possibility than they will plan and think about ways to develop their relationship.

For example: Mr. and Mrs. Jorge, being members of an orthodox religious sect, felt that it was absolutely necessary that they stay married and make a perfect success of their sex-love relations. Whenever, therefore, the slightest thing went wrong between them, they tended to become thoroughly panicked by the idea of a possible estrangement. Particularly when (as a result of worry) Mr. Jorge became impotent, and it seemed that they would remain childless (which was also considered catastrophic by their religious sect), they became still more frantic. Soon they were both so tense that the slightest mishandling of a situation by either one would tend to set first one and then the other mate off; and bickering and self-recrimination became their continual marital diet.

When this couple was helped to see, as a result of several marriage counseling sessions, that although it was *highly desirable,* it was not *absolutely necessary* that they have perfect sex relations, bear children, or even have a wonderful relationship together, they calmed down considerably, and were then

46

able to tackle the practical problems involved in actualizing their desires.

Similarly, anyone who sets desirable goals for marriage, and then calmly and steadfastly works at trying to achieve such goals, but does *not* convince himself or herself that utter disaster will ensue if he somehow fails, will usually have an excellent chance of achieving his ends.

There is an old verse, attributed to a student at Oxford University, which runs:

> A centipede was happy quite,
>   Until a frog in fun
> Said, "Pray, which leg comes after which?"
> This raised her mind to such a pitch,
> She lay distracted in the ditch
>   Considering how to run.

Translated into marital terms, this means that the more one worries, catastrophizes about one's attempt to satisfy one's partner and to have a good marriage, the more one is likely to end up in a ditch. *Doing* something about possible marital problems is fine; being over-concerned about *not* doing things or about doing them *perfectly* is invariably self-defeating.

After one stops catastrophizing about the possibility of one's failing at marriage, the next step can be a realistic attempt to maximize marital compatibility. Here the first and foremost point, perhaps, that one can make to oneself is that one must fully accept the fact that love and compatibility are not necessarily the same thing; indeed, they often differ widely.

You and your spouse may love each other dearly and look with real trepidation at the possibility of being temporarily or permanently separated. But that mutual love does not mean that you are indubitably compatible living partners—any more than your love for golf makes you an excellent golfer or your

47

love for highly seasoned food makes it and your stomach highly compatible. While you and your spouse's basic incompatibilities may be a constant source of irritation, two other mates, without loving overly abundantly or trying very hard to have a successful marriage, may be luckily sufficiently compatible to get along far more peacefully, or even ecstatically, than you and your marital partner.

Marital compatibility, like individual talent for art, science, or mathematics, is a condition which varies enormously. Often it has relatively little relation to the degree of love between a couple. It is not something that automatically follows upon being in love; nor is it something that can always be willed into existence by all-out effort. Nonetheless, there are certain things which can often be done to increase (though not necessarily perfect) domestic compatibility in marriage. For example:

1. You can, first of all, realistically *expect* and *accept* a fair degree of incompatibility in virtually any marriage. So your wife is over-fastidious, while you incline to be reasonably sloppy; or your husband is a chain smoker, while you think the filthy weed is evil-smelling and cancer-producing; or your mate speaks with an intonation that somewhat grates on your ears. Is it really so odd and so heinous for him or her to behave so differently from you? Can you truly not stand her sloppiness or his smoking? Are you actually being done in by the other's "undesirable" behavior?

Happiness, as has been pointed out by several profound thinkers for many decades, is a ratio between what you expect and what you get. If, in marriage, you expect your mate to do everything you want, to be everything you would like him or her to be, you are bound to be disappointed. If your marital expectations are reasonable, disillusionment with your spouse will be virtually impossible.

2. Incompatibilities of temperament, physique, or tastes can, to a moderate extent, be worked at and changed. If your

48

spouse immensely enjoys spaghetti, and you are unenthusiastic about seeing people eat spaghetti, it is unlikely that any amount of effort on your part is going to induce him to start disliking spaghetti, or even to forego eating it in spite of his liking for it. It is possible, however, that your own lack of enthusiasm in this regard is the result of an arbitrary prejudice which you could well, for your own sake, surrender. Perhaps you could work on *your* prejudice instead of *his* tastes.

Again, if your spouse is unusually sloppy about his personal habits, perhaps his acquiring neater or cleaner habits is not impossible; probably it would even do him some good, in terms of increased enjoyment, if he did discipline himself better in this respect. If, without nagging or blaming him in any way, you *calmly* proceeded to try to teach him to be neater or more cleanly, his preferences in this connection would gradually become closer to your own, and this kind of "incompatibility" between the two of you would vanish.

The main trick here, however, consists of picking on a habit of your spouse which *actually* is doing him some harm and which he would benefit from changing and then calmly, unpunitively, and uncritically persuading him that it really *is* for his good, and not merely for yours, to change. Moreover, the more you love your spouse *in spite of* his obnoxious habit, instead of hating him *because of* it, the more likelihood there will be that he will be in a changing mood. Out of love, husbands and wives will frequently do much; out of being nagged, they will more frequently stew much.

3. Incompatible tastes and interests can sometimes be limited in their obnoxiousness by careful planning and mutual consent. Thus, a husband who adores deafeningly loud music may be encouraged to listen to it when his wife is visiting or may be induced to construct a specially sound-proofed room in the house, where he can play away as loudly as he likes.

A wife who is careless about putting away her underthings may be tactfully induced to confine these wandering undergar-

49

ments, at most, to the bedroom instead of the whole house.

A spouse who enjoys nothing more than going to the theater at least once a week may, by mutual consent, be catered to in this respect once every other week or once a month; or may be encouraged to go sometimes with another person than his or her mate; or may be catered to once a week provided that the mate is also allowed to do what he or she desires—such as buying a boat or redecorating the house.

Compromises in these respects are frequently feasible and worth the trouble of talking things out and coming to mutually accepted terms. Sometimes, this just will not work; for the mate who gives in to the other may build up enormous resentment in doing so. But in many respects every marriage must be a matter of live and let live, of give and take, of compromise and forgiveness. Otherwise, marital domesticity is not likely to work out with *any* mate that the non-compromiser may choose.

4. Perhaps the very best way to make the proper allowances for marital incompatibility is to place a much greater emphasis on mate *selection* than is usually done in our culture. Marriage, as we said before, consists of more than love; and although it is rather silly for most individuals, today, to marry anyone whom they do not love, it is equally silly for them to marry everyone whom they do. It is far wiser instead for one to choose, out of the many possible mates that one could and perhaps even does already love, that partner who, quite naturally and spontaneously, has a high degree of temperamental and preferential compatibility with one.

Stated a little differently: if, before you marry, you make quite certain that you know your potential wife or husband as thoroughly as possible; if you regretfully but firmly eliminate all those candidates who, however madly attached you may be to them, just do not seem to have the qualities that you would like to *live with* for the next fifty years or so; and if you virtually live with your final choice or choices for at least several months before you take him or her to the altar;—under these conditions of strict selectivity, you are far more likely to wed someone who is naturally and easily compatible with you than if you approach marrying in a less discriminating way. Even under the most rigorous circumstances of premarital scrutiny —even, for example, if you literally live with a would-be mate for a year before marrying him or her—you may still make a serious error in picking a highly compatible partner. But this way, at least, your chances of so doing are measurably reduced.

5. Another prophylactic mode of minimizing possible incompatibility in marriage is for the courting couple to de-emphasize romance. Thus, those who are going steady or are engaged can spend a good deal of time together in situations which take romantic expression out of the main spotlight. Love-making is the most enjoyable of recreational activities; but, if courting couples spend most of their time making love, they will learn relatively little about many personality traits of each other that are important to close day-by-day living. Fun-spoiling as it may sound, couples who are seriously thinking about getting married would often do well to budget their love-making time and, instead, spend considerable time and effort getting to know each other non-romantically *in a wide variety of social experiences.*

6. Marital compatibility can and often should be tested, during the premarital stage, *in action* rather than only in words. Although two romantically attracted individuals can easily maintain various verbal pretensions, it is much harder for them consistently to fool themselves when the chips of real activity are down. If Sue, for example, is interested in drama and if George professes great pleasure in reading Shakespearian tragedy aloud by the fireside, it might well be best for Sue to get George to start reading, rather than to take his romance-inspired word for it. When it comes to the showdown, is George full of excuses and quickly bored with the Shakespearian declamations? Would he rather kiss Sue's pretty little mouth than listen to her interpretation of Prince Hamlet's

psychosis? Sue needs to know; and she darned well better —*before* the announcements are sent out.

Action is apt to be most revealing of basic compatibility for marriage (or its lack thereof) when the interested couple experience pursuits and surroundings which, in the usual course of courtship, they may rarely encounter. If Ed has always ducked going to formal teas, that is precisely the kind of affair to which Sally should take him. He is likely to be awkward and ill at ease, and Sally should see how she likes this smooth fellow when he's ruffled or embarrassed. And as for sweet, beautiful, and well-mannered Sally, Ed should preferably discover how she behaves at novel as well as familiar situations. If she has never bowled, for example, Ed should take her to the nearest bowling alley. How does he like that cool number as she shows difficulty in even lifting, let alone rolling, the bowling ball? Is this awkward, perspiring, possibly peeved Sally still the girl for him? Or does it take a few straight shots of romance in the moonlight of lover's lane for Sally or Ed to feel again that the other is all the sweet things of life? If this is required, this couple may have reason to suspect that its marital compatibility would not be independently strong but might well be a feeble thing which leans upon the love-sex drive for support.

7. There is another old-fashioned, but fairly effective, aid in testing for potential compatibility in marriage: *time*. Especially if a couple keeps trying out a good variety of unromantic action experiences together, time works well in exposing character traits and habit patterns that are somewhat less than ideal. Even young romance can not perpetually maintain a blinding razzle-dazzle. The very best of "lines," given time, shows its cracks. The most even-tempered people, tested by time and unromantic experiences, often reveal deeper and less even feelings. The most lovable more than occasionally appear unlovely at the seams. The curtain of romance is made of wispy

silk, not iron, and time permits glances behind the curtain to see whether intimations of secure companionship are lurking solidly behind.

8. Any couple that really wants to be honest about testing for compatibility in marriage can recruit wonderful allies from families and friends. Relatives and old associates know the least endearing traits of the individual even better than he or she sometimes does. They can be helpful in revealing undesirable characteristics in several significant ways:

a. Like it or not, we have all been molded by our family and friendly associations. Something of what your prospective marital partner sees in your relatives and associates, he is likely to meet with sooner or later in you. Right now, romance may be clouding his view of your family-inculcated traits; but will it cloud his view of the same traits when your sisters and your cousins and your aunts display them? Quite probably not.

b. The revealing of pre-romance friendships is often helpful to the prediction of post-marital compatibility because such associations have usually been built about long-standing interests and personality preferences of the individual. If Jack spent most of his time with people of the poolroom, beer-joint, rock-'n-roll variety whom Lillian finds repulsive, the chances are good that he may turn to similar associations after marriage, when he becomes less preoccupied with romance. If Lillian's friends prior to Jack's inspiring entrance into her life were largely of the gossipy, superficial, inane category, it is probable that she will revert to type again after marriage.

c. Families and friends can help bring out the relaxed habits and manners of the individual as distinguished from his or her "company manners." If one observes one's prospective mate over a period of time in casual settings with his or her own friends, the personality characteristics thus exposed are more likely to resemble those that will appear after marriage than the traits that he or she tends to exhibit on dates. If a potential husband or wife has been putting on the dog during courtship, his or her family and friends will be apt to strip away any such phony pretenses.

Tests of compatibility such as those we have just been outlining can certainly become tedious. However!—they are often considerably less tedious than living for a few decades with an individual with whom one lacks real compatibility. Granted that, trying though they are, these tests (as we previously noted) carry with them no guarantee for making a marriage gloriously compatible, the fact remains that they may well improve a couple's chances of discovering in advance whether or not they will get along well together after the marital knot has been tied.

5

Problem Solving in Marriage

Let us suppose that, through following some set of procedures similar to those just outlined for picking a reasonably compatible mate, or by using some magical hunt-and-peck system of your own, you have managed to marry a mate who is in many respects ideal for you, and whose relatively few basic incompatibilities you somehow are able to accept. Will, under these admirable circumstances, problems still be likely to arise in your marriage? They definitely will.

The difference between an unsuccessful and a successful marriage is not that the former includes serious problems and the latter lacks them. Rather, it is that successfully married couples begin with some degree of basic compatibility and then go on to develop skillful ways of handling problems that inevitably arise. The unsuccessful couples, on the other hand, become increasingly snowed under by their problems—which, in content, are likely to be little different from the problems that successful couples learn to handle.

Methods for dealing adequately with marital problems often develop spontaneously and unconsciously in successful marriages. There are probably no general, sure-fire rules which, if memorized and applied, will invariable lead to problem-solving bliss. It is possible, however, to delineate certain methods that have proved helpful in many relationships.

First and most important of these, perhaps, is the specific concept of problem solving itself—or the idea that human beings, usually, *are* able to control their so-called feelings and emotions and to regulate their own lives, instead of being driven by organic, unconscious, social, or cosmic forces.

As we pointed out previously, when discussing the main irrational ideas that lead to marital disturbance, one of the main and most pernicious of these notions is the belief that most human unhappiness is caused or forced on one by outside people and events, or by inner drives that are uncontrollable, and that one has virtually no control over one's emotions and cannot help feeling badly on many occasions. This belief, when translated into the idea that married couples cannot really control their feelings, and cannot approach their difficulties in an objective, problem-solving manner (much as they would approach any other practical life difficulty), is especially self- and marriage-defeating.

It is fortunately true, however, that virtually all the disturbances, upsets, and difficulties of marriage *are* nothing but problems—that is, questions and issues proposed for consideration and solution. And it is equally true that man, when he has realistic faith in his own powers, is the greatest problem solver that has yet been invented, and that even complex marital hassles and irritations can usually be resolved by him when he puts his information-gathering and reasoning powers to good use.

Consider the predicament of Jane and Ivan Orlanski. Although they both felt that they cared considerably for each other, their marriage, from the beginning, was no bed of roses, no bowl of cherries, and no great shakes. Jane had two miscarriages before she bore a rather sickly child; and she had to spend a great deal of time nursing her mother, who lived in a nearby apartment. Ivan, in spite of constant plugging away at his small importing business, had several unfortunate setbacks. Since Jane, because of tiredness, physical disability, and some amount of disturbance over her two miscarriages, was not too often sexually receptive, and since Ivan was just as highly sexed at the age of thirty-eight as he had been during his late teens, he had a continually roving eye, and only with great difficulty kept himself from roaming into the beds of willing secretaries, waitresses, and neighbors' wives who kept becoming attracted to him. Jane, who sensed what was going on, was often depressedly jealous.

When Jane and Ivan came for marriage counseling because of their predicament, they both had the same basic question to ask the counselor: *Could* anything be done about Ivan's propensity to have a roving eye? They both seemed to assume that their sex problem was caused by the fact that, biologically, Ivan was highly sexed and promiscuously inclined; while Jane was only moderately interested in sex, and her desires could easily be killed by physical or emotional upsets. Viewing their sex difficulty in this light, they saw no possibility of changing or controlling it because of its physical basis. Consequently, they dreaded even facing this important issue in their lives, and only with great hesitation had come for counseling.

As soon as the counselor insisted, at the very first session with both Jane and Ivan, that all they had was a *problem* and that virtually all problems are soluble once one devotes enough time and energy to examining and working on them, both

57

these partners were immensely relieved. They knew that they loved each other and that they *wanted* to work at solving their difficulty. Once they began to view it as a problem that could, theoretically, be solved, they felt confident that they would eventually understand it fully and resolve it.

With this new *attitude* toward their sex differences, it was not difficult for the counselor to show Jane and Ivan some alternative ways of behaving in their marriage.

Jane was shown that Ivan's roving eye was natural enough under the circumstances, that it did not in any way prove that he loved her any the less, and that it was at least in part caused by her own giving up too easily on satisfying him sexually. When she understood this, she became much less depressed and was able to give Ivan more than sufficient sexual release by non-coital techniques when she herself was uninterested in having intercourse. She also became more interested on more occasions in having it.

Ivan, when he began to accept the fact that he was not a monster or a pervert for appreciating the charms of many of the women with whom he came into contact, stopped blaming himself for so doing, lost his obsessive guilt, and became considerably less interested in these women. As his non-coital and coital relations with Jane increased, he began to be even less absorbed in adulterous thoughts and he was able to devote more concentrated thoughts and energies to his business, which began to flourish.

Within two months after they first came for marriage counseling, Jane and Ivan both felt that their sexual problem was almost entirely solved and that their love for each other was stronger than ever.

The concept, then, that one *can* approach marital difficulties in a problem-solving manner is, in itself, one of the best possible anxiety reducers. Once one firmly believes in this idea, it often becomes only a matter of simple choice to pick this or that alternative which may solve a serious marital situ-

58

ation. Eventually, if such alternatives are calmly selected and given an honest try, one is almost bound to work reasonably well and the "great" or "terrible" problem is solved.

In going about the actual solution of marital difficulties, once the husband and wife fully conceive of these difficulties as being potentially solvable, probably the most important of all methods is effective communication between the mates. In a later chapter, we shall discuss in detail various communication problems which often develop in marriage and ways of dealing with them. Here we shall more generally note that modern marriage depends upon good communication in much the same fashion as do so many other aspects of contemporary life.

There is an old saying that it takes two to make an argument. But it is also true that it takes two to make a discussion, to work out a solution to a problem, to learn a workable compromise for a difficulty. If, by going silent or in some other way failing to cooperate, one party to a marriage fails to communicate adequately, the relationship starts to disintegrate. When disturbances ruffle a marriage, silence is not golden but destructive.

Just being willing to talk about a marital problem is not, of course, all that is needed to face it squarely and to do something constructive about it. Two other rather obvious (yet often ignored) essentials of problem solving must be met. First, each partner must admit the existence of a difficulty about which communication is required. This may sound silly, but there is often a tendency, especially early in marriage, for individuals to deny marital rifts and to ignore them until they have developed to threatening proportions. This is because many couples feel insecure and find it easier, like the legendary ostrich, to hide their heads than to face their anxieties.

The second requisite for unraveling a marital problem is to determine as accurately as possible its particular nature and sources. This again sounds simple enough, but is easier said than done. One obstacle to understanding a problem is that

59

its roots are often largely hidden—are not available to the couple's conscious awareness. This is one of the most important reasons why even exceptionally intelligent and basically well-adjusted couples sometimes need the professional help of a counselor or psychotherapist to get a clear understanding of the true nature of their problems.

Take, by way of illustration, the case of Sid and Joan Masterson. They realized that they kept getting terribly angry at each other, but were not quite certain why. Sid knew that he did not approve of Joan's over-attachment, as he thought it was, to her mother; and Joan realized that she did not like Sid's thorough-going absorption with his legal work. But each acknowledged that the other's involvements had some degree of legitimacy and could not explain why they were *so* angry about these involvements.

It was not difficult to determine, after a half dozen marriage counseling sessions in which Sid and Joan, at their own request, were seen simultaneously, that Sid was really disturbed not so much by Joan's attachment to her mother as by the fact that he could not get along at all with his own mother. Being guilty about his own poor relations with his mother, he was constantly reminded by Joan's closeness with her mother that he was not doing the "right" thing himself. Then he would become inordinately jealous of and angry at Joan and would go out of his way to try to interfere with her filial devotion.

At the same time, Joan, who was actually proud of Sid's professional activities, felt insecure about her own role in life. Their only child was away at college and she had not bothered, over the years, to acquire any vitally absorbing interest outside of raising this child. Now, in her late thirties, she really had nothing essential to do around the house. Sid's long hours at the office, and the work which he often took home, left her with still more idle time on her hands. In the circumstances, she was just as jealous of his professional activity as he was of her good relations with her mother.

When these underlying wishes, guilts, and jealousies of Sid and Joan were brought to the surface—which was not difficult even though they were "unconscious" or (more accurately) unobserved—much of their anger against each other began to evaporate.

Instead of Sid's telling himself, as he had been doing, "There goes my goddam wife, again, nauseatingly giving in to her mother!" he was now able to say to himself, "If Joan can understand and get along with her mother so well, why can't I make a little more effort to understand and get along better with mine?"

Joan stopped inciting herself with, "Damn it, why must he be so intent on getting back at work again, leaving me all to my lonesome?" She now was able to say to herself, "What am *I* going to do while Sid keeps so marvelously busy? I'd better go out and find some enjoyable interest of my *own.*"

Within several weeks of talking to themselves in this radically different way, Sid began to get along better with his mother and Joan became absorbed in producing a play for her local sisterhood group. They both had become consciously aware of the real reasons for their previous hostility to each other. In becoming so conscious, they had been able to do something effective to undermine these reasons.

Another difficulty in determining the nature and source of a marital problem is that the problem is seldom, if ever, one-sided. Both husband and wife, in trying to face and get at the root of a difficulty, must look at disagreeable things not only in relation to the other but also to themselves. Almost no one enjoys discovering unpleasant facts about himself, and some people seem unable to endure the anxiety which arises in the process of such discovery.

Facing marital problems squarely is not the relatively simple and detached process of peering through a microscope at the genes of a fruit fly. It is more appropriately likened to looking into a set of front and back mirrors as one tries to probe a boil

61

on the rear of one's neck. Highly nervous and subjective people do not tend to do too well at this kind of self-confrontation.

Relatively mature and less disturbed marital partners, however, can work at achieving some degree of objectivity in discussing their marital difficulties. They can stand off from themselves to some extent, accept the view that they each doubtlessly have made and will keep making mistakes and that it is no crime or catastrophe to fall into error. Because they are thereby rendered less defensive and more willing to accept responsibility for their own blunders and shortcomings, they are then able to listen to and try to understand the partner's point of view, to make an active and consistent effort to acquire additional information and skills (which may include professional consultations), and to get more and more practice in viewing themselves, their partners, and their marital relationships with considerable objectivity.

Propensity toward self-blame, in other words, is probably the greatest single barrier to open-minded marital communication. Spouses who think that it is terrible and frightful if they themselves are in the wrong will naturally tend to assume that the other is to blame for existing difficulties. Starting with this other-blaming assumption, they will, of course, not really listen to the mate's side of the discussion; and intercommunication becomes abnormally restricted.

Spouses, on the other hand, who are willing to accept full responsibility for their own failures and mistakes, because they truly believe that to err is human and that human beings largely learn by trial and error, will much more unprejudicedly view their mates' side of the story, and will thus be able to bring to light the true facts of major marital differences. Moreover, if and when such facts are brought to light, and their partners are shown to be mistaken or misled, they will then tend to accept these mistakes as normal instead of heinous, and will make more ado about rectifying than carping about them.

Another most important aspect of problem-solving in marriage (as in any other aspect of life) is that of persistent and consistent effort. Love and hard work, as we previously implied, may sometimes not be enough to assure marital success; since, where there is an unusually great initial incompatibility between the mates, all the work in the world may not be sufficient to overcome it. When some goodly degree of basic compatibility exists in a marriage, however—as it probably exists in most contemporary matings—problems may usually be solved by persistent effort. The married partner will do well to seek perpetually new and alternative solutions, instead of quickly giving up after a few cavalier attempts at resolution.

Many couples become too easily discouraged. When their first somewhat random efforts to face and handle a difficulty fail to bring dramatic positive results, they assume that they *never* can achieve such results and give up. Their efforts, or lack of them, are somewhat reminiscent of the person who picked up a book as a child, saw that he could not read it, and so never wasted his time with books again. Marital problem solving is a much more complicated skill than reading and cannot be acquired in a few easy lessons. Often the uninstructed newlywed is about as well prepared for marriage as the uninstructed five-year-old child is prepared for reading.

Even when the sources of a marital difficulty have been accurately determined, strong desires on the part of the mates to make the changes agreed upon do not necessarily assure rapid success. Old habits, backed by old ways of thinking, persist; and new ones are sometimes difficult to acquire. Patience and persistence are unavoidable requirements for marital problem solving.

Harry and Sandra Browne were able to see fairly quickly and easily that their quarrels over how to raise their son, Theodore, stemmed largely from the fact that Harry had been pampered as a child and did *not* want to spoil Theodore; while Sandra had been rather deprived as a child and leaned over backward to see that their son was not deprived. But when it came to

63

putting into action the middle-of-the-road policy of child-raising on which they both apparently agreed, they found that Harry still tended to be over-severe and Sandra over-liberal with Theodore. Only by patiently working out a system where they both *objectively* watched each other's behavior with the child and *calmly* reminded each other of too positive and too negative extremes that were taken, did they finally, months after their initial perception of and agreement about the problem, manage to adopt a fairly moderate policy of interacting with Theodore.

Good counter-balances for patience and persistence in marital problem solving are good humor and temperance. Some young couples try to tackle too many problems at a time in a spirit of grim, do-or-die earnestness. These couples tend to compound the everyday tensions of marriage in the very process of trying to reduce them. They have to learn to be more moderate in their demands on themselves and to realize that home isn't built in a day.

The old adage that a couple should "never go to sleep on a problem" is, at times, misleading. Some problems are far too complex to solve in one sitting and a bleary-eyed and irritable couple at 3:00 A.M. is less likely to see a solution than the same couple well-rested eight, ten, or forty hours later.

Sometimes, instead of being promptly arrived at in the course of discussions, marital solutions are formulated and worked out unconsciously in the daily living which follows such discussions. Stages of attack can at times be scheduled. First there can be discussion; then a period for contemplation and possible action; then perhaps a review of the situation some time later.

Marriage, moreover, should not normally be one continual round of discussion following discussion following discussion. As much fun as possible should be had during and in-between the problem sessions. A light touch, a little laugh at one's own mock-tragic seriousness, a refusal to let a yet unsolved problem spill over into the rest of life, a resisting of the temptation to feel sorry for oneself and to pout or rage—all these help. If the modern married couple must have a maxim to live by in this Age of Anxiety, a most appropriate one might be: Take it easy! Tomorrow will be another, and just possibly a brighter, day.

More and more couples in contemporary America are finding that their best efforts to handle their own problems are ineffective. Some of these couples are too proud, ignorant, fearful, or indifferent to seek help. Sometimes one partner is willing and the other is not. But, increasingly, both husbands and wives are showing a willingness to admit their need for help, and to seek the counsel of a psychologist, psychiatrist, social worker, marriage counselor, clergyman, or other specialized and qualified person. This certainly makes just as much sense as their seeking, at various times of crisis in their personal and married lives, the aid of a competent lawyer, physician, or accountant.

Some couples who look for help with their marital problems fail to find it. Some unwisely lean upon the willingly offered but often ineffective and biased aid of their relatives or friends, who, very likely, have seriously unresolved marriage problems of their own. Still others fall into the hands of quacks. But a growing number are getting professional assistance, which is usually available on a private basis in most sizable cities of the country, and which may also be obtained through family agencies, clinics, universities, churches, and other groups. A directory of marriage counseling services will be found at the back of this book.

The main point is that, in seeking help for their marital problems, husbands and wives should (a) look into their own hearts and stop blaming themselves, (b) non-critically try to communicate openly and frankly with their mate, (c) calmly persist at considering all possible alternative solutions to their difficulties, (d) take a relatively relaxed, not too serious attitude toward themselves and their partners, (e) get all possible relevant psychological and marital information they can discover (from lectures, group discussions, and books like this one), and (f) finally, if serious problems still persist, go for professional aid. With this kind of a multifaceted attack on their marital problems, they are almost certain to go a long way toward solving them.

6

Can We Be Intelligent about Marriage?

The man who was sitting in front of my desk had a handsome, determined, intelligent appearance. He was twenty-eight years old and had two children, aged five and three. He worked nights as an orderly in a hospital and attended medical school during the day. He ate, slept, and saw his family in occasional quick snatches between his job and his studies. In two more years he would be finished with medical school and this rigorous routine. He asked his wife to be patient about the whole thing. But she was tired of being patient; she had fallen in love with another man.

I heard Mr. Medic's story out and asked just a few questions. I offered him no advice other than the suggestion that he

67

practice the patience he had been preaching until I had a chance to talk with his wife.

Mrs. Medic was a pretty girl. She also appeared intelligent, calm, and poised.

"I tried to keep this from happening," she said, "but it happened anyhow. Arnold and I married eight years ago when he was twenty and I was only seventeen. He was just out of the Army and had a year of high school to finish. But he had this big-deal drive to be a doctor. So he did his year of high school in one semester and started to college on the G.I. Bill. I worked those first three years until Kenny was born.

"At first it was fun. I felt a part of the big deal, and there were a lot of little ways I could help Arnold. But when I had to stop working because of Kenny, and he had to take on a full-time job, things began to get rough. When he got through pre-med and entered med school, life got *really* rough. Since he's been in med school, I almost literally never see him. And when I do, during the summer, he's poring over something like an anatomy book and is always as cross as a bear.

"I don't really blame him. I understand. But he's not a husband or a father or a companion or even as good a friend as the milkman or the letter carrier. Living with what he may some day become is like living with a ghost in reverse. And, besides, how do I know that things will be any better after he gets out of med school? Then he'll work day and night in his internship and his years of residency. And even then he'll have a book in his hand when he makes love to me—if and when, I should say—because he'll want to take his Boards in surgery a year sooner than anybody else. And he'll have to know something anybody has ever written on anything even vaguely connected with anything they might ask him in his exams—even if it is impossible to know it. Or especially if it's impossible. Oh, he'll make a fine surgeon; but as a husband and father he just plain stinks.

"Am I getting too long-winded? Well, anyhow, so what did

I do? For eight years I was a model wife. Make that seven years. This past year I've complained. Bitched, I believe, is the proper word. I've tried to get Arnold to ease up. I told him that if he didn't, something would have to break. I told 'the great doctor' that something had to give. Well, something did. It was me.

"What happened was scarcely unique, I know. You must make a chalk mark on a mental blackboard every time you hear about a triangle; and I'll bet you, in your business, have a darned well marked-up blackboard! Anyhow, I met this man. I don't like to call him 'this man,' although, believe me, he's been called worse than that lately. For drama-kicks, his name is Ken, the same as my older boy. Anyhow, I met him at the YWCA, of all places. He's really an awfully nice guy. He and I both fought falling in love, but it kept happening to us. Sounds corny, doesn't it?

"I really didn't go out looking for love, although I suspect you and Freud wouldn't believe me. But because I knew I was love-hungry, I picked a nice safe spot like the YWCA. I felt I'd go stir crazy if I didn't get out of the house. So I picked a harmless place like the Y, and I picked a harmless activity like a course in short-story writing. I've always liked writing and I thought it would be something I could do to express my own personality in the lonely times without Arnold. But, you know the rest—the 'harmless activity' boomeranged. Enter from the backstage, center, the handsome villain in the role of the instructor of the course in short-story writing. Only he's not particularly handsome. And, if he's a villain, he's the kind of villain I'd like to live with the rest of my life instead of a hero like Arnold."

What should a marriage counselor do in a situation like this one? Persons who believe that divorce is always wrong, or right only under circumstances of some horrible wrongdoing, would have a ready answer: the counselor should force Mrs. Medic to return to her husband. But return to what husband? A kind of phantom of the possible future, as she herself suggested? Even if I could so persuade her (which is doubtful, for a counselor can't just magically reverse major trends in people's deep-seated feelings), would it be best for her? For the children? Even for Mr. Medic? I doubted it, but reserved judgment until I had another interview with the husband.

"It is true, as she is frank to admit, that your wife has been emotionally unfaithful to you," I said to Mr. Medic. "But neither of us, nor for that matter anyone else, is in a position to judge her. This is something that she has to work out in terms of her own attitudes and feelings. The practical question that you and your wife and I must work with right now is: Where do you go from here? Is the marriage still workable? And, if so, under what conditions?"

"I think it is workable," said Mr. Medic. "And whether Grace likes it or not, she can't trade me in for a professor who drools a lot of sweet words at her."

"Let's try to forget the merits and demerits of the professor for the time being," I said, "and look at what you have to offer your wife. The thing she seems to want most from you—or formerly wanted from you, since she is frankly indifferent at present—is love and attention for herself and the children. Can you supply this?"

"No, I can't," he said. "There's no time to do it right now, and you can't give love and attention without time. It's not that I don't feel it. But, as I've told Grace a thousand times, there's only two more years of this, and then I'll be through med school."

"What about the amount of time you'll have for five years or so after you're out of school?" I asked. I paraphrased for him the dim outlook taken on those years by his wife.

"Yeah, I suppose she's got something there," Medic said. "If you're going to be a really good surgeon, and I intend to be, you really don't have any time to relax even after you knock off your Boards. But other doctors' wives settle for this deal. Why can't Grace?"

"There are a number of answers to that question," I said. "First of all, there are many wives of physicians who do not 'settle for this deal.' Divorced physicians are by no means a rarity and unhappy-though-still-married wives of doctors are even less scarce.

"Secondly, some doctors have wives who both give to and expect less from life than your wife does. We have to think in terms of the kind of person *she* is and not the kinds of persons other physicians or medical students have as wives. Some seem to get more satisfaction from the prestige associated with their husband's work; some seem to want less love and attention; some are probably basically more fearful of critical judgments of other people than your wife seems to be.

"And thirdly," I continued, "some men are either more fortunate or more capable of carrying both a medical career and a family. I don't mean this in any derogatory way. I know you have done exceptionally well both in supporting your family and going to medical school. And maybe it is mainly because you are less willing just to get by in school than are men who have equal family responsibilities. But the fact remains that you have neglected your home life much more completely than some of your colleagues. Matters directly related to your career always seem to come first with you and to push everything else, including your wife and children, out of your life. If you had a wife who accepted this, or at least was not too unhappy putting up with it, you wouldn't be facing a showdown now. But the fact is that she is the way she is. Let us face this fact."

"What you say is true enough. And it's also true that this is the way I'll always be. But it seems unfair that I have to lose my wife and children because I'm conscientious about my career."

71

"What's so unfair about it? Throughout human history men driven by single purposes have had to give up many things to pursue their goals. If medicine is that kind of purpose with you, then you have no great ground for complaint about giving up a family you'd enjoy mainly by theoretical possession. If, on the other hand, you can honestly state that your family means so much to you that you are willing to ease up—not give up, but ease up—on your medical career, I can help you keep your wife and children."

"I'd like to say I'd ease up," Mr. Medic said, "but I know it would be just words. I couldn't, even if I wanted to; and I don't honestly want to. Even if I quit my orderly job and let Grace go to work (she's wanted to, but I've been against it), I'd pour the new time that would be available into more study, not give it to her or the children. There's enough to keep me busy twenty-four hours a day for the next hundred years. I can't be just a so-so surgeon. I've got to be the best."

"Then I think you've solved your own problem," I said. "You certainly have a right to decide that you will give your life to a medical career. Even if it were a less worthy project, you'd still have that right. Nor do I think that anyone has any business trying to divert you from your purpose. But do you have the right to try to force your wife down this road with you? This I question. Anyhow, my question is theoretical —she's made it clear that she's not taking the trip."

"But she married me for better or worse, didn't she? And if she sticks with me, half the credit will be hers."

"Such credit, in terms of *her* outlook on life, would be like blood from a stone. Nothing to it. No satisfaction for her. Her main purpose in life seems to be to have a home with a loving and attentive husband and father for her children. She married you with the expectation that you would be that kind of person. Perhaps she was mistaken in having that expectation; but she did have it. You aren't now and don't intend to become the kind of person she expected you to be. That is your own prediction as well as hers. So she made a mistake. A very serious mistake, if you will. But what you're now saying is that the mistake she made at the age of seventeen is one she should be stuck with the rest of her life. Isn't that what you're saying?"

"You don't make it sound very pretty."

"I'm not trying to make it sound any particular way. I didn't write this script. I didn't compose this symphony, or cacophony, of marriage. You and your wife did. I agree that it doesn't 'sound pretty.' The question is whether or not the marriage, sounding less and less pretty, should go on for a lifetime. You say 'yes.' Your wife says 'no, I've had enough.' She believes she has the right to a second chance at her main life purpose. You seem to feel that she should remain chained to her original mistake. You can certainly make it difficult for her to divorce. I doubt if you can permanently prevent it."

"I don't believe in divorce."

"Forgive me, but that's about as sensible as saying: 'I don't believe in surgery.' I wouldn't be this blunt with you if I didn't know the church to which you nominally belong has a very liberal attitude toward divorce."

"I guess I just don't believe in failure in anything so important as marriage. And parenthood, too. It's true I don't really know my kids, and I haven't slept with my wife since sometime last August. Most of the time during the week I sleep at the hospital. And when I'm home on the weekend, I want literally to sleep, not make love. But I hate failure, and I hoped that Grace and I could still work this thing out."

"Perhaps you still could," I said. "But the only way you could do so would be through your own willingness to sacrifice certain aspects of your career. You've already said you can't, or won't, do that. Maybe even if you would, your wife wouldn't want to go on now. She may be beyond the point of emotional return. Sometimes when we say we refuse to fail, we have already failed and really mean that we hate to *admit* we failed. I think possibly this is your situation now."

"Maybe so," Medic said. "So now where do we go from here?"

Where we went from there was into an exploration of all sides of the triangle. I had some additional talks with Mr. and Mrs. Medic. I also talked with the professor. His course at the YWCA was a side issue with him, and he had a substantial position on the staff of a nearby university. He was himself divorced from a short-lived wartime marriage and seemed, indeed, to be what Mrs. Medic had described as "an awfully nice guy." He was not only eager to marry Grace but wanted to adopt and take over the support of the Medic children.

Mrs. Medic continued in psychotherapeutic counseling with me for several months. She wanted to work through some of her personal problems, including those connected with her unsatisfactory marital experiences and the shock of making an actual break. Although it might appear from the material quoted from the first interview with her that she was a most confident and self-contained person, much of her verbalization was bravado and a flare for drama. Underneath, she was a scared, but nevertheless courageous, young woman who needed help in working out a clearer conception of herself and her life role.

Once Mr. Medic was over the hump of admitting failure in his home life, his resistance to a divorce melted. His love for his wife and children was more theory than practice. His real passion was medicine, and he came soon to welcome the additional time he was given to devote himself to this first love. Relieved of the financial support of his family, he could drop his heavy full-time work and support himself with an easy part-time job, thus giving himself more time for study.

A relatively quick divorce was arranged. The last I heard

74

(two years later), there was a happy English professor's family which had just expanded from four to five members, and a Dr. Medic, who had just started a well-placed internship.

The Medic divorce may sound quite immoral to some readers. The school of thought which holds that divorce is *never* right is by no means dead. There is an organization, for example, which calls itself Divorcees Anonymous. Its leaders have been quoted as saying that they feel any divorce is a mistake. The organization is dedicated to saving people from the alleged horrors of divorce, somewhat analogously to the fashion that Alcoholics Anonymous is out to save habitual drunkards from the very real (for them) horrors of drink.

The comparison of divorce with alcohol is, we think, an inaccurate and unfortunate one. Both, it is true, can be misused in such a way that they become evils. But an alcoholic is one who has persistently demonstrated his inability to make proper use of alcohol, and most of those who are considering divorce are doing so for the first time. They (unlike the drunkards in relation to alcohol) have not *habitually* failed at marriage. If they had, it might make more sense to keep them from getting married again than to keep them in their present marriages against their will.

We shall discuss divorce in more detail in a later chapter. Let us get back to marriage right now. In the course of my last interview with Mr. Medic, he asked: "Can a person be intelligent about marrying?" My answer (which I amplified for him) was: "No, not very."

What Mr. Medic had in mind was the fact that he and Mrs. Medic had married when they were both immature emotionally and chronologically. Could, under those circumstances, the Medics have been more intelligent about marrying? Perhaps; but it would have been most difficult for them to see ahead and predict in advance the emotional and social difficulties that were going to occur—particularly when, a few years after they married, they were really different individuals, with quite different goals, from what they were when they were a seventeen-year-old bride and a twenty-year-old groom.

The fact is, as I said to Mr. Medic, none of us can be *too* intelligent about marrying. In our society, we tend to follow our feelings into marriage—to marry for love—rather than contracting what might be, from a social, economic, or intellectual point of view, a "worthwhile" relationship. But feelings are both the cause and effect of actions; and as our active experiences change, our feelings change. They, in turn, lead us into still different actions.

If the basic trend of events in our lives moves in such a way as to lead us apart in marriage, to develop in us feelings which are antagonistic to our mate, then it is not very realistic or intelligent for us to stay married. If, on the contrary, the basic course of events in our lives is favorable to our marital partnership, and strengthens our feelings of love and companionship, it is realistic and intelligent for us to stay married. To contend, however, that the application of our intelligence was the main determining factor in those marriages where the trend of events led to positive results is to delude ourselves. This is somewhat comparable to giving full credit to the intelligence of the people who pick the winning horse in the Kentucky Derby. They are, perhaps, intelligent in their choices; but also awfully lucky.

It is possible, to a limited degree, to make intelligent choices of both horses and spouses—both of which, at times, may pay off quite well. A person who is well-informed about the records and conditions of the horses in a race, the jockeys who will be riding, the nature of the weather and track conditions, etc., can be more intelligent than a person who is completely uninformed. If, however, the race is an honest one, all kinds of circumstances, unforeseen and uncontrolled by information and intelligence, can intervene to make the winner some other horse than the one so "intelligently" chosen by the bettor. It

76

is similarly possible to use one's intelligence to increase the odds of success and reduce the risks of failure in marriage. But nothing even close to an "unbeatable formula" exists for either horseracing or marrying.

What are some of the things which help people to be more intelligent than average about marrying? We have already discussed some of the ways of getting to know more about the person you may be thinking of marrying and of pretesting some elements of your mutual compatibility.

Even more important, in many respects, is getting to know more about yourself. What kind of person are you? What are your major life goals, values, interests? Which of these are really most important to you? Not *supposed* to be important, but truly of greatest importance to you? How do some of your ideas of what you want for yourself in marriage match, or fail to match, with some of your non-marital ambitions? What experiences have you had in life that make you feel that your answers to such questions as the foregoing are reliable and valid?

Stated differently: are you confident, from observing yourself in action in a variety of life situations, that you really know what you think and feel about yourself in and out of marriage? Or are you merely mouthing conventional ideas, borrowed thoughts about what a person presumably *should* think and feel and do? If the latter, then don't you think it about time that you discovered what *you* really want to do in life, what *you* would truly enjoy?

This especially goes, as far as marriage is concerned, for your vital or main interests. Every marital relationship, as we pointed out previously, has to be something of a compromise, has to include some sacrifices of interest. If many of your minor interests—such as eating Chinese food or looking at the late late show in television—have to go by the board because your mate won't share them and objects to your participating in them very often, that may be too bad, but your marriage will

77

probably survive. If, however, even a single one of your most vital interests must be sacrificed to marriage, beware! If, for example, you do not merely enjoy Chinese food, but are an outstanding authority on it, and are compiling a massive tome on Chinese cooking; or if your one main enjoyment in life is viewing the late late television show—then you really have a serious problem if your spouse objects to these pursuits. Like our Mr. Medic of several pages back, you may have to choose between your vital interest and your marriage.

The better you know yourself and your own life bents before you marry, and the more knowledge you have of your beloved's possible objections to you and those bents, the safer you are likely to be in making a marital choice. The more ignorant you are about yourself and your potential partner in these respects, the more disaster you are courting.

Speaking of self-knowledge, what about your own degree of emotional maturity? As we also noted previously, one of the greatest blocks to a good marriage is the emotional disturbance of the participants. Well—how about your own disturbance? Are you realistic, patient, forgiving, and unfearful enough to risk your marrying anyone? Mr. Medic, as we saw, held faster to fantasy than he did to reality. Although the events of his marriage had accumulated considerable proof to the contrary, he kept dreaming that he could be the kind of husband and father his wife expected *and* the kind of physician and surgeon his ambition compulsively demanded. He immaturely refused to see that these extreme goals were incompatible and had to be helped to the point where he could face giving up or modifying one or the other goal.

How about you? Do you want to be a great husband *and* a self-made billionaire? a terrific father *and* a world-explorer? a devoted wife *and* an outstanding clubwoman? Are your basic goals compatible with what you, your spouse, or your children really want? Look into your own heart. Don't avoid this most important issue.

Knowing oneself is a lifelong process. Emotional maturity is similarly never complete. But to some extent you can know yourself and attain emotional maturity *before* you seriously consider marrying. And to some extent you had better! Marriage, rather than solving any problems, usually creates two or more where there previously was one. Are you *really* prepared for thus adding to your difficulties and concerns? If so, you may well, in the process of being married, add appreciably to your self-knowledge and your maturity. But it is still advisable to start from scratch! That is why, these days, so many thousands of couples and individuals go for premarital counseling and psychotherapy—to make certain that, even before they attempt a marital partnership, they have some significant degree of self-knowledge, and freedom from disturbance.

In addition to self-knowledge, a married person also needs a high degree of self-love and self-respect. You can know full well how to drive a car but refrain from turning on the gas, pushing the proper buttons, and swinging down the highway. You can also know a great deal about yourself without putting this knowledge to *good use*. Self-love and self-respect are gained not only by knowing yourself and your potential and actual mistakes—but by your acquiring a sane, non-blaming philosophy of life so that you can calmly and unmasochistically correct your blunders, prevent yourself from perpetuating them indefinitely.

Self-love and self-respect are particularly important in marriage; since few, if any of us, can truly care for and help others when we loathe ourselves. There is an all too human tendency for us to get irritated with others in direct proportion to our irritation with ourselves. Sometimes, we may even refuse to acknowledge our own errors, and project them, and the blame for them, onto others with whom we intimately associate—particularly our spouses.

Self-love and self-respect are phrases that carry many different meanings, some of them invidious, to many badly brought up individuals. Thus, some of us are raised to feel that it is conceited, immoral, "selfish" to think highly of ourselves and not to keep sacrificing ourselves for others. Yet to the psychologist it is clear that a person who does not distinctly love and respect himself cannot truly love and respect, or fully see the point of view of, another human being.

Perhaps this point can be understood better by looking at the case of Mrs. Kayl. Mrs. Kayl had been divorced twice at the time she came to see me. Her third husband had just moved out of the home to a hotel the night before she called me for an appointment. The departure of this third husband induced Mrs. Kayl to think (at least tentatively) that there might be something wrong with *her*. What, though? She was a beautiful, seemingly intelligent, emotionally warm-appearing woman in her late twenties. She looked like the kind of woman men would fight for, not desert.

"I have always devoted myself to the man I was married to," Mrs. Kayl said, "for I never believed in any sort of marriage with reservations. Even when their demands seemed unreasonable, I tried to meet them. I also tried to anticipate their desires and do all sorts of extra things for them. I was most economical, and did my own sewing and fixing over furniture to save them money. I never put my own interests ahead of theirs.

"And what did I get for my trouble? My first husband began drinking more and more until he finally had to be institutionalized. When he was drunk, he would swear at me and revile me and sometimes even beat me. Even then, though, I didn't leave him. I forgave him. But when he came out of the sanitarium, he insisted on a divorce and went to Florida and got one.

"My second husband didn't drink. I made sure of that before I married him. At first he was wonderful to me, but then I found out from a friend that he was having an affair.

He told me he was working late nights, but he was really having this affair with a girl at his office. And it wasn't because he didn't have sex at home. I never turned him down, even when I was dead tired. But he became less and less interested in me sexually. He turned *me* down. I forgave him this affair and said we could make a new start. But he vulgarly told me what I could do with my new start. He said he wanted to sleep with a real woman, not with perfection and forgiveness. I didn't know what he meant. I pleaded with him. But he stopped coming home nights and wouldn't sit down and talk things over with me the few times I would see him. After about six months of that kind of life, I divorced him.

"Then Charlie, that's Mr. Kayl, came into my life. His name is really Edward, but everyone calls him Charlie because —oh, I guess it doesn't matter to you. Anyhow, Charlie was absolutely perfect. He never drank anything except an occasional beer, and he was certainly no lady's man. He was very kind and understanding and devoted. I knocked myself out for him in marriage even more than I did for the first two. And then, after only three months, and when I thought everything was just lovely, he packed himself up and said he was leaving.

" 'Leaving!' I said. 'What have I done? What's wrong?'

" 'Everything's wrong,' he said. 'I feel as if I'm doing a stretch in a mental hospital for the criminally insane or for imbeciles or something. You're not going to drive *me* to drink or to sleeping with floozies the way you did your first two husbands. I'm getting the hell out while I know what I'm doing.'

"And out he walked. And I know he really means for good. And I honestly don't know what I did wrong. Is he right? Did I drive Dick to drink and Marvin to other women?"

"No," I answered. "No one is *driven* to drink by the behavior of his wife. Or to other women, either. Your first two husbands were responsible for their own particular reactions. You weren't.

81

But they, like your present husband, were evidently reacting to something they didn't like in you. It is up to you and me to find out what this something or these somethings are."

I already could see what the general problem was. Mrs. Kayl was what has come to be popularly known as a "shrike." She lacked basic self-liking and self-esteem. She felt insecure in her relations with others because she was overly concerned about their accepting and loving her, and therefore could not feel secure within herself. Her method for dealing with her feelings of insecurity was to "knit a net" of kind services around the man she was unconsciously always fearful she would lose.

Mrs. Kayl smothered her own individual desires—and hence her interesting individuality—and tried to serve every need of her husband in the hope of pleasing and holding him. But each husband would himself feel smothered, strangled by the net of his wife's devotion. Each then struck out at this strangling influence in his own way. Finally, Mrs. Kayl would be left not only with her original feelings of insecurity and worthlessness, but intensified feelings of inadequacy stimulated by each husband's rebellion. Feeling increased insecurity, she would sacrifice her own desires still further, knit an even tighter net of service and devotion to the current husband, and set the stage for his fighting free of the net by the best method he could find.

If all this sounds complicated, it must be remembered that it is really an oversimplification of the involved emotional processes of a shrike-like personality and the kind of reactions she encourages in those who are closely entwined with her. Both the smothering type of behavior of Mrs. Kayl and the responses of her husbands took place, it should be realized, largely at the unconscious level—that is to say, they all knew that something unpleasant was happening, but could not put the finger of clear awareness on just what was happening to themselves and their mate.

I spent many psychotherapeutic hours with Mrs. Kayl. I

came to understand the childhood circumstances out of which her underlying feelings of self-rejection sprang and I helped her to develop a good measure of self-esteem and self-love. How? Mainly by helping her to think, feel, and act in essentially opposite ways from her familiar self-defeating patterns.

I encouraged her at first to be what she considered selfish, demanding, and conceited. She was given specific assignments in standing up for what *she*, rather than what others wanted; in frankly acknowledging her good points and successes instead of hiding them out of fear of jealous disapproval of others; and in having sex relations because she wanted satisfaction rather than just because she wanted to satisfy and please her partner. Her deep and twisted patterns of self-sacrifice were ruthlessly exposed to her and tracked down to the irrational ideas of martyrdom which she had learned with her parents and kept reindoctrinating herself with ever since. She was re-propagandized, by the therapist and by her newly encouraged activities, with stiff antidotes of self-expression, ego-assertion, and individuality, to rid her system of the poisons of phony self-abnegation. Some of the rethinking and reliving that she underwent was undertaken right in the therapist's office; but much of it had to be done in Mrs. Kayl's real-life situations, especially those which occurred when she had any contact with her husband.

Mr. Kayl, who seemed quite willing to come in and speak about his relations with his wife, turned out to be a reasonably strong and capable individual. When I explained to him the nature of his wife's problems and how I intended to try to help her to change, he reconsidered the permanence of his walkout and offered to cooperate in her planned rehabilitation. He was himself relatively free of neurosis (unlike Mrs. Kayl's first two husbands, his reactions to the "net" had been quick and healthy) and he patiently started to help his wife in her painful movement toward self-understanding and self-realization.

The Kayl family is now a sound one into which two children

have entered. Mrs. Kayl has become first a person, second a wife, and third a mother. This, not the reverse, is the proper priority. An individual must first be true to his or her own deep inner needs as a person in order to be able to give love to and accept it from his or her spouse and children. It is only when life is going well for parents as individuals and as marriage partners that they are able to give the love, emotional stability, and unfettered guidance which their children need for healthy development. When we hear a person say, "I sacrifice myself completely for my wife (or husband) and children," we do *not* think: "My, how noble!" We are more likely to think: "Poor husband (or wife) and poor children! This person needs psychotherapy."

Summing up: to be as intelligent as we can about marrying and marriage, we have to develop our self-knowledge and self-respect. This will not guarantee success in marriage, but it increases its probability. Even with much progress in knowing, respecting, and loving oneself, the individual will keep making mistakes. Consequently, we shall continue to have divorces and separations: but we need not continue to make them deep and twisting tragedies. We can learn from divorce, rather than condemn it as a social holocaust. We can come to think of it as the expected and accepted price for a free and democratic approach to marital living.

Can we, then, be intelligent about marrying? No, not very. But every little bit helps. Let us see, in our next two chapters, how we can apply at least a little bit of intelligence and understanding to the questions of love and infatuation and to whether or not an individual should marry.

7

Love or Infatuation?

"Do you think I really love him?" she asked me. "Or is it just an infatuation?"

She had, just the day before, attempted to commit suicide by taking an overdose of sleeping pills. She had gone to her lover's apartment while he was supposedly at work, in order to decorate his place for a surprise birthday party. Noticing the light on, and being afraid of burglars, she had tiptoed into the bedroom and found him fast asleep—with another girl tightly wrapped in his arms.

She had tiptoed out again, gone directly to her own apartment, and immediately taken half a bottle of sleeping pills. By sheer accident, her mother had come to see her, had noticed the half-empty bottle and the disarray of the room, and had sum-moned a physician who soon restored her to consciousness. Now, at the physician's insistence, and with his promise that he would not notify the police if she went for some help with her emotional problems, she had come to see me.

"Tell me," she pleaded. "Do I really love him? Can it be possible?"

Seven years ago, at the age of twenty-two, she had met Roger and had fallen violently in love from the second she saw him. Friends had introduced them at a party and he had im-mediately started telling her what was wrong with her: that she was too heavy, didn't dress sexily enough, and had no poise. He boasted about the other girls whose sex favors he was en-joying, said that he could never go for her type, but offered to teach her some of the facts of life. He took her to his apart-ment that night, forcibly stripped and assaulted her while she dumbly offered little resistance, and kept her there all night, not letting her call her parents to tell them that she would not be home.

Since then she had clung to Roger in spite of everything. He rarely had a kind word for her and only when drunk (which he often was) would he show her any affection. Then, as soon as he sobered up, he would deny that he ever had been affec-tionate. He shamelessly exploited her, borrowed considerable money which he never returned, and used her in every way.

Marriage, of course, he never mentioned—except to say that it was a stultifying, bourgeois institution and he could not see how any man could be fool enough to get trapped in it. Other girls, of all descriptions, he continually had and often flaunted before her. But if she so much as looked at another man, he got drunk, beat her, and called her a whore.

Through all this, Josie never once complained or thought of leaving Roger. Whatever he wanted, she did. When she got pregnant, she unhesitatingly had an abortion because he wanted her to have one. When he beat or cursed her or told her not to come back any more she cried—and always crept back. When he teased her sexually and for weeks refused to give her any real satisfaction, she cried some more—but did nothing else.

Almost every time she saw Roger, he got drunk and Josie ended up in tears. But she never thought of not going back to him. And she daydreamed about him incessantly. At work, where she carried on with surprising efficiency, his image was before her almost every minute. At home, where she had much contention with her parents, who violently opposed her relation with Roger, she would lie on her bed for hours, almost every chance she got, just thinking about him.

When Josie moved to her own place, it was mainly to get away from parental and other interruptions in her thoughts about Roger. She would slide around her small apartment in a coma-like state, thinking of him while cooking, doing her dishes, washing her hair, or doing a hundred other household tasks. If the phone rang, except if it were he (it rarely was, since he almost never called her), she took it as an annoying interruption and was impatient to get back to her trance-like state, her thoughts of him.

Even when Josie stopped asking outright questions, her pained eyes continued to beseech. "Was it really love?" she wanted to know. Desperately, searchingly, her closed lips and her confused eyes continued to ask this question. I knew, from long experience, just the answer she wanted. "No," she wanted me to say, "of course what you have felt, what you still may at times feel for this man is not true love. It is sickness, a mere infatuation, and like all infatuations it will soon pass away and leave you whole, no longer sullied. It will go, just like a bad dream, and soon you will hardly even remember his name."

This is what Josie wanted me to say; but, in all honesty, I could not. This is what scores of counseling and psychotherapy clients wish the counselor to say: that love and infatuation are completely different; that true love remains and infatuations pass; that it is not difficult to distinguish the one from the other;

and that it is therefore relatively easy to avoid getting too deeply entangled with those with whom you are infatuated and to remain maritally free until you meet, at long last your true, true love.

Instead of perpetuating this solacing myth, however, the honest counselor is professionally and scientifically obligated to tell his clients the truth about love and infatuation. He is morally obliged to tell them something along the following lines.

There is no such thing, first off, as "true" love. *True* means conformable to what is actual, real, factual, or existent. In this sense, all love, in that it is an emotion that actually exists, is true. *True* also means faithful, trustworthy, loyal, honest, reliable. But virtually all loves, *while they last,* are faithful, loyal, and reliable. After love has faded, it naturally is no longer existent, faithful, loyal, or reliable. But this cannot gainsay the fact that during its heyday it *was* true.

In societies like our own, where enforced monogamy is the rule and non-monogamous forms of union are disapproved and discouraged, love commonly is confused with marriage, and "true" love is defined, as is "good" marriage, in terms of its being enduring. Similarly, devotees of various creeds attempt to define "true" love in terms of their own prejudices: so that, it often comes to mean to members of these creeds legitimatized, Christian, family-centered, "mature," non-sexual, "pure," or some other qualified form of love. All these qualified modes of "true" love are obviously arbitrary; and none of them is fully accepted by all observers.

Realistically, therefore, we must acknowledge that *all* love is *true* love—as long as, even for a moment, it actually exists. Having said this, we must immediately also note that there are innumerable kinds and degrees of love and that, whenever anyone asks whether he is in love, or is truly in love, what he means to ask is: "What kind and degree of love am I now experiencing?"

Love is a more or less intense emotional attachment, affection, or involvement with another individual. If one suspects, therefore, that he is in love, he may be certain that he is. The only question is how much and in what manner he loves.

One may, for example, love mildly or violently; sexually or non-sexually; for a day or a decade; heterosexually or homosexually; sacredly or profanely; monogamously or plurally; romantically or non-romantically; conjugally or non-conjugally; etc. The suicidal patient, Josie, if one should attempt to diagnose her feeling for her lover, may be said to have loved him violently, sexually, enduringly, heterosexually, profanely, monogamously, romantically, and conjugally. She also could be said to have loved him obsessively, neurotically, masochistically, and foolishly. The pattern of her feeling state, while radically different from that of the attachments of many other girls, nonetheless constitutes a decided, if aberrant, type of love.

What, then, of infatuation? Was this girl not infatuated with her lover? Technically, yes. The dictionary defines infatuation as "a foolish and extravagant passion." In this sense, she was certainly infatuated. Actually, however, infatuation has come to mean a kind of love different from this, and in so doing has lost most of its meaning.

Several years ago, one of the authors of this book did a study of the love emotions of five hundred college girls, all of whom were questioned on many aspects of their heterosexual "loves" and "infatuations." It was found that these girls, instead of using the term *infatuation* to cover their foolish or extravagant attachments, were employing it to cover virtually all their past or unenduring affairs.

In our monogamously oriented society, evidently, we make our young people so ashamed of falling in love frequently and then falling promptly or eventually out of love again—which my study showed that they actually do most of the time—that they are loath to confess, even to themselves, how often they do love. They consequently divide amorous attachments into "loves" and "infatuations," and call their *past* loves infatuations and their *present* infatuations loves.

To make matters still more confusing, I found that a great many of the girls I questioned tended to speak of "passing" or "mild" infatuations. By this they meant that whenever they loved a boy for a short while or loved him in a mild manner, they considered this an infatuation. This is quite at variance with the dictionary definition of the term *infatuation*—which implies that, although this kind of attachment may be brief, it is usually an extravagant, impassioned affair.

Considering the confused manner in which the term *infatuation* is now employed by so many young people—and college-level young people at that—in our society, it would appear that, in all honesty, the best thing we might do about the term would be to drop it entirely. Even when it is correctly employed to mean foolish and extravagant love, it tends to become meaningless: since many kinds of love appear foolish and extravagant to everyone but the lovers involved; and, alas, even to the lovers themselves, once their passion has waned. Love is love. However transient, mild, profane, plural, or foolish it may be, let us acknowledge it as a real, often enjoyable, and true experience.

Another reason for acknowledging love as love, and not trying to categorize it arbitrarily as "true" or "infatuated" or some other "good" or "bad" type of love, is that modern psychological research and clinical experience is increasingly discovering that love is not an isolated part of human life. It is intimately related to basic human desires, to personality as a whole, and to the familial upbringing of the lovers. Our own study of five hundred college girls, for example, showed that there was a tendency for these girls to have more satisfying love relationships when they had good relations with their fathers than when they got along badly with them. And several contributors to Ashley Montagu's volume, *The Meaning of*

90

Love, stress the important connections between childhood conditioning and later heterosexual attachments.

Let us return to the suicidal client, Josie. That she was obsessively and neurotically in love with her boy friend was perfectly clear, when she came for psychotherapy, even though she wondered whether her feeling for her lover should be called "love" or "infatuation."

What was not clear to her, and what required a good many sessions of intensive therapy to help her understand, was that her obsession had relatively little to do with her lover and much to do with herself and her own distorted and irrational attitudes.

Josie came from a home where her mother, an exceptionally critical and embittered woman, endlessly censured her for almost everything she did, particularly for her sex acts. From early puberty onward, if she went out with a boy, or wore a low-cut dress, or alluded in any way to sex activities, her mother would call her a strumpet. She would say that she only had sex on her mind, and predict that she would end up in the gutter, illegitimately pregnant and syphilitic.

Josie's father, at the same time, would tell all kinds of sex jokes and would comment salaciously on her developing female form. He would often walk into her room when she was undressed and would jest with her about her shyness and her not being more sexually affectionate to him. This would incense the mother still more and she would accuse her daughter of seducing the father and would hint strongly that they were actually having sex relations behind her back.

Under these circumstances, Josie grew up with a horror of sex. At the same time she was covertly attracted to her father and secretly excited, as well as appalled, whenever he touched her. She kept thinking about her mother and father having intercourse; strongly wanted to take her mother's place in her father's bed; and often masturbated with the image of her father in mind. On one occasion, when he had embraced her when they were both dressed in bathing suits, she had felt his erect penis and had had an orgasm, followed by a hysterical outbreak of tears and a violently upset stomach.

When Josie met her boy friend, she had already convinced herself (by internalizing her mother's negative propaganda) that she was the lowest kind of creature imaginable and that no good man would ever love or marry her. Although Roger did not outwardly resemble her father, he did have many of the father's cruel, teasing ways. Often when she was having sex relations with him, particularly when he was being sadistic and was refusing to satisfy her, she would fantasize being with her father and taking him away from her mother. She then became all the more guilty; and, to assuage some of this guilt, ran toward instead of away from Roger's sadistic treatment.

Josie's sex-love problem, in other words, was directly derived, as are virtually all love-sex problems, from her general attitudes toward herself. She believed that she *should be* a nice, pure, lovable, virtually perfect girl and that she actually *was* a nasty, impure, unlovable, horribly imperfect creature. She believed that, at the very least, any worthwhile person would be fully accepted by her own mother and father; and, knowing that her mother did not accept her and that her father lusted after her sexually but had no real respect for her, she "logically" concluded (in the light of her groundless premise) that she was valueless.

Believing that she was generally "bad" and worthless, it was another "logical" step for Josie to conclude that she was sexually reprehensible. Her mother specifically taught her this, again; and her father more subtly gave her the idea that she really did lust after him and that this was not "proper" or filial. Or, rather, by his jokingly derisive attitude, her father gave her the notion that (a) it was great that she was sexually attracted to him and (b) it was also ineffably wicked. As pointed out in one of our books, *The Folklore of Sex,* this is a common result of the "dirty joke" attitude toward human sexuality: to give the hearer the double-edged, utterly contradictory notion that sex is both a nasty *and* a tasty dish, and that he or she is both frightful *and* delightful for thinking about this dish.

Once she began to feel so sexually inadequate and "bad," Josie could not afford to look her own sex desires frankly in the face. Instead, she acquired unconscious, defensive attitudes that precluded her enjoying a normal sex relationship. She could only allow herself to accept sexual gratification when it was accompanied by a sufficient degree of pain to assuage her underlying guilt feelings.

Roger, because of Josie's masochistic tendencies, became, in a perverse and yet for her a logical way, an almost ideal sex partner—because he sadistically treated her as a person and as a bed mate. Thus, he would caress her passionately and bring her to a frenzy of excitement, and then he would suddenly stop his caresses and refuse to "bring her off," saying that it was not good for her to have so many orgasms or that he was too tired to continue. Josie would then have to beg and cajole him and humble herself in every possible way before he would consent to give her an orgasm. She thereby felt that she had really worked and suffered for her pleasure and was consequently not very guilty about receiving it—as she doubtlessly would have been had it come easier.

Perhaps even more importantly, Josie's general or moral masochism, as distinct from her specific sexual masochism, was catered to by her relationship with Roger. Feeling that she was utterly worthless and not deserving of a "good" boy friend or husband, and yet not wanting to be entirely without male companionship, she was able "logically" to fit herself into the "bad" relationship with Roger—to have her cake with her punishment, but at least to have *some* of the cake.

Josie's obsessive-compulsive love for Roger, then, seemed utterly senseless on the surface but was actually motivated by some very "logical"—or at least psychological—expectations and longings. Love, as we have noted above, is normally based on the (conscious or unconscious) perception or expectation that one's beloved can and will satisfy some of one's fundamental desires or "needs." It does not especially matter what these "needs" are, since they differ widely from individual to individual. Nor does it matter whether the "needs" are "real" ones or whether (as is actually the case with most so-called human "needs") they are nothing but strong desires which the individual arbitrarily and unchallengingly *defines* as "needs."

It doesn't even matter if the lover's "needs" are, in point of fact, truly satisfied by his beloved. As long as he thinks that his ardent desires are satisfied or that in the future they will be, he will usually be moved to love. In Josie's case, her desires to have a relationship with a man like Roger were distinctly masochistic and neurotic. They were based on the most irrational assumptions and beliefs about herself. But as long as she kept creating these "needs" to immolate herself with a lover, her affair with Roger "logically" was sufficiently "satisfying" to keep her madly attached to him. It was, in a very real sense, a "normal" result of an abnormal initial set of premises.

How was Josie's neurotic love—or, if you will, silly infatuation—finally resolved? Only by working through to the very bottom of her basic philosophies of life and the general character structure, defenses, and conflicts which resulted from these philosophies. She was helped to see, first, that she did have a basic set of false premises about herself, and that these originated with the negative indoctrinations of her mother and father. She was shown that she did not have to accept, at face value, their attitudes toward her, even though they were her parents; and that, without hating them for being negative, she could refuse to be influenced by them in her adult years as, unfortunately, she had been virtually forced to be influenced when she was younger. She was induced to look upon both her parents, not as ogres or idiots, but as poor disturbed individuals (who themselves had been unduly influenced by the irrational attitudes of their own parents) who could be accepted the way they were without being taken too seriously.

In particular, Josie's self-critical and self-punitive attitudes toward herself were rigorously and consistently questioned and attacked by the therapist. She was shown that there was no reason why she *should be* completely nice, pure, and lovable; that she *could* afford to make mistakes and failures; that it was *not* terrible when other people thought her wrong; that she *was* able to do many of the things she wanted to do in life if she stopped concentrating on doing them perfectly.

As Josie's general self-defeating philosophies were being unearthed, challenged, and assailed, she was also induced to look clearly at and to question her specific sex assumptions. She was shown, in this connection, that she was not wicked because she was interested in boys and at times wore low-cut dresses; that neither her father's obvious sex interest in her, nor her returned interest in him, were abnormal and heinous; that sex is not both nasty and tasty, but is good in, of, by, and for itself, as long as it does not needlessly harm other human beings; that sex activity need not be deodorized with romance or atoned for with masochistic elements in order to make it edifying.

As Josie's general and sexual attitudes toward herself and others significantly changed, as her feelings of unworthiness and of terrible sexual guilt waned, she was able to accept love and sex gratification, on a realistic, non-masochistic basis. She came to her therapy session one day highly elated.

"I never thought I'd be able to do it," she said, "and I'm terribly happy I did. I saw Roger last night and he expected things to be just as usual. Was he surprised! First thing, I refused to have anal intercourse, as he usually wants me to do. Not that I think it awful anymore, or anything like that; but I just don't enjoy it. So I just refused. He almost tried to force me, but I'd have none of it. He saw he couldn't get anywhere, and that ended that. Did I feel good!"

"You really liked yourself for standing up for yourself, didn't you?"

"Yes, for just about the first time in my life in things like that, I really did. Then, again as usual, he started leading me on, making love and then stopping in the middle—you know, his usual sadistic way. But this time I stopped him cold.

" 'Look, Roger,' I said. 'You know perfectly well that that doesn't do anything for me—except leave me hung up and angry. Now either you do it the right way, *my* way, or let me get the hell out of here. I've taken enough of this crap from you too long. But no more!'

"You should have seen the look on his face! Like I struck him with a baseball bat or something. But he came through, just as I asked; and, sexually at least, it was fine. I can see right well, however, that there really isn't anything in this affair and it's almost as if I'm hanging on, at present, just to right things a bit, just to get my own bearings. Roger's on the way out, and I think he knows it."

Within several weeks more, Roger was out. Josie's mad, obsessive-compulsive attachment to him was at the end of its rope and she could hardly remember what she had seen in him in the first place. Since the relation with him no longer satisfied any of her basic desires or "needs," her "infatuation" with him collapsed. Nor is it likely that she is going to become similarly foolishly obsessed with any other man of his stamp.

So-called infatuation, then, is nothing but a form of love, even when it is neurotic, foolish, exaggerated love. And it stems, like all amative manifestations, from the basic desires of human beings. More usual kinds of love originate in a person's reasonable desires to have good companionship, enjoyable sex relations, shared parenthood, comfortable domesticity, and other satisfactions with a member of the other sex, and his (conscious or unconscious) expectations that these desires will be nicely fulfilled with the person with whom he is in love.

More unusual kinds of love, such as mad infatuations, frequently result from a person's unreasonable desires—or "needs" —to compensate for or atone for his own "worthlessness" by becoming inordinately attached to someone else. The individual who truly likes himself, respects his own aims in life, and has long-range, vitally absorbing interests toward which he is working will not tend to become wildly infatuated as often as the one who has little self-respect. Even when he does become highly enamored of a member of the other sex who is obviously sadistic, stupid, or otherwise clearly unsuited for a long-term relationship with him, he is ordinarily well able to control his feelings (by changing the thoughts that lie behind and give rise to them) and to keep on a fairly even love keel.

Real infatuation, in other words—meaning foolish or self-defeating love—is largely the product of self-loathing and the "need" magically to make up for one's own (actual or imagined) lacks by clinging or bowing down to another. It is almost invariably a derivative of general emotional disturbance rather than a unique thing in itself. Nonetheless, even inordinate infatuation is a form of "true" or "real" love. It indubitably exists; and it has significant meaning for those who experience it. It also, like any other form of human behavior, has experiential qualities that may lead to valuable learning on the part of the infatuated lover. It may be crazy; but it is still *true*.

8

To Marry or Not

That many men have qualms about marrying is a well-known fact and is not surprising in view of the additional social and economic responsibilities a man must assume with a wedding band. What is perhaps more interesting and startling is the frequency with which many girls avoid marrying.

Sally Lawlis is a case in point. Sally is a good-looking, intelligent private secretary. She makes enough money to live in fair comfort, but has to struggle to save for certain luxuries. She likes her job, but is by no means in love with it. At the age of twenty-eight, she has had several minor and three major affairs with males and has not seriously considered marrying any of them.

Sally has high sex urges and has always had a lover of one sort or other since she was nineteen. She lives by herself, is an efficient but unenthusiastic housekeeper, and tends to get lonely when she is not with others for any length of time. She has mild interests in reading and art, but is not devoted to any hobby or interest.

Theoretically, Sally should be eager to get married. Her parents and relatives make a tremendous issue about each of her passing birthdays. She herself feels, and with some reason, that she is not getting any younger or better-looking. She has no financial resources on which to fall back in case of serious ailments. She requires steady sex satisfaction and companionship. She would like, within a few more years, to have children.

For all this, Sally has distinct anti-marital leanings. Why? First of all, she doubts whether she would like to assume all the normal responsibilities of marriage—caring for her husband and children, sacrificing time and energy, doing things she might not like to do. Secondly, she does not want to be sexually or amatively restricted. Thirdly, she wants companionship but also frequently wants privacy. Fourthly, she doesn't want anyone telling her what to do or not to do.

Sally, in a word, deplores the possible restrictions and confinements of marriage. She admits that being mated has certain advantages, but does not want to assume its concomitant disadvantages. Eventually, she feels, she will probably marry; but she is in no hurry to do so, and even may end up by never marrying.

Is Sally, then, abnormal? Is her opposition to marriage peculiar or neurotic? No, not necessarily. Granted that her present life is not entirely satisfactory and there are notable gaps in it. Although marriage may, on the one hand, fill some of these gaps, the chances are that it will also, on the other hand, interfere with some of the satisfactions of her present free existence.

If Sally suddenly should fall violently in love with one of her boy friends, and experience unusual satisfaction in being with him on a more or less permanent basis, she would have some incentive to risk the dangers and restrictions of marriage. But, as long as she is not intensively enamored of any male, or loves on a temporary basis, she has relatively little incentive to enter the state of matrimony. There is nothing too illogical about her wariness of marriage, and, if she never marries, her life may be little the worse.

Take, on the other hand, Marcia. Marcia is just about as intelligent and good-looking as Sally. She is twenty-nine, and also works as a secretary. Marcia, too, lives alone, has had several lovers, is reasonably highly sexed and has no outstanding interests or hobbies. But Marcia's reasons for not marrying are different from Sally's. Marcia is afraid to marry.

She would like nothing better than to form a deep, warm, permanent attachment to a man. But she feels that she has absolutely no ability to stay sexually faithful (as she would like to stay); that she could not possibly be an efficient housekeeper; that she is incapable of raising children; and that no man could love her for more than a very short time.

Marcia, for the most part, is right about her incapacities for wifehood and motherhood—neurotically right. Because she *believes* that she is woefully promiscuous, inefficient, and unlovable, she invariably acts in a promiscuous, inefficient and unlovable manner. Her actions then antagonize and disgust the males with whom she has intimate relations and they sooner or later leave her. Their actions are then taken by her as "proof" that she is as uncapable and disapprovable as she thinks herself to be.

Marcia, obviously, avoids marrying in a neurotic, self-defeating way. Underneath, she would love to be a wife and mother. Frequently, however, she will say: "Marry? Me? Why, don't be ridiculous! What would I do married? I just couldn't stand it. All those restrictions! Who wants it? I'd have to be crazy to do a thing like that!"

Desperatedly, she tries to convice herself that what she says is true. But it isn't: she does want to marry, probably always will. Her avoidance of the proposals she keeps receiving is a tragic, disturbed flight. Her case, though on the surface similar to Sally's, is actually much different.

With Marcia, I have had quite a counseling job. First, I have had to trace down the fundamental reasons for her enormous feelings of inadequacy. Thus, Marcia and I have unearthed such important factors as a mother who greatly favored Marcia's older sister and a father who first gave Marcia considerable support but who later deserted her and her family by running off with another woman. We have also turned up the fact that Marcia began masturbating at the age of seven, was caught by her mother several times and was viciously threatened, and to this day has had a low estimation of herself for having autoerotic ideas.

Marcia's experiences with her mother and father, as well as with others who were important to her in her younger years, have led her to believe, quite falsely and yet strongly, that she is worthless, hopeless, and impossible, and particularly that she is not a worthy object of love. To make matters infinitely worse, she has been perpetually repeating to herself, for about twenty years, the same negative propaganda that her parents originally said or implied. Her own repetitions of this nonsense, together with the blunders or ineffectualities which have resulted from her continually telling herself that she could not possibly do well in various aspects of life, have convinced her of her "worthlessness" far more thoroughly than have the originally promulgated parental hypotheses.

Thus, Marcia is now quite aware that her mother was wrong in favoring her older sister and severely criticizing her for masturbating. She now recognizes that her father had his own severe problems and deserted her and the family because of these problems rather than because of anything wrong or bad that she, Marcia, may have done. But she has been most reluctant

101

to admit that her *own* poor behavior (her promiscuity, hostility, and irresponsibility) is not heinous and blameworthy. Because she has internalized her mother's basic blaming philosophy, she takes an unholier-than-thou attitude toward herself, and looks upon her "sins" as great crimes instead of as problems to be tackled and solved. Consequently, even though both her mother and father are now deceased, *she* still ceaselessly berates herself.

I have had quite a time, then, with Marcia. Getting her to see that human beings are *essentially* worthwhile, and that they do not have to "prove" their value by being perfect, by achieving great things, by never making a mistake, has been difficult and time-consuming. Finally, however, my efforts (at reeducation) and hers (at rethinking) have begun to pay off. Marcia is now ready to admit that she is not loathsome, is not a criminal—either because the adults who were significant in her early life dogmatically said so or because she herself has continued to say so for the last twenty years.

Now Marcia and I are working on her specific problem of marrying. Since she has begun to feel less unworthy, she readily admits that marriage might be a good thing for her and she for it. Her affairs with men have now taken a different turn; and as soon as she discovers that a current boy friend is not, nor probably never will be, a good prospect for matrimony, she quietly but firmly ceases to see him. With the better prospects, we discuss in detail what she feels about them, how she reacts to them, and in what ways she may possibly be hindering her relationships with them. In consequence, her relations with males have immensely improved and it would seem to be only a matter of time when we shall be getting Marcia into a satisfying marriage.

The lesson of what has so far been said in this chapter is that there are two basic reasons for an individual's resisting marriage in our society: logical and illogical, non-neurotic and neurotic.

On the logical side, it should be forthrightly pointed out that not everyone, by any means, should marry. There are some individuals, and perhaps not too few, who just are not suited for marriage. Some of these, for example, are dedicated persons, such as outstanding scientists, artists, or politicians, who are so vitally interested in some cause that it would be most difficult to dovetail this cause satisfactorily with ordinary marriage.

Other individuals—such as some unusually beautiful women or handsome and talented men—get along so well in the single state that they would have little to gain, and perhaps considerable to lose, by marrying. Still other persons are too sensitive, too finicky, too highly sexed, or too something else to be able to find almost any mate or marital relationship quite satisfactory. Finally, some persons are too inadequate, too neurotic, or too disorganized to be a satisfactory marital partner to almost anyone.

For various sound reasons, then, marriage is not for everyone. At the same time, many individuals who logically should marry never do so because of various illogical or neurotic reasons. Some are, for no valid cause, simply afraid to be married. Some are still too tied to their parents or other relatives. Some are afraid to take a chance on any risky affair, including marriage. And so on. . . .

It is quite appropriate that those who do not wish to marry for neurotic reasons actually avoid marrying. For marriage, as is often pointed out in psychological texts, is no happy berth for most neurotics. Occasionally, a neurotic marries someone who complements himself so well, and who in effect gives him adequate psychotherapy, that he becomes less disturbed as a result of marriage. But not often. More often, marriage adds measurably to neurotic doubts, conflicts, crises.

Almost by definition, a disturbed individual is one who cannot get along adequately with himself. If so, there is no reason to believe that he will be able to harmonize well with another human being in an intimate marital relationship. Stated differently: marriage usually doubles or quadruples an individual's

103

responsibilities and difficulties. Hence, it is more likely than not to make it easier for a disturbed person to become even more disturbed.

Neurotics, then, should preferably not marry: they first should be treated. Anyone, in fact, who is most reluctant to marry should normally keep away from the altar and should first work through his objections.

I had, for example, a female patient, thirty-five years of age, who had been married and quickly divorced at the age of twenty-two. Since that time she had gone with one boy after another and had become engaged to several of them. Each time she was about to marry, however, she panicked, and somehow broke the engagement.

This patient came to see me when she was engaged to a man two years older than herself and had been going with him for two years. He seemed to be an excellent prospect for marriage—had money, good looks, and emotional stability. He knew about her past history, accepted the fact that she was rather neurotic, but still wanted to marry her. The wedding day was set for six weeks ahead. She, as usual, was becoming panicky.

I went through this girl's life history with her and quickly turned up some aspects of her background which seemed to influence her marital fears. Her father and mother had never been happily married and, when the patient was a child, the father kept leaving the mother and returning, after a few weeks or months for some more bickering. Her parents finally were divorced when she was seventeen; and both had made rather miserable second marriages.

To make matters worse, the patient's mother was a critical woman who kept pointing out how good-looking her daughter was, and what a fine external appearance she gave, but how she was exceptionally shallow underneath, and could easily be found out by anyone who got to know her well. The implications for the patient's marrying any solid individual were, of course, clear.

When the patient first married, she made a poor choice by taking as a husband a man who was completely attached to his own parents. He gave her little love or support, and divorced her as soon as he discovered that she was not going to mother him. In the course of the divorce, he blamed her for all their difficulties, flaunted his relations with other women, and acted in a generally obnoxious manner. She never forgave herself for selecting him as a husband, but also felt that if she had been a better person, he might not have acted the way he did.

In these circumstances, my patient, though wanting desperately to remarry and to make up for her past mistake, was morbidly afraid that she would repeat (a) her parents' marital failures and (b) her own. She felt that her fiancés would find her out, soon after marriage, and would leave her, as her first husband had done. Consequently, she left them first—almost literally at the altar.

I showed this patient the pattern of her past behavior and how it was importantly related to her present indecision and inaction. She saw this clearly enough, but was still loath to take the marital plunge. This is true of many patients. They may come to understand quite fully (or as psychologists and psychiatrists say, get sufficient insight into) the origins of their present disturbances—and still remain just as disturbed as ever.

Then, using the technique of rational psychotherapy, I concentrated on showing the patient how she was *now* telling herself irrational sentences and ideas, and reindoctrinating herself with the nonsense that her mother and others had originally led her to believe. I demonstrated, by a detailed examination and analysis of her present thoughts and behavior, that she still believed (a) that *it was terrible* if she made a mistake in any major endeavor, especially marriage, (b) that *she was worthless* if, after one unsuccessful try at marriage, she failed again,

105

(c) that she positively *had to* succeed in her next marital relation or else risk the "horrible" censure of others, and (d) that her feelings of panic, which occurred when she was about to marry, were utterly uncontrollable, stemmed from deep-seated "emotional" reactions, and could not be effectively managed.

After showing this patient that she had these basic beliefs or philosophies, I then kept analyzing, attacking, ridiculing, and challenging these beliefs—forthrightly showing her that mistakes are *not* terrible (but are human and often, from a learning standpoint, fortunate); that failing at a task does *not* prove that one is worthless or hopeless; that, although it is *preferable,* it is not *necessary* that one succeed at marriage; that *it doesn't really matter* what one's friends think, as long as one respects one's own activities and risk-takings; and that even the most pronounced feelings of panic are not uncontrollable "emotional" reactions, but actually stem from silly ideas and can definitely be, as these ideas are changed, controlled.

After a month of steadily pounding away at this patient's irrational fears of failure, of not being able to please others, and of inability to control her own emotions, I was able to a considerable degree to undermine her illogical self-recriminations. She began, at least at times, to question and challenge her own panic-creating thoughts. On one occasion, she came to me and said:

"I'm sure you're right about most of my doubts about marrying arising out of my own fears and feelings of inadequacy, but there are some other good reasons, too."

"Such as?" I asked.

"Well, there's one thing that my fiancé doesn't know about me, that I haven't told him yet; and if I marry him and then he finds out, he may be quite upset about it. Or if I tell him now, before the marriage, he may not want to marry me."

"What is this thing he doesn't know?"

"About my inner organs," she said. "I only have one ovary. I had to have one removed several years ago."

106

"But how do you know that he would object to that?" I asked. "Maybe he's not interested in having children. And if he is, as you know, you are perfectly capable of having them with one ovary."

"I know. But I am sure he would object and would not want to marry me."

"How are you sure?"

"I don't know. I just am."

"But aren't you just saying to yourself, again, as you almost perpetually do: 'With this one ovary out, I am a poor, imperfect creature, that no man worth his salt would want to marry'? Aren't you also saying: 'Look how I've lied to him, so far, about this ovary business. This proves what a horrible, false creature I am. How could he ever want such a worthless person as me?' "

"You really think I *am* saying those sorts of things to myself?"

"Well, *aren't* you?"

"—uh . . . I . . . you know, I guess I really am! And also, now that you bring it up, I guess I'm saying: 'What good *is* a woman with only one ovary? I probably won't be able to have children at all. And then what good will I be as a wife?' Yes— I'm saying that, too!"

"Right. Bringing your own so-called worthlessness to your attention, up and down, in and out. Convincing yourself, merely by your own unchallenged repetition of balderdash, that you *are* no good, you *are* a terrible, lying individual. But where, actually, is the *evidence*?"

"The evidence?"

"Yes, where is the proof that no man would want to marry an imperfect creature, that people who avoid telling their fiancés certain pertinent facts are horrible liars, that women who might not be able to produce children have no real role in life, no good reason to be married?"

"Oh, I see what you mean. These are all propositions that

107

I keep making to myself and accepting without any proof. I see them as self-evident—and yet they really aren't."

"Right. That's the story of your life—seeing as 'self-evident' propositions that are highly questionable; then acting on these highly questionable propositions; then, of course, tripping yourself up and falling on your face; then, finally, using your self-recriminations and consequent failures as further 'self-evidential proof' of how awful and hopeless you are."

"Quite a vicious circle, isn't it?"

"Quite!"

In this manner, as my patient kept bringing up one reason after another why she should not marry, I showed her how her "reasons" were actually rationalizations for her own deep-seated feelings of inadequacy and worthlessness and how these feelings were based on groundless, endlessly repeated assumptions for which she had no evidence whatever. Then, acting on these false assumptions, she would keep behaving in a panicked, incompetent manner—and falsely use this behavior as further "proof" of her original assumptions of inadequacy. As soon as I was able to induce her to question and challenge her groundless assumptions, she began to feel less inadequate and less indecisive.

As part of this patient's "homework" assignments, I had her face her fiancé, quite squarely and honestly, with some of the things she had been hiding about herself, including having only one ovary. Each time she did this, she could see in practice, as well as in theory, that there *was* nothing horrible or frightful about being rebuffed or about failing at a task.

When, for example, her fiancé at first took a dim view, not of her having one ovary, but of her having previously kept this fact from him, and when it looked for a time as if he might possibly break off the engagement, she discovered to her surprise that she *still* felt quite well and strong. *She,* for once, respected herself, and didn't need his love or approval that much while she had her self-respect.

108

As she said to me at the time, "Perhaps this is the end with Tom; I don't really think so, but it may be. But it doesn't *matter* that much, even if it is. For I now, for the first time, am beginning to have *myself*, to like *me*. And as long as that is so, I am sure that there are always other Toms to be had. And even if there aren't, I'll *still* have me—which is more than I've had since ever I can remember!"

As the date of the wedding approached, the patient still had some qualms; but these tended to be, now, in the normal range. And since every marriage involves some risk-taking, and the patient's qualms were as much about her husband's thoughts and behavior as about her own, she decided to plunge in, anyway, and go through with the wedding.

I felt that her decision was a wise one and that, with some continued psychotherapy after the marriage, there was little doubt that she would come through—no matter how the marriage itself turned out. As it happened, both she and the marriage came through; and, after five years, she and her husband are enjoying a remarkably good marital relationship, even though their desire for children seems to have been permanently thwarted.

All's well that ends well. But let us emphasize that this case is an exceptional one, and that it probably was concluded successfully only because the patient was flexible enough to admit that she had a serious problem and needed professional help. The fact remains that neurotics are not good marital risks and should avoid marrying, in most instances, until they have worked through a good part of their neuroses prior to taking marriage vows.

To return to our main theme: Not all people should marry. But, in this society, most probably should. Marriage, for the average male and female raised within our culture, seems to be at least the lesser evil, if not necessarily the greatest good. This is particularly true for the American female. Marriage affords her, among other things, the possibility of having and raising children, a measure of affectional security, social status, economic stability, and steady companionship. All these things she may be able to achieve outside of marriage, but it is highly unlikely that she will.

We are talking, remember, about the *average* young woman or man. The above-average individual may be able to achieve many advantages of life without marrying. The below-average individual may not be able to take marriage, however much he or she may want it. But the average person has relatively little choice. To him or her it is an expected and almost necessary way of life.

Even though modern marriage has many distinct disadvantages, it still appears to be, at the very least, tolerably satisfactory for most men and women. It can, of course, be much more than this. It can be a sheer delight, a mystic luminous joy. Statistically, however, we know that it rarely is. And clinically, our counseling and psychotherapeutic experience tends to show that marriage is usually not so bad as it may often seem to be—especially when it is compared to the non-marital state.

Many married couples, not realizing this, go for needless divorces. They see, while they are mated to each other, all the common disadvantages of their union. What is more difficult for them to see, because human beings tend to accept as commonplace and to take for granted many of their day-to-day satisfactions, is that their marriages have many real advantages. They consequently get divorced—only to find, when they do not remarry, that they are often worse off than they previously were. In some such instances, they frankly acknowledge their mistake and remarry each other. Most of the time, they do no such thing—even though they may often contemplate it.

Since, logically or illogically, most of us will and do marry, let us move on to consider some of the problems that are frequently met in marriage and some ways of meeting them more effectively.

9

Sexual Preparation for Marriage

One of the most important—though not by any means necessarily *the* most important—aspects of marriage is sex relations. Few couples marry without some degree of expectation of satisfaction in the sex area. Relatively few, alas, seem to attain that degree commensurate with their original expectations.

Courses and books giving the facts of life to would-be marital partners are common today. What is more needed, however, is a few *un*common courses and books that refuse to beat around the bush and get down to cases pithily and objectively. Take, for example, the usual high school or college course in marriage and family relations that is given today. Is it given in a

111

truly objective, dispassionate, and meaty manner? Not as far as sex preparation is concerned. Not by a long shot!

Imagine, if you will, a bright young college student, who may perhaps be a senior and already of voting age, saying in class, "Let's have it straight, Professor. Is it all right if I practice oral-genital relations with my girl friend?" Or, "What would you say is the most effective method of contraception and how, exactly, do I go about employing it?" Can you imagine this student getting a straight and unequivocal answer?

There are several reasons why many classes in preparation for marriage do not get down to the fundamental, personal, more sexual aspects of marital adjustment. First, the instructors in these courses are often themselves ignorant or emotionally disturbed and just could not handle down-to-earth teaching.

Secondly, the academic setting in which most marriage courses are given is more conducive to grade-giving and rote learning than it is to personal-emotional discussions and experiential learning.

Thirdly, instructors are limited by heavy enrollments, research and extra-curricular commitments, the ever-watchful eye of censorious authorities, and so on. Finally, many instructors are hogtied by personal, religious, professional or other prejudices which prevent them from being ruthlessly objective about love-sex matters.

Articles and books on sex have their own special limitations. Articles for mass media, such as newspapers or magazines, are subject to unusually heavy censorship and can rarely say a great deal. Books allow greater leeway—but not as much as you might think. To have a large circulation, and particularly to be accepted as a textbook in the many courses that are given on marriage and family problems, a sex manual must usually lean over backward to be evasive, romantic, and noncommittal on many essential points. It cannot be fully explicit about birth control details; it dare not frankly say that premarital sex relations are fine and dandy; it frequently never even mentions non-coital sex relations; and it is generally much more restrained than its author is when he is speaking to a small group of his associates or friends.

One of the best ways in which sex-love education can be given is in the course of intensive psychotherapy—assuming that the therapist is himself undisturbed, well-informed, and open-minded. Since, however, individual psychotherapy tends to be time-consuming and expensive, and many about-to-be-married couples want a goodly degree of sex preparation in a reasonably quick and inexpensive form, a good compromise can often be had by resorting to group therapy that is especially centered on problems of marital adjustment.

In a group therapy session of this kind, conducted by one of the authors of this book, a part of the session consisted of the following interchange between the therapist and members of the group:

Therapist: Our first and second sessions will deal mainly with sex. Why sex first and longest? Because it's one of the biggest and roughest of all factors that lead to marital difficulties. Sex is, to begin with, a central focus of the husband-wife relationship. It's one of the main reasons why people marry and it is an intrinsic part of reproduction—to which most marriages lead. Take away sex and reproduction and marriage tends to become somewhat meaningless.

Mary K.: Aren't you being a little extreme? Lots of couples do not have any children and yet they seem to have good enough marriages.

Therapist: Quite so. In fact, some marriages without children are healthier and better than some with. But can you imagine a marriage that, from the start, contemplates neither sex nor children?

Mary K.: Well . . . no. I suppose not. Except in very unusual cases.

Therapist: Quite unusual! Not that I'm trying to say that

113

nothing but sex matters in marriage. Lots of other things do. But many or most of these things would probably cease to matter *in the whole pattern of marriage* if you removed sex. After all, people can go out together, be friendly, even live under the same roof without marrying. And they probably never would marry, most of them, if they didn't desire each other sexually.

John M.: I, for one, certainly wouldn't think of it!

Selma F.: I might think of it; but I doubt whether I'd ever go through with my thought!

Therapist: Agreed. So sex is the heart of most marriages, and troubles tend to center around the heart. When things go wrong elsewhere, the problems head toward the heart— toward the sex relations of the married couple. Sex is a sort of collector of troubles from other sources.

Mary K.: You mean that, even when the sex itself is good and other things are wrong, the sex then tends to go sour?

Therapist: Exactly. Not always, I must hasten to add. Occasionally, couples can hate each other's guts and still get along very well sexually. But not often! In addition, however, to being a repository where other troubles seem to accumulate and to affect its tone, sex is also a source of difficulties in and of itself.

Selma F.: Why is that?

Therapist: Why? Because, in large part, our society mishandles the whole matter of sex from infancy onward. We are confused about sex. We have recently emerged from a hush-hush approach to it, a kind of ostrich-like attitude of pretending it didn't really exist. We have somewhat moved away from this viewpoint today; but we don't know exactly how far to go. Many people still act like ostriches in regard to sex. Some others act like peacocks and flaunt sex and their defiance of the ostriches. Still others sit back and just look confused about both the ostriches and the peacocks. The ostriches convey the

114

notion that sex is bad and dirty. We've all had some ostrich conditioning. The peacocks, though, by their very defiance, show that they haven't really worked out a relaxed, comfortable, and happy sexual adjustment. Unconsciously, they have a lot of the ostrich left in them. And the confused ones quite evidently have no answers. Most of us enter marriage these days with our own particular mixture of attitudes about sex: part ostrich, part peacock, always more or less confused.

Leonard L.: You can count me in as one who used to be an ostrich, but is now frankly and honestly confused.

Marjorie S.: Ditto here!

Therapist: We can't expect, in this limited number of group sessions, to solve all the problems that come from sexual malconditioning, let alone all those that feed in from non-sexual sources. But perhaps we can, in these discussions, manage to give you a few useful hints about organizing your sex feelings.

As we enter marriage, what should be our basic expectation about sex? The most important attitude to have, perhaps, is that sex is fun of the most wonderful kind. It's a delightful plaything. We have legal permission and social approval, once we are married, to enjoy sex. So let's make the most and best of it. Sacred feelings about sex, like the dirty feelings for which they are a kind of shield, are for the birds—the ostriches and the peacocks of the strange and unhappy world of neurosis.

Mary K.: But aren't you being a little extreme, this time? *Isn't* sex a sacred thing, and shouldn't we try to keep it so?

Therapist: I'm glad to see, in a sense, that some of you, such as Mary here, are a little shocked by my words. This proves to me that you aren't simply reacting passively to what you may consider my entertaining performance. If you are, then I know that I'll never get anywhere in my attempt to launch a process of sexual reconditioning. Anyway, my answer to Mary is: No. Sex is *not* a sacred thing but a very earthly, very human, and, in fact, very animal thing. And the fact that

115

we insist on making it into some kind of sacrament only proves, as I said before, that we are really not ready to accept it for what it is.

Mary K.: But what about the dignity of the human being and the spiritual aspects of sex?

Therapist: Well, what of them? I didn't tell any of you, as far as I can recall, to be unkind, rough, inconsiderate, insensitive as you relate to your mate sexually. I said to have fun—both you and your spouse have fun. To have fun together, you have to be sensitive to the desires and feelings of the other. But dignified? Not in sex activity! Spiritual? Man in search of his soul? Not in bed. Dignity and spirituality can be incorporated in other than sexual situations. Love and respect for each other, yes. But you don't ask for dignity and spirituality in the midst of a watermelon-eating contest or a game of charades, do you? Are sports bad and dirty because they are undignified and unspiritual? Sex is a sport. Sex is fun.

John M.: Hear, hear!

Therapist: Nature has given us sex as a means of reproduction, you may say. Yes, so she has. But nature has also quite definitely given us the equipment to have fun with, too. Nature didn't, fortunately, just make the birth process a dreadful and dreary business. It made sex the outstanding built-in fun apparatus. Playing with sex, without proper contraceptive procedures, of course, may lead to the procreation of children. Since this is so, society has traditionally placed as many obstacles as possible in the way of our sex play—except in the marital situation, where we are generally set up to deal with the appearance of offspring. But because we must be prepared for the responsibilities of parenthood when we engage in sex play does not mean we are wrong in playing or wrong in having fun when we play.

Leonard L.: To read some of the sex manuals I've been trying to wade through recently, you'd think that sex wasn't fun at all—but one great engineering project! Do things *have* to be the way these manuals put it?

Therapist: I'm glad you raised that point, Leonard. I was just going to say that in enjoying yourself sexually, often one of the first and best things you can do is to disregard many of the well-known charts and manuals. As you note, they suggest that sex is something of an intellectual pastime, like playing chess or building the Boulder Dam. As I said before, the "gutter" type of approach to sex play, which regards it as a shameful and dirty activity, is certainly deplorable. But as undesirable and misleading as this "behind-the-barn" type of sex conditioning may be, it is often more realistic that the scientific chart approach. At least it recognizes feelings—sensual and emotional feelings—as the essence of sex relations; at least it implies that sex is a matter of experimentation and psychological commitment rather than just a question of intellectualization and anatomical maps.

Selma F.: But I've found some of the sex manuals very helpful. I'm not sure whether I would have ever known where some of my essential organs were without their help. Don't you think they can ever be helpful?

Therapist: Oh, yes: don't mistake me. A good sex book can be just as helpful as a good cookbook. But, just as fine cooking must, to some degree, be a creative act, a sensing, a let's-try-this-fantastic-thing-and-see-if-it-works process, so must fine sex. Sex manuals, particularly to the young and inexperienced lover, can be great; but not *sufficient unto themselves*. They can well map out general territories or give some specific ideas which two sex mates possibly might not think of themselves. But these sex books should be used as primers, not as encyclopedias; as outlines, not as work books. By the same token, the gutter approach can be used as a kind of primer, too—for it at least recognizes the healthy animal-like basis of sex relations. But it has its distinct limitations, since it also

117

views sex as something that is bad, immoral, and guilt-ridden. Even the strongest and healthiest sex urges can be inhibited by such moralistic attitudes.

After this introductory session, the group then went on to a consideration of many specific sex problems, some of which we shall treat in later chapters of this book. The point to be made here is that down-to-earth love-sex education for marriage is usually sadly lacking in our culture. Theoretically, it could be given in the home and the school; actually, of course, it is not. Parents are too biased and inhibited in their own sex attitudes to be good educators; and teachers and educational systems, as we have said previously, are distinctly limited. Working through sex problems in individual or group psychotherapy is perhaps one of the best methods now available and should be employed far more often than is presently true.

In any event, sex is an integral part of nearly all marriages, especially in our basically antisexual society, a part that presents many serious problems. In the following chapters we shall try to tackle some of these sex problems in more detail.

118

10

Impotence in the Male

Because both the authors of this book are known to specialize in the psychological aspects of sex problems, we see a good many men who are, or who think they are, impotent. But even more numerous than these are the many males who come to us for entirely different reasons—marriage difficulties, neurotic symptoms, or even business difficulties—and who, in the course of our questioning them, reveal distinct signs of impotence.

Sometimes, after seeing several such men in succession, we begin to wonder whether virtually all disturbed males in our culture are not, in one degree or other, sexually inadequate. This, fortunately, is an exaggeration; but there is also some measure of truth here.

Perhaps it would be well to define, at the outset, what impotence is. A male may be said to be sexually inadequate when he is afflicted with one or more of these conditions: (1) When he has little or no desire for sexual relations or has a distinct dislike for them. (2) When he has little or no sensitivity or experiences virtually no pleasure when his sex organs are directly stimulated. (3) When he is specifically oversensitive or experiences pain during sexual contact. (4) When he obtains an adequate erection but is not able to experience orgasm. (5) When he achieves an orgasm but receives little or no satisfaction or release through achieving it. (6) When he has great difficulty achieving an erection or easily loses his erection (by quick ejaculation or by its subsiding without ejaculation) once he has attained it.

Of the various types of male inadequacy, the last named one is far and away the most prevalent—or, at least, the one most complained of by males. Actually, the other types seem to be more common than is usually supposed.

Generally, however, males who do not desire sex relations, who are not easily aroused, who have oversensitive organs, and who have good erections but little pleasure in orgasm do not frequently become concerned about their difficulties. Frequently, they do not realize that they are afflicted; and, when they do, they often have little incentive to do anything about their affliction.

On the other hand, the male who has normal desire but who cannot easily get or maintain an erection is virtually always disturbed about his inadequacies and frequently will try to do something about them.

It is too easy for the psychologist or marriage counselor to assume that all forms of male impotence are the result of psychological factors. This is not true. Many organic, physiological, or constitutional causes of sexual inadequacy exist, including inborn defects, hormone deficiencies, lesions of the central nervous system, malnutrition, over-indulgence in alcohol and drugs, and various organic ailments and diseases. By and large, however, most males who seek help because they are partly or completely impotent are, when medically examined, found to be in just as good physical condition as most men who are fully potent. And it is generally agreed by urologists and other medical authorities, that male inadequacy is, in some ninety-five per cent of all cases, largely caused by psychological disturbances.

A case which will reveal some of the psychogenic causes of impotence is that of Mr. Poole. This client came for counseling, not because he was impotent, but because his wife had left him for another man. He was profoundly shocked by her action and wanted to do everything possible to get her back. When I questioned him about his sex relations with her, he readily admitted that he had been almost completely impotent for the entire ten years of their marriage. He felt, however, that this was unimportant; that his wife knew that he really loved her; and that she certainly would not have left him merely to gain more sex satisfaction with another man. Mr. Poole, in fact, was so convinced that his sexual inadequacy was unimportant that he had steadfastly refused to do anything about it for many years; although Mrs. Poole had frequently begged him to get some help in connection with it.

Mr. Poole's impotence took one of the most common forms: that of extremely rapid ejaculation. He would have no difficulty in achieving a firm erection; but just as soon as he attempted to enter his wife's vagina, or at best within a few seconds after entering it, he would ejaculate. He was then through for the evening and could not obtain another erection. In the circumstances, particularly because both he and his wife were prudishly afraid of all other forms of noncoital sex contact, his wife was completely unsatisfied and had never had a single orgasm in their entire married life.

121

It was not difficult to discover why Mr. Poole was impotent. In the first place, as has already been indicated, he was unusually Puritanical. He had been raised by a very religious (Baptist) mother and father, in a family circle where all demonstrations of physical affection were absolutely taboo. He had rigorously refrained from masturbation during his adolescence and early manhood and had castigated himself mercilessly whenever he even had a nocturnal emission. When he first started to date girls—after reaching his twentieth birthday—he treated them with the utmost respect and never even tried to kiss one good night. The first time he kissed his wife was after he had dated her steadily for two years. That was the night they became formally engaged; and he had never embraced her before their wedding.

In the second place, Mr. Poole was unconsciously afraid of having children, although consciously he said that he wanted very much to have them. He had had so little overt affection in his own home that he was desperately hungry for affection from his wife. He concentrated on the most romantic kind of relationship with her: bringing her home flowers every night, surprising her all the time with little gifts, telling her how much he adored her, etc. His aim was to obtain a similar, ultra-romantic, never-dying affection from her; and he was unconsciously afraid that, if they ever had any children, that would be the end of their romantic togetherness. Consequently, he did not really want to penetrate his wife sexually and thus risk pregnancy.

In the third place, Mr. Poole, while at first not greatly disturbed about his premature ejaculation, soon became terribly anxious and apprehensive about it. Although his fears of intercourse and of pregnancy were unconscious, his fear of impotence—of being incompetent, not being manly, not being able to satisfy his wife—was quite conscious, and somewhat overwhelming. He tried to employ the rationalization that sex was unimportant to marriage and that, because he showed his wife love in so many other ways, she could well forego a certain amount of sex satisfaction. But, underneath, he could not deny to himself the fact that he was a distinct sexual *failure*.

Being raised, moreover, in a society where manliness is considered next to godliness and where sexual adequacy is considered almost synonymous with manliness, Mr. Poole could not help looking upon himself as a weak, feminized individual. To compensate for this self-concept, he tried going to a gymnasium, playing poker with the boys, and being somewhat of a tyrant with his subordinates in the office. To no avail. He still felt like a weakling; and every time he had another quick ejaculation, he felt even more so.

At this point an utterly devastating secondary neurotic reaction set in on top of Mr. Poole's primary neurotic symptom. His primary reasons for being impotent, as noted above, were his deepseated prudishness and his fear of being affectionally replaced by his own (potential) children. But once these primary fears led to his sexual inadequacy, his perceptions of this inadequacy led to an obsessive secondary fear: the fear of continuing to be impotent. And this secondary fear, as is so often true in this kind of affliction, became worse, more perniciously powerful, than his primary anxieties.

After a while, Mr. Poole would start saying to himself, as soon as he even thought about having intercourse with his wife: "I wonder what's going to happen this time. I'll bet I won't last any longer than I ever do: not even a minute. I know I'll fail, just as I have always done. Why must it always be this way? But I'm just no good at this, no good. I know, I know I'll fail again. I just can't do it, can't keep it up. I'm just a weakling. No damned good!"

Then, being this negative about his potency, and suggesting to himself over and over again that he would fail, Mr. Poole invariably did. Each failure made him still more anxious, more negative, less self-confident. Each one led to further reindoctrination of the concept that he was weak, inadequate, impotent.

Finally, he got to the point where, even had his original reasons for (unconsciously) wanting to be impotent—his fear of sexuality and of having children—even if these had somehow vanished entirely, his secondary reasons for being impotent—that is, his very fear *of* so being—would have kept him quite inadequate.

This, unfortunately, is what almost inevitably happens to neurotics. The primary reasons for their symptoms of disturbance may indeed be important factors in the causation of these symptoms. But once the symptoms start—once the obsessions, compulsions, phobias, psychosomatic complaints, or other neurotic results are well established—the patient becomes so disturbed about the symptoms themselves that his neurosis becomes quadruply intensified. Thus, fear of criticism may originally produce stuttering; but then fear of stuttering may produce still more, and more, and still more stuttering. Unsatisfied and conflicting sex desires may originally lead to insomnia; but then fear of insomnia may easily lead to worse, and worse, and still worse insomnia.

So particularly with male impotence. Just because, in our culture, impotence is conceived of as being such a *horrible*, such a *heinous* symptom, it gives rise to secondary fears and anxieties which almost inevitably deepen and worsen the impotence. Just because the male ego is so viciously attacked and positively devastated by the mere thought of being sexually inadequate, the afflicted male is thoroughly panicked, shocked, and almost paralyzed by perceiving that he has this particularly neurotic symptom. And he becomes, in consequence, more self-condemning, more generally and sexually inadequate.

Mr. Poole, for example, had quite enough problems to face in life without being impotent. Because his parents rigidly eschewed overt affection, he grew up with the belief that he was unworthy of love and he felt relatively worthless. Because his family stressed "goodness" and anti-sexuality, he believed himself to be wicked and perverse whenever he had normal sex desires. Because he was not the brightest, most talented individual in the world, and had been raised to believe that he *should* be, he felt incompetent in business and social areas of life.

In many ways, then, Mr. Poole was having a normally difficult time keeping his ego above water, maintaining a decent estimation of himself. Then, when his underlying feelings of inferiority resulted in a specific neurotic symptom—as it could have well been predicted that they eventually would—and when his particular symptom, impotence, itself was culturally viewed as a terrible blot on a man's sexual-amative and general escutcheon, this was just about the last straw. His self-hatred increased while his self-confidence proportionately decreased. Fear of not being potent led to virtual certainty that he never could be. This, in turn, reduced his feelings of adequacy and self-confidence still further. The usual neurotic vicious circle was then nicely whirling, whirling, whirling.

What could be done to help Mr. Poole? One logical first step was to give him some insight into the original causes of his impotence. This was not easy. He had, at first, no inclination whatever to admit that he was unusually Puritanical; nor that, if he was, Puritan notions could be at the bottom of his sexual disability.

Mr. Poole brought up some material that indicated that his prudishness had not merely been directly acquired from his parents but that it had partly been erected as a defense against his incestuous urges toward his beautiful young mother. Particularly at this point, he tended to resist probing and interpretation.

At this juncture, were I a well-trained "non-directive" therapist or an orthodox Freudian, I would have beat a hasty retreat, would have very gently (over a period, say, of several hundred analytic sessions) worked through Mr. Poole's resistance, or would have otherwise been afraid to go on with my probing. Not, however, being orthodox in any respect, and always feeling obliged to keep at least one eye on the patient's

125

pocketbook, I persisted in grappling more directly with his resistance, and soon was practically beating his Puritanism over its repulsive head.

I showed the patient, in other words, how and why his (and other people's) prudishness originated; what dynamic purpose it served; how unscientific and idiotic it was in this day and age; what tremendous harm it was doing him; and how, like other superstitions he had understood and tackled in the past, he should and could get rid of it. My frontal attack was unequivocal and sustained. It often is in the process of rational psychotherapy.

"But how," asked Mr. Poole at one point, "can you expect me to change my ideas about sex, when I have had them so long and have always assumed that they were the correct views, and have acted accordingly on them?"

"The mere fact," I replied, "that you have eaten horse manure for thirty years, without ever quite realizing what kind of food it was, is no excuse for continuing to eat it forever. If you *enjoy* being a sexual Puritan, and derive notably good results from being one, well and good. But, obviously, this is not quite true, is it?"

"No, I am afraid that I have to admit that it is not," ruefully replied Mr. Poole. "But do you mean to say that just because I don't enjoy some aspects of my behavior and see that they are defeating my own ends, that I can stop them—just like that?"

"Theoretically, yes. If you can *do* a thing—such as tell yourself that sex is horrible stuff and that it would be awful to have a child who would compete with you for your wife's attentions —you can obviously *not* do that same thing—that is, tell yourself that sex is *not* horrible and that it would *not* be awful if you did not have your wife's sole attention."

"And will I then, if I tell myself that sex is good and having a child with my wife is great stuff, will I then automatically get over the fears that originally, as you have been showing me, led to my impotence?"

126

"No, not automatically, unfortunately. It's not quite as easy as that. Besides, don't make the mistake of thinking that I am teaching you some kind of Couéism or 'power of positive thinking' method of saving your soul—for I am not. Telling yourself that sex is good and having a child with your wife is great stuff may not necessarily be true in your case—for perhaps you *don't* really like sex that much or care to have a child. And even if you do, this kind of 'positive thinking' is not going to get you very far. At the most it may serve as a temporary diversion from your difficulties. It cannot really correct them as long as, together with this 'accentuating the positive,' you are *still* unconsciously or unawarely emphasizing the negative."

"I don't quite get that. You mean that I am actually doing, or can do, two kinds of thinking at once, and that as long as I do both, there will be a noticeable—uh—conflict and I won't very well be able to rid myself. . . ? "

"Precisely! There is no reason whatever why human beings cannot, at almost the same time, or at least within, say, that same minute or hour, think *two* kinds of quite contradictory thoughts. And that's exactly what you, and most other disturbed people, have been doing all your life. I don't have to tell you, for example, that sex is good or that having a child may bring great joys—you already know that, don't you?"

"Why, yes. I've often thought just that."

"Right. You *know* it. Unfortunately, however, you *also* 'know' quite the opposite. That is, you 'know' that sex and children are horrible. And most of the time, and with much deeper conviction, you 'know,' and keep repeating to yourself, the so-called horrors of sex and child rearing. While only a small percentage of the time—perhaps two to five per cent—you 'know' and keep convincing yourself that genitality and reproduction are *not* horrible."

"So if I can reverse the process, then, and most of the time convince myself of the latter—that having intercourse is *not*

127

awful—instead of the former, I will then get over my sex trouble?"

"Yes, you will then get over your *original* sex blockings—the ideas and inhibitions which *first* led to your incapacity. But, remember, it's not quite as easy as it looks at first blush: for you must not only *tell* yourself, over and over again, that intercourse and child rearing are *not* awful, *not* terrible, *not* frightful; you must actually *convince* yourself that this is so. Without such conviction, all the word-parroting in the world will not help change your ideas."

"But how *can* I convince myself?"

"How did you convince yourself that various other superstitions that you once believed—such as a belief in the horror of spilling salt or seeing a black cat—were not true? By *thinking* about them. By *working* at getting rid of them. By weighing, time and again, the so-called evidence supporting them and finding it wanting. In other words, as I tell my patients almost ad nauseam, you can only get rid of a superstition or false belief—such as your belief that sex is horrible—by continually *questioning, challenging, contradicting* it, by doing what we do in scientific experiments: marshaling the factual evidence against this highly implausible hypothesis."

"So if I keep questioning and challenging my notions that sex and child rearing are terrible, they will eventually begin to change or go away."

"Right. And, if you really work steadily and faithfully at such questioning and challenging, you might be surprised how quickly this self-eradicating process can take."

"But don't I have to understand fully the origins of my false beliefs, find out exactly how I first acquired them."

"No, actually you do not. It's nice to know their origins in detail. It sometimes helps you in the process of questioning and challenging them. But as long as you are willing to accept the fact that these antisexual superstitions of yours did have an origin, that you were not born with them but were directly and indirectly indoctrinated with them by your parents and your culture, it is not really necessary to know all the details of how you originally acquired them. Interesting and informative, yes; but not necessary.

"If, for example, we never can determine, even after hundreds of sessions of psychotherapy, exactly how you were originally indoctrinated with the black cat superstition you can still, today, challenge, question, and contradict it, and thereby rid yourself fully of it. If we discover that your mother specifically had a violent fear of black cats, or of perhaps all cats, this may help you undermine your present superstition; but you can still do so, and quite effectively, *without* such detailed information about how you originally acquired it."

"Instead of 'positive thinking,' you want me to work hard at 'contradicting the negative' and then you are sure I will lose my Puritanical outlook."

"Right. Since *you* originally acquired this outlook, and *you* have been unwittingly maintaining it by reindoctrinating internal sentences ever since you acquired it, *you,* of course, can rid yourself of it. By *work,* I insist—by effort, practice, energy. By energetically and consistently *contradicting* the nonsense which you have been, and even at the present moment still are, needlessly feeding yourself."

In this manner, over a period of several more weeks of therapy, Mr. Poole's basic antisexual and anti-child-rearing concepts were directly tackled and he was encouraged and persuaded to challenge and question them himself, in between the sessions. This, in a workmanlike way, he proceeded to do.

At the same time, and even more importantly, his attitudes toward the horror of failure and of deeming himself worthless unless he succeeded at sex and other tasks were also brought to his awareness and forcefully attacked. He was convinced that he need *not* blame himself after any sex failure; that it was only normal and natural for human beings to fail, at first, at complex tasks like having mutually satisfying sex relations;

and that a sex failure was merely that, a sex failure, and was no indication whatever of an individual's intrinsic worth.

In addition, Mr. Poole was specifically taught non-coital methods of bringing his wife to satisfactory orgasm if and when he was unable to do so coitally. With his new-found lack of tension because he had stopped blaming himself for possible failure and because he realized that coital ineptitude need not necessarily deprive his wife of her full satisfaction, he soon took a radically different attitude toward sex relations and began, at first at times, later with regularity, to be fully potent. On several occasions, moreover, he was able to have multiple orgasms for the first time in his life and he was quite surprised at his own hidden talents.

Also to his surprise, even though relatively little time was given during his therapy to the discussion of his relations with others, he voluntarily realized that he was acting tyrannically at the office, because of his "need" to lord it over others and "prove" his masculinity. Then he became a considerably more relaxed and efficient worker in his business surroundings. Although I have not seen him now for several years, he keeps referring new patients to me from time to time, and they often indicate that he is a remarkably changed and happier individual.

Mr. Poole's case illustrates some of the most salient factors in male impotence: specifically, Puritanism, generalized feelings of inadequacy, fear of losing something (such as the affection of one's wife), and panic about the state of impotence itself. These factors are not, of course, present in every single case of male inadequacy. Indeed, in virtually no neurosis is any one causative factor necessarily present; and multiple causation is much more likely to be the rule. Nonetheless, in most instances, the so-called "sex" problem is not really that at all. It is a general personality problem, and usually has deepseated roots in the individual's general background and philosophies of living.

130

As Alfred Adler pointed out many years ago, and as the modern psychoanalytic theorists are increasingly accepting, most human problems are not sex but ego difficulties. The troubled person, instead of being truly concerned with his own preferences and attempting to see how he can best get out of life what he really wants (such as love, sex, and work satisfactions) is inordinately concerned with comparing himself to *others* and thinking of himself as worthless unless he conforms to, and at least equals or surpasses, *their* standards and values. Consequently, he loses the proper focus on his own tastes and desires and incompetently and unhappily chases himself around the tree of life instead of enjoying its fruits.

Even the so-called specific and psychodynamically deep-seated "causes" of impotence are almost invariably related to the individual's estimation of himself and others. Thus, a man may consciously or unconsciously dislike or hate his wife, and consequently be unwilling to be potent with her; or he may view her as a mother rather than a sex partner; or he may be strongly influenced by her sexual inhibitions and inadequacies; or he may have unconscious homosexual leanings; or he may be guilty about premarital or extramarital affairs; or he may have an Oedipus complex and fear that he is going to be castrated by having intercourse; et cetera.

In all these instances, the male, at bottom, feels threatened about being dominated, losing his manhood, standing on his own two feet, performing a "wrong" or "wicked" act, and so on. And his feelings of being thus threatened are directly consequent to his taking other people's opinions too seriously and being afraid stoutly to stand up to his own basic desires.

Again, impotence is sometimes caused by poor sex techniques, such as coitus interruptus; or lack of confidence in the contraceptives being used; or fear of acquiring venereal disease; or other technical or informational deficiencies. But if the individual really likes himself and is determined to do something about his sex inadequacy, these difficulties can, with relatively little effective counseling, easily be overcome. When he does not sufficiently have his own self-respect and instead worries endlessly what *others* may think of him, he rarely will take the required remedial steps. So, once again, his "sex" problem really is one of personality inadequacy.

When one realizes that perhaps the vast majority of males in our culture have more or less serious feelings of inadequacy—because they were raised to have them in the first place and were sent out into a highly competitive world in the second place—it is hardly surprising that many of them should ultimately display their general feelings of incompetence by becoming impotent in the sexual area. It is only to be expected that general inadequacy, or feelings in regard to such inadequacy, will frequently induce sexual insufficiency; and it does. Consequently, the treatment of the impotent male rarely involves the treatment of his sexual symptoms alone. Rather, it involves the treatment of the whole individual—of his general as well as his specialized neurosis.

It might even be said that sexual impotence is something of a boon to many men just because it causes them sufficient discomfort so that they may go for therapeutic help, which otherwise they might never approach.

John Katt, for example, came for therapy because he found it impossible to achieve a full, rigid erection. Otherwise, he said, he was getting along fine. But he soon began to admit, after a little questioning, that this was not exactly true. In spite of a fine academic record, he was failing in his profession of dentistry. In his family circle, where he very much wanted to be a big shot, his opinions were largely ignored and he was treated as if he were a nonentity. Although he tried to become an active participant in social groups he found himself virtually tongue-tied when in any group and felt most uncomfortable.

Dr. Katt's sexual impotency was not difficult to track down to its sources. His wife looked upon him in much the same manner as his acquaintances and family members—that is, as a big lummox, totally inept. He became impotent because (a) he was living up to her picture of him (and his own picture of himself) and (b) he unconsciously wanted to get back at his wife for having such a low estimation of him, and was consequently going on a sort of sitdown—or, rather, liedown—strike against her.

The truly crucial point in this case was not that John Katt was sexually impotent but that he was generally impotent and that he probably never would have done anything about his general inadequacy unless he had been plagued by his sexual debility. Coming to therapy because of sexual failure, he was ready to be shown the whole pattern of his life and to work on his general as well as his sexual inadequacy.

When, in the course of psychotherapy, he was soon enabled to become fully potent sexually, he felt that he did not want to stop at that point, but spontaneously insisted upon going on with the treatment until his general inadequacy feelings were rooted out, challenged, questioned, and overcome. He was then able to make a satisfactory adjustment in vocational, family, and social as well as in sexual areas.

Summing up: sexual impotence is an important neurotic symptom and can usually be cured by psychotherapy; but it is a symptom of general neurosis in most instances; and it is more important that the victim's underlying disturbance be worked on and overcome than that his sexual symptom be ameliorated. Feelings of inadequacy are feelings of inadequacy no matter how you slice them. They merely become more dramatically provoking when they take the form of sexual disability.

11

Frigidity in the Female

As is true of sexual impotence in the male, which we have just been examining, frigidity in the female is a term that has often been used to cover a multiplicity of sexual disorders and disabilities. Women have been called frigid when they were anesthetic, indifferent, incompetent, and inorgastic. Also: women who are not easily stimulated; who have pain or displeasure in intercourse; and who have little or no satisfaction even when they do achieve a climax.

The issue of female frigidity has been particularly confused because many early sexologists, including most orthodox Freudians, tended to consider a woman frigid, no matter how high her sex desire or how climactic her performance, if she did not achieve full sexual release "vaginally" or during coitus. As both the present authors have noted on many previous occasions, this narrow concept of frigidity is not backed by any scientific data. As long as a female is able to achieve, with a fair degree of regularity, a satisfactory orgasm in *some* manner—whether through intercourse, digital manipulation of the clitoris, supplementary anal stimulation, or any other method—there is no legitimate reason for labeling her as frigid.

Although there are many individual causes of frigidity in the female, virtually all of them may be subsumed under three main headings: organic causes, relationship causes, and psychological causes. Organic causes are generally held to be unimportant in most instances, but they *do* at times exist. Thus, a woman may be sexually unresponsive because she has inborn hormonal deficiencies; defects or injuries of the sex organs; serious nutritional lacks; lesions or defects of the central nervous system; general organic ailments or diseases; fatigue and low vitality; or normal aging processes. Before it is cavalierly assumed that her frigidity is of emotional origin, she should undergo a thorough medical examination to uncover any possible physical causes of the problem.

Relationship causes are particularly important in female frigidity (rather than in male impotence, where they usually play a less important role) and are connected with the fact that human sex proclivities frequently become disorganized and unfulfilled when one partner in a sex, love, or marital relationship becomes disturbed about her mate's attitudes or actions. Thus, a woman may become sexually inhibited because she does not love her husband or feels that he does not sufficiently care for her; because she resents him for things he has or hasn't done; because she is not physically attracted to him; because his sexual technique or capacity is, in her eyes, deficient or insufficient; because she thinks his sex demands on her are too great; or for a host of similar reasons concerned with her personal and sexual relationship with her husband.

135

In addition to or instead of relationship difficulties between mates, there may be a number of other psychological reasons why a particular woman is frigid. Thus, she may have been raised to have severe feelings of shame or guilt about all sex relations, even including marital intercourse. She may be consciously or unconsciously afraid to become pregnant. She may have homosexual tendencies which block her interests in heterosexual relations. She may have deep-seated attachments to her father or some other male relative which arouse guilt reactions and inhibit her letting herself go sexually with her husband or lover. Or she may be so generally disturbed—that is, severely neurotic or psychotic—that she is incapable of focusing adequately on sexual stimuli and coordinating her physical movements sufficiently well to achieve full sexual arousal and climax.

Deep-seated psychological disturbances, such as some of those just listed, frequently lie at the root of frigidity. But it is questionable if the *main* causes of *most* cases of contemporary female sexual inadequacy are to be found in highly complicated and deeply hidden unconscious motives that have to be discovered in the course of hundreds of sessions of intensive psychoanalysis or psychotherapy. The two primary causes of frigidity today are probably of more superficial psychological origin.

The first of these is ignorance, by apparently millions of women in our culture, of the fact that sexual arousal and satisfaction are not a matter of proper physical stimulation alone, but are also very much a brain function. They are a result of what the woman *thinks* and *imagines* while she is engaging in sex relations. Women, in particular, appear to need to *focus persistently* on sex-love objects and relations while their bodies are being adequately stimulated in order to achieve full responsiveness. When they fail to do so, and focus instead on non-sexual things while engaging in sex acts, they frequently set up insuperable psychological blocks to satisfaction.

A case in point is that of Mrs. Patrice Murphy, who came for therapy because she had never, in her whole life, experienced a sexual orgasm. She seemed to have adequate sex desires and had even rather avidly had sex relations with several males before meeting and marrying her husband. Although she had enjoyed these relations to some degree, she had only come close to but never quite achieved climax. She said that she loved her husband and also enjoyed intercourse with him; but, again, without climactic result. One of the first interchanges between Mrs. Murphy and the therapist went as follows:

THERAPIST: You say that you almost reach orgasm on many occasions, but that you never quite make it. Is that right?

MRS. M.: Yes. It gets very frustrating after a while, too! Just as I think I'm about to get there—and, bang, down I come to zero again. Sometimes I could almost scream.

THERAPIST: What do you think about when you are having sex relations and trying to achieve an orgasm?

MRS. M.: Think about? I don't really know. Nothing, I guess.

THERAPIST: It's pretty hard for a human being to think of literally nothing. Almost impossible, in fact. Now try to remember: what do you actually think of at those times?

MRS. M.: Hmmm. It still seems to me—But no: maybe you're right. I probably do think of—Hmmm.

THERAPIST: Yes? Of what do you think?

MRS. M.: I guess I think of *it*. Of orgasm, that is. Of not getting it.

THERAPIST: Of how terrible it is that you don't get it, you mean?

MRS. M.: Yes! That's it, mostly. Of "am I going to be able to get it this time?" And "my God, how close can one be and still not get it!" And things like that.

THERAPIST: In other words: you keep *worrying* about not getting an orgasm, this time, just as you were worrying about not getting it last time; and you're using the fact that you did not get it last time as presumptive "proof" that you probably won't get it this time, again. Is that it?

MRS. M.: That's exactly it! I just *know* I won't get it this

137

time, because I never have before, and I'm afraid that I won't get it ever.

THERAPIST: You're right: that exactly *is* it. And it's just that kind of worrying, of being certain that you never had it before and won't ever get it this time or in the future, that keeps you from focusing properly on the pleasure, the joy of getting it right now. Naturally, with your mind out of focus in that manner, you're going to knock off any possibility of getting an orgasm.

MRS. M.: You mean there's something *else* I should be thinking about while having relations?

THERAPIST: Right. I mean just that. Sex satisfaction is as much or more a product of the mind as of the body. And even though you're doing just the right things with your husband—and from what you tell me he's quite a good and considerate lover—you're hardly doing the right things *with yourself*.

MRS. M.: Can you be more specific? *What* am I not doing? *What* am I not thinking that I should be focusing on?

THERAPIST: On what I just said before—on pleasure, on the joy of having relations. You should be focusing on whatever excites you sexually; on your own physical sensations; on the stimulating quality of your husband; on the feelings in your loins and genital area; on the allied sensations in your lips and breasts and internal regions; on the emotions you are having along with your physical contacts; on anything and everything that focuses your pelvic musculature toward the sexual peaks and contractions which eventually culminate in orgasm.

MRS. M.: But can I really *do* such a thing? Can I help myself, physically and mentally, to come to climax? Can I strive and strain at it?

THERAPIST: You certainly can—just as you can, and I am sure do, help yourself to focus on a complex musical symphony, and derive almost orgiastic joy, at times, from it. Just as you strive to enjoy a party, when you begin by having a dull time at it. Sex is often something to be worked and strained at—as an artist works and strains at his painting or sculpture. Not

138

worried about (as a neurotic artist does about his creations); not catastrophized about lest your effort to achieve sex satisfaction possibly fail. But creatively, actively, pleasantly striven for, focused upon, concentrated on.

MRS. M.: You are distinguishing, then, between my trying, fairly hard, to achieve a climax and my worrying, equally hard, about the possibility of my *not* achieving it?

THERAPIST: Exactly. Work, effort, creative straining, productive tension—these are all good things, without which human beings would attain little that is worth attaining in life. Art, science, even business would hardly exist without this kind of dedicated activity or creative commitment of oneself to short-range and long-range goals. But this kind of productive tension should not be confused with unproductive, self-sabotaging *hypertension*: which really amounts to worrying over possible failure, catastrophizing a potential lack of goal attainment.

MRS. M.: So I should work at focusing on achieving an orgasm but not work myself up into a lather at the possibility of failing to achieve it? I should strive for success without catastrophizing the eventuality of failure?

THERAPIST: Right! Try every physical and mental trick in the books to focus on your climaxing. Commit yourself, all out, to the *trying*, the *activity* of sex. But not to the "dreadfulness" or the "horror" or your own assumed "worthlessness" or failure. "If at once you don't succeed, try, try again." *Trying* never hurt anyone. Nor, even, did failing. Only your own *false belief* that failure is horrible, your own groundless *assumption* that you are to blame for not succeeding—only this *makes* the horror exist. And, of course, deflects you from the pleasurable, creative focusing on your own orgasm.

Mrs. Murphy got the point. She did, for the first time in her life, try focusing on her own sex pleasure, rather than on how horrible it would be it she failed to achieve this pleasure. First through masturbation; then through clitoral massage by her husband; and finally even through coitus, she was able to achieve major breakthroughs and obtain occasional orgasms. As she got more practiced at the proper kind of focusing, and more expert at turning off her own fears of failure, her orgasms became more and more regular.

After four months of therapy she was having two or three climaxes a week, and sometimes two or more a night (especially around her periods, when she was more sexually excitable). From a completely non-orgasmic woman she became a thoroughly enjoying and satisfied sex mate, and she and her husband were highly gratified by her progress.

Mrs. Murphy's case not only illustrates the first of the two main psychological barriers to sexual fulfillment which afflict so many American women—that is, their ignorance about how to focus on their own climaxing—but also is a good example of the second main barrier which today is so prevalent: namely, worry and catastrophizing about orgasm. As soon as a woman tends to believe that she must be sexually competent and begins to tell herself how frightful it would be if she did *not* achieve a tremendous state of desire and climax, her very exaggeration of the *necessity* of her being sexually successful will frequently prevent her success. Any time an individual believes that she *must* succeed in some endeavor, rather than that it would be *preferable* if she did, disaster in that endeavor is very likely to befall her. This is particularly true of women who feel that they *have to* succeed at achieving sex orgasm and that it is utterly disastrous when they do not.

Thus, Mrs. Murphy not only *wanted* to be able to come to climax, she unconsciously *demanded* that she be able to do so. But as soon as one demands anything, the possibility always exists, and must on some level of consciousness be acknowledged, that one may *not* get one's demands fulfilled. By definition, however, a demanded thing is a necessary one; and if there is a possibility that one will *not* get a necessity, one must almost inevitably be anxious about this.

If, on the other hand, one merely *wants* or *prefers* something, the recognition that it is possible that one will not get it produces merely irritation or annoyance or disappointment rather than deep-seated anxiety.

When Mrs. Murphy gave up her demand that she achieve orgasm, and concentrated instead on her preference to obtain it, the work and the practice she did to obtain this preference soon attained her goal. Work and practice almost always, when they are not accompanied by anxiety, help an individual improve at psychomotor tasks—such as playing the piano, cooking a meal, or achieving orgasm.

Are there any practical steps, aside from non-anxious sexual focusing, which a woman and her mate may take in order to facilitate sexual arousal and lead, finally, to satisfactory orgasm? There are. First, in regard to arousing a female who usually is quite difficult to bring to a high point of sexual excitement, the following steps, which are discussed in more detail in *The Art and Science of Love,* by Albert Ellis, may prove to be useful:

1. The woman who is not easily arousable should engage in sex relations at a time best suited for excitability: for example, when she is relaxed, well-rested, not pressed for time, and away from troubling circumstances.

2. The woman's partner should make overtures at a time when the mates have been getting along excellently together and when there is a minimum of strain and hostility between them.

3. Kindness, consideration, and love by the mate is likely to be more effective than any rougher kind of treatment.

4. Special care should be taken to locate and to stimulate adequately the special erogenous zones of the woman after these have been experimentally explored and determined.

5. Considerable direct genital stimulation before any vaginal penetration is attempted is required by many females who are not easily aroused. In many or most women, the vagina itself is not a particularly sensitive organ, except for its first inch or so (or introitus). But the clitoris, the inner lips, and the region

of the urethra are usually quite sensitive, and should be adequately massaged or kissed for maximum arousal, and often for orgasm itself.

6. Coitus itself, even though at first not too stimulating, may lead to arousal in some instances. Often, however, women find coitus distinctly anti-arousing if it is engaged in before other forms of arousal are utilized. As in all sexual regards, frank experimentation in this respect is most desirable.

7. Periods of rest in between arousal attempts may sometimes be desirable. A woman who is not easily aroused at her mate's first attempts may, five or ten minutes later, be in a more receptive mood—especially if her mate has been attentive and considerate during the interim.

8. The application of ointments or hand lotions (such as camphor-menthol ointment or commercial lotions) to the woman's external genitals may sometimes be desirable.

Assuming that a woman with a tendency toward sexual anesthesia has achieved sufficient arousal, there are several techniques which she and her mate may employ to help her attain full climax:

1. If the woman is found to have special areas of sex sensation, such as the clitoris or the upper wall of the vagina, her partner should exert steady, consistent, rhythmic pressure on these areas until she approaches or achieves climax.

2. In certain instances, special kinds of strokings—such as intermittent, irregular ones or very forceful massage—of sensitive parts will be desirable and perhaps necessary.

3. Verbal or attitudinal expressions by the woman's partner —such as protestations of love—may sometimes be needed to bring a woman to fulfillment.

4. Deep, forceful penile-vaginal penetration, which can best be obtained in certain coital positions (such as the position where the two partners are seated facing each other) may sometimes help bring a woman to climax.

5. Multiple physical contact is desirable in many instances.

Thus, the male may kiss or caress his wife's breasts or caress her clitoris while they are having coitus.

6. A variety of non-coital stimulations and coital positions is often desirable, since a relatively low-sexed woman may today become bored with the same technique that yesterday was terribly exciting.

7. There is no law against a woman's stimulating herself at the same time that her husband is also endeavoring to help bring her to climax.

For all the usefulness of such sexual techniques as have just been listed, it must again be stressed that, exactly as is true of the impotent male, the frigid female very frequently has general problems of emotional disturbance which far outweigh in import her sexual incapacities, and which in many instances are the main cause of these sexual ineffectualities.

Only a few weeks ago, for example, I saw a thirty-three-year-old unmarried female who, in spite of considerable petting and several affairs with a variety of highly eligible males, some of whom she was deeply fond of, was quite unable to achieve orgasm. It became clear, after just two psychotherapeutic sessions with this woman, that her entire pattern of behavior with her male consorts was that of serving them in every possible way, letting them often exploit her in order to win their affections, and never standing up for her own rights or desires.

This pattern of emotional enslavement, motivated by her dire need to be loved by others, was quickly revealed to this patient. After it was forcefully attacked for several more sessions by the therapist, the patient almost miraculously began to stick up for herself for the first time in her life. She asked one of her current boy friends several pertinent questions about himself which she had hitherto been afraid to broach. She took another suitor firmly to task when he inexcusably came very late to an appointment with her. She refused to be bulldozed any longer by one of her girl friends to whom she had been nauseatingly kowtowing for several years.

143

Although specific sex matters were only lightly and briefly discussed with this patient—largely because so much time was spent in discussing her general problem of self-immolation—she began to have terrific orgasms with the suitor whom she had taken to task for being late (and with whom, previously, she had only managed to become sexually excited but never fulfilled).

As she herself put it during the fifth therapeutic session: "It's amazing, the things I've been doing these last few weeks. I never thought I could ever do anything like that. And the way I'm beginning to like myself, now, when I always simply loathed myself before—that's even more amazing! As for the sex, I really think that that's coming without my hardly trying. I know that you told me to keep focusing on my own satisfaction. But even if you hadn't, I think I would be doing it anyway. For I really *like* myself now, and I *want* to do good by me. I think, for the first time, that I *deserve* to get full satisfaction. So I try, I really try these days. And—well, much to my surprise at first, it's there! But no, it really isn't that much to my surprise. I sort of *expect,* now, that I will be satisfied—that I deserve to be. And *that's* what's doing it, I think—my new expectation. I think I will be satisfied—and I am!"

This attitude—that one deserves to be and will be satisfied, that one is *worthy* of orgasm, is almost the nub of the whole matter. Once a human being feels *that* way, and then keeps actively trying, practicing to be satisfied, it is usually only a matter of time when sexual orgasm (or virtually anything else she really wants to achieve) will come her way. Work and worthwhileness—an almost unbeatable combination for a human being's getting what she really wants. Put these in your sexual-social armamentarium and the fine results may well be positively amazing.

12

Sex "Excess"

Not all our clients who fear that they are engaging in sexual "excesses" are men. One female, who thought that Martin Luther's rule of couples' copulating twice a week was to be taken literally, was inclined to have dizzy spells and blackouts when she and her husband had intercourse four or five times in a single week. She was easily cured when she was reassured that the father of the German Reformation had made no allowances for widespread individual differences and that, while semi-weekly coitus is more than sufficient for many couples, it is a starvation diet for many others.

Other women, with more logic, often ask whether having multiple orgasms nightly is "too much" or "unhealthy." Again, we invariably tell them no. We have seen woman after woman

145

who has six, ten, fifteen, and more climaxes a night, and sometimes for weeks or months on end, with little or no effect on her health and well-being. If any, the effect is usually decidedly favorable.

The fact seems to be that the human sex drives have their automatic feedback regulators or governors: so that when they begin to become "excessive," they also become pleasureless and temporarily nonexistent. If you happen to be, normally, a three-or-four-orgasm-per-week individual, you may occasionally push yourself to five or six. But not for long! You will soon begin to feel sexually irritated, listless, and disinterested and will quickly tend to desist and return to your normal quota.

Not that it is always easy to determine what your particular orgasmic quota actually is. Too many other factors than the strictly biological enter here. A man or woman, for example, may usually be a once-a-day copulator. But many physical factors (such as illness, vitamin deficiency, malnutrition, and cold) and many psychological factors (such as hatred of one's mate, sex guilt or fear of "excess") may reduce this person to a once-a-week routine. Or an individual with moderate sex capacities may be enabled to exceed his normal rate as a result of violently falling in love, having numerous changes of sex partners, or losing his neurotic sex guilt and fear. What a person's "normal" sex capacity is, therefore, is considerably influenced by the kind of life he lives, physically and psychologically.

Nonetheless, sex desires are partly biological and each individual appears to have a more or less physiologically based sex capacity which may be considerably reduced by various circumstances but which cannot easily be appreciably increased for a long period of time. A once-a-day copulator may, merely as a result of a change in his ideas and attitudes, quickly be brought down to a once-a-month frequency. But to increase his copulatory rate to, say, a frequency of three or four times a day, for even a period of a few weeks, is in most instances quite impossible.

146

It is interesting, in this connection, to note the attitude of one of my patients. When he first came to see me, he was able to have sex relations only about once a week. After a few months of treatment, he was able to have them from ten to fifteen times a week, and often three or four times a night.

"Maybe," he said, "you're just talking this into me and that's why I've been able to do it so often recently."

"Nonsense," I replied. "If I were able to talk sex into anyone as you think I may be doing in your case, I wouldn't be wasting my time doing marriage counseling and psychotherapy. I'd simply go around talking sex into this man and that man and, in no time, considering the vast sums most of them would be more than willing to pay for this service, I'd be a millionaire ten times over. The only reason I can 'talk sex into' you is because it was always there, in the first place, and you've simply squelched it all these years with your neurotic guilt feelings. In helping you get rid of your silly fears about sex, I am merely helping you to actualize the sex drives you've always had. I can't create any such drives, no matter how deaf and dumb I talk you or anyone else into it. If I could, I'd be the greatest benefactor of mankind—and womankind—of the ages!"

In this man's case, he had been seduced by his older sister when he was eleven years of age, and had had intercourse with her two or three times a day for a whole year. At first, he had naively accepted this incestuous relationship, but later had tended to become increasingly guilty about it. He tried to stop, but couldn't. He became still more disturbed and was only able to resolve his difficulties by becoming less capable of having erections and orgasms. He convinced himself that daily copulation was "excessive" and he cut down to once-a-week sex relations with his sister.

Ultimately, he was able to find other girls with whom he could have intercourse and he discontinued the relations with his sister. When he married, at the age of seventeen, he was utterly convinced that he was a once-a-week copulator, and that any greater frequency of intercourse was injurious to his health.

At the age of twenty-five, this patient came to see me, not because he felt he had sex problems but because he was having violent disagreements with his wife over how they should raise their children. I was soon able to show him that his concepts of sexual "excess" were directly related to his defense against his incestuous relations with his sister and that actually he had no reason for fearing such "excess." Very quickly, as noted above, he was able to increase his coital activities with his wife considerably.

I had much more difficulty in getting him to stop blaming his wife for the way in which she was treating their children; but when I finally convinced him that, even though she was mistaken about many of her child-rearing notions, she was not a criminal for being wrong and that he could reeducate her much more effectively by being calm and non-critical than by being savagely fault-finding, their sex relations were qualitatively as well as quantitatively bettered and their marriage notably improved.

Another interesting case has, with minor variations, been repeated several times in my practice. A twenty-two-year-old graduate student's fiancé had first come to see me to complain that she was worried about marrying him because he seemed to be capable of sexual interest only about once a month. He admitted that this was true, but said that he didn't see anything unusual about it. Many males, he said, had told him that they rarely had intercourse with their wives; and one of his best friends, in fact, only had it twice a year. Why, then, was he abnormal?

In talking to this patient, I soon determined that nearly all the men of low sex range whom he was quoting were much older than he. Indeed, he seemed to have a special propensity for making friends with males who were as much as twenty or thirty years older than he and who—coincidentally enough—

were low-sexed even for their age group. I pointed this out to him and at first he was taken aback by the idea that there was anything unusual about his becoming friendly so often with considerably older men.

I took out Dr. Kinsey's volume on sexual behavior in the human male and showed him some of the norms of male activity. This surprised him still more—despite the fact that he was a graduate student in the social sciences and should have been well aware of some of the Kinsey data.

After considerable resistance from this patient, I finally was able to show him that infrequent copulation was neither statistically normal nor desirable: that sex was a good thing and that more sex was often still better. Then—*after* I had started forcefully re-indoctrinating him with more permissive ideas about sexual participation—my patient began to unbend and to bring out several dire sex fears. He had learned, while still a child, the old folklore saying that "to lose a drop of semen is like losing a drop of blood." He essentially believed at this time that semen was "white blood" and that it should be conserved at all costs. As he grew older, he toned down his beliefs in this connection, but he still held onto another bit of folklore: that each man has within him a limited number of orgasms and that the earlier he uses these up, within his lifetime, the earlier he becomes completely impotent.

This patient's adherence to folklore—which was somewhat startling to discover in a social science graduate student—was partly inspired and sustained by his relationship with his mother. She had been exceptionally close to him during his childhood and had jealously guarded him against all female wiles. She spoke about girls as voracious man-eaters and encouraged him to read several of D. H. Lawrence's novels in which females are depicted as virtually sucking out the male's life blood through exploiting him sexually.

My patient had consciously and unconsciously absorbed his mother's ideas and had bolted from several potentially inten-

149

sive relationships for fear that he would become too involved and squeezed. When I saw him, he had managed to become engaged to a girl but was still resisting her sexually and trying to form a much more "spiritual" attachment to her than she—a considerably healthier individual than he—desired.

As is not unusual in my handling of this kind of case, I attacked this patient's antisexual superstitions full blast. I showed him that semen has nothing to do with blood; that the more orgasms one has during one's lifetime, the *longer* one is likely to remain potent; and that few, if any, females are out to drain men sexually and then cast them to the wolves.

Said I, at one point in the therapy, to this patient: "What are you afraid of, anyway? What can your fiancée or any other woman actually *do* to you?"

"Well—uh—I don't know. Nothing, I suppose."

"But if you actually supposed that women could do nothing to you, you'd have no problem. What you really suppose, away down deep in your mother-fed thinking processes, is that they can, they damned well can, do something horrible, something awful to you. They can't, of course. But you suppose, really, that they can."

"I believe on one level that women can't do anything to me, but I believe, on another level, that they can. Is that what you're trying to tell me?"

"Precisely. Just as you believe, on one level, that sex is good and pleasant—and on another that you will lose your life's blood by engaging 'excessively' in it. You have the old set of beliefs, mainly given you, and almost quite deliberately, by your mother; and you have the newer and more scientific set of beliefs, mainly worked out by you, with the help of your scientific education, since your late adolescence. But the new, objective set of beliefs is still very much smothered by the old, superstitious set. And you *act,* sexually, mostly on the old rather than the new assumptions."

"But *are* the old beliefs really superstitions?"

150

"Well, *aren't* they? *Is* an ounce of semen equal to an ounce of blood?"

"No; of course not."

"And *are* women, as your mother indicated, ready to gobble you up sexually?"

"Well—no."

"See! Even then you hesitated. Just a moment ago you said that you supposed women could not do any damage to you; now you're half-supposing again that perhaps, maybe, it just could be that they might harm you in some way."

"Well, they might—might they not?"

"Sure they *might*. They might cut off your testicles while you are sleeping, literally stick a knife in your back, or hire some bruiser to beat you up. But what are the *chances* of any of these things happening?"

"Pretty slim, I have to admit. But how about mental harm? Couldn't my fiancée, Edith, or some other woman harm me that way?"

"How? By criticizing you? Showing little faith in you? Deserting you?"

"Well—why not? Any of those things could happen, couldn't it?"

"Sure it could. The thing—the criticism or the rejection, for example—could happen. But could, without your actually creating it yourself, the *harm*?"

"What do you mean?"

"I mean just what I asked. Granted that Edith or some other woman could criticize or reject you, would that criticism or rejection actually harm you, in any way whatever, unless *you* made it harmful, unless you said to yourself 'Oh, my God. How terrible it is that she is criticizing me or rejecting me. I can't stand this. How awful!'?"

"I see what you mean. She, this woman, could say things to me, but only I, myself, could hurt myself by taking her statements seriously. And in this way *I* hurt me rather than *her* doing so."

"Exactly. *You* hurt you—as a human being always does when he is harmed by the words, gestures, or attitudes (as distinguished from the actual physical blows) of others."

"And if *I* hurt me, then I can *stop* hurting me—stop taking a woman's criticism or rejection seriously?"

"Exactly. What *you* do to yourself you can *not* do to yourself. If *you* terrorize yourself sexually, as you (with your mother's original help) have been doing, you can *stop* this self-terrorization."

"Hm. I never saw it that way before."

"Don't you think it high time that you did?"

After several months of this kind of rational psychotherapy, it was possible to work through this patient's attachment to his mother, his fear of women, and his superstitions regarding the dangers of orgasm. He gradually improved in his sex powers and, at the time I stopped seeing him, was capable of having five or six sex outlets a week. He married his fiancée and to my knowledge they have made a satisfactory union.

Another variation on the theme of sexual "excess" is the one psychotherapists often hear of "weakness" versus "strength." Maximilian Guttman was a case in point. A thirty-two-year-old taxi driver, who was most concerned about his masculinity, Maximilian reversed his sex and food desires by downing the former and augmenting the latter.

In spite of the fact that he was considerably overweight and that his physician had insisted that he reduce, he continued to ignore his diet and to overeat voraciously. At the same time, he rigorously refrained from having sex relations with his wife, though he immensely enjoyed having such relations, and he only reluctantly "gave in to the Devil," as he put it, once every fortnight.

Maximilian had been specifically raised by his doting mother to believe that food was "strengthening" and that sex was "weakening." He literally felt that he weakened himself whenever he had an orgasm; and he would feel terribly tired and strained after each sex encounter—until he ate a substantial meal. There was virtually a one-to-one relationship between his eating and his sex activities—if and when, as occasionally happened, he let himself go. The more he ate, the less he would have sex relations; and the more he had sex relations, the less hungry he would be. Nevertheless, even though not hungry, he would eat immediately after copulating because he felt that food was "strengthening" and that he could not do without it.

When this patient was authoritatively informed that there was little intrinsic connection between sex and food and that sexual climaxes were certainly not, by themselves, weakening, he was able to lose some of his fears and to copulate at least ten times a week. When having regular sex relations, he could go without food almost all day—provided that his fears of sex were downed. But as soon as he became worried about "excessive" sex activity, his craving for food returned and his copulatory activity decreased drastically.

Maximilian was finally cured only when his general attitudes toward "strength" and "weakness" were forcefully brought to light and he was induced to face and attack them. He believed that he was a worthwhile human being only if others thought him physically "strong" and "masculine" and that he was utterly worthless if he was "weak" and "feminine."

Personally, he enjoyed sedentary and somewhat esthetic pursuits (particularly the writing of song lyrics). But he was ashamed of not being the great outdoorsy type of male whom he had looked up to in his youth, and whom his mother had tended to deify. And his attempts to gain physical strength through heavy eating and semi-continence were compensations for the hard physical exercise which he thought he should engage in but actually did not enjoy.

When Maximilian was induced to question the validity of of his urge to be a he-man, and to ask himself *why* it was neces-

153

sary that he make like Tarzan if he were to consider himself a worthwhile human being, he of course could find no legitimate reason why he *should* be physically powerful. Further questioning and challenging of his childhood-imbibed assumption that to be "strong" and "manly" was a mark of human value led him, finally, to see that this was an untenable hypothesis. His surrendering this highly questionable premise, and replacing it by the assumption that he was a worthwhile human whether or not he was physically mighty, took away all his need to eat instead of copulate.

Still another variation on the theme of sexual "excess" is that shown in the case of a good many males and an occasional female who have physical pains or discomfort after intercourse. Thus, a twenty-eight-year-old husband had no difficulty having intercourse with his wife two or three times each night. But as soon as he did so, he had pains in his penis, testicles, groin, and chest. He had innumerable medical examinations, all of which conclusively showed that he had no physical reasons for these pains. Still, he insisted, there was something physically wrong with him and he kept having still more medical examinations.

When this patient was seen for psychotherapy, it was quickly obvious that his postcoital pains were simply excuses to forego intercourse and that he was exceptionally worried about his "overdoing" his sex activity. In addition to believing several of the same kind of superstitions about the weakening effects of coitus that we have been previously noting in this chapter, he was terribly guilty about his promiscuous sex desires. From early manhood, before and after his marriage, he had lusted after scores of women whom he encountered and he had always felt that his desires for these women were abnormal and perverted. Feeling thoroughly ashamed of them, he had done his best to repress them from conscious awareness.

To penalize himself for his non-monogamous urges, and at the same time to protect himself against the possibility of ever giving in to them (which he had never once done in the course of seven years of marriage), this patient had convinced himself that he was engaging in "excessive" activity and had done his best to stop this "excess." His postcoital pains were one of his best devices for reducing his sex outlets.

When this individual's guilt about his promiscuous desires was brought to light and directly attacked by the therapist, it was amazing to see how quickly and drastically his coital attitudes changed. Once he was willing to accept the fact that virtually all normal males, no matter how happily married, frequently lust after other women than their wives, and that there is nothing in the least perverted or abnormal about their lust (although there may be something self-defeating and neurotic about their unwisely or compulsively giving in to this lust and thus jeopardizing their marriages), he largely lost his postcoital pains. The more he copulated with his wife and the more he acknowledged the normality of his having non-monogamous urges, the more his pains lessened, until eventually they vanished.

In several different ways, then, males and females in our culture acquire erroneous ideas of sex "excess" and begin to use various neurotic symptoms to protect themselves against such "excess." Actually, where the individual is in good physical health, it is almost impossible for him or her, except most temporarily, to have "excessive" sex activities. In a few instances, where the individual suffers from a heart ailment or some other physical condition, frequent coitus may be medically contraindicated. But where he or she is quite healthy, the sex drives tend to have their own automatic controls and are very difficult to abuse.

Males, when they have orgasms that are too frequent for their own capacities, lose the power of erection or become unable to have further orgasms when they achieve tumescence. Females, when they approach the line of sexual "excess," become disinterested in further activity, or are unable to have further orgasms, or feel an irritation in their genital region.

155

When such symptoms as these do not occur and males and females are perfectly capable of pleasurable climax, and have continued desire after orgasm, they continue to enjoy themselves without any fear of "excess."

Both men and women may, of course, on occasion indirectly sabotage their health by staying up too late, failing to eat, or getting insufficient fresh air and sunshine because they are devoting so much time to the pleasures of sex. But the chances of their directly harming themselves by frequent sexual engagements are infinitesimally small and should create no cause for worry. Sex, when enjoyed up to the limit of one's individual capacity, is one of the most harmless, beneficial, and healthiest of human acts. It is also fun.

13

Controlling Sex Impulses

Men and women continually come to see us to complain that they have uncontrollable or compulsive sex desires and that they are literally forced to do sexual things that they do not want to do.

"It's not that I want to be exhibitionistic (or homosexual, or promiscuous, or sadistic)," they say, "but I just don't know what happens to me, and I suddenly find myself being forced to do what I don't want to do. I've tried to stop it many times but I just *can't!*"

We listen to their stories carefully, these compulsive-obsessive sex participants, and usually conclude that they are seriously disturbed individuals who are in need of intensive psychotherapy. But not always. For we have found, after being more than once fooled, that some of them are pseudo-compulsives or that, once having been in the throes of uncontrollable sex desires, they are now insisting that they are still compulsive when actually they are not.

Consider, in this connection, three married females—a Lesbian, a so-called nymphomaniac, and a prude.

The Lesbian came to therapy because she was, according to her description, compulsively seducing the girls at the settlement house at which she was a group leader. Her attraction to these girls was distressing on several counts. Firstly, she loved her work and knew that sooner or later her sex relations with her female charges would be discovered and that her career as a group worker would be wrecked. Secondly, she was keenly aware of the fact that she might be doing distinct psychological damage to some of the girls, particularly those whom she virtually forced to have relations with her against their will. Thirdly, she was married to a man whom she considered a well-nigh perfect husband and whom she loved; and she was fearful of jeopardizing her marriage by her Lesbian activities.

For these reasons, Pamela said, she had tried for several years to overcome her homosexual tendencies, but had miserably failed. Not only did she continue to seduce many of her young charges but she would from time to time stay out all night with older girls as well. She would vow that she had to stop this Lesbian activity and would return to her husband and swear off the girls with whom she worked; but she would, within a few weeks, find her sex tensions rising so tremendously that she said she couldn't stand it any longer—and she would compulsively return to her homosexual activity.

For several weeks, when I first saw this twenty-three-year-old girl, she kept insisting that hers was a true sexual compulsion—that there was something about her body which absolutely craved and cried for physical contact with another female and that therefore she could not conquer her compulsion.

I wouldn't buy this idea at all. For one thing, as I explained to her, there are no biological, instinctive heterosexual or homosexual drives as far as can be scientifically determined. There are merely undifferentiated or plurisexual biological drives, which are caused by the secretion of our sex hormones and which incite sexual nerve endings and tissues—particularly the nerves and tissues of the male penis and the female clitoris—to want to be stimulated until a climax or orgasmic release of tension occurs. But these biological drives are non-directional; and humans only *learn* to direct them into certain channels, such as masturbation, heterosexuality, homosexuality, or bestiality, as a result of their experiences and attitudes. No one is born homosexual *or* heterosexual; we all learn to be one or the other (or both).

Moreover, as I showed Pamela, in her particular case there was no question that sex was not the paramount issue in her "compulsiveness." She got little real satisfaction from the girls with whom she had relations, since they were largely inexperienced and would allow her, at most, to satisfy them, while rarely fully satisfying her. On the other hand, in her relations with her husband, she experienced full satisfaction and orgasm—and yet she kept avoiding relations with him.

Again: it gradually became clear that the main satisfactions Pamela received with the girls were basically ego and not sexual gratifications. She liked having power over her charges. She used them as substitutes for her younger sisters, with whom she had never been able to be close. She decidedly enjoyed the adventure, with all its risks and dangers, of seducing the girls under the most difficult circumstances (almost literally, for example, right under her director's eyes). She used her Lesbianism as a medium to express her deep-seated, partly unconscious rebelliousness against authority.

Little by little, largely because of my direct therapeutic insistence, my patient saw this. At first, she kept insisting on her sex uncontrollability.

159

"But it must be physical," she would say, "because I can actually *taste* it. It's entirely unlike my relations with my husband. I guess I was just born like that. I know, from my psychological studies, that this just isn't right, that people are not born this way. But I *feel* that it is right. Can't sex just be different? Can't we just be born with a sort of chemical attraction to one sex rather than the other?"

No, I insisted, it wasn't different. Sex desires, like food desires, have a strong physiological basis, but they are also importantly influenced by learning. And although an individual's hormones may drive her to *some* kind of sex satisfaction—just as her hunger drives will propel her to *some* kind of food satisfaction—there is nothing in the hormones, as far as can be determined, which makes a particular kind of sex activity necessary. Biologically, orgasm is orgasm, and the method of achieving it matters little. One human being may, on a fairly physiological basis, *like* one type of sex activity (or food) better than another; but, on a biological basis alone, she is not going to *demand* that type. Demands are much more likely to originate in the cerebral cortex than in the sexual tissues.

It was a hard fight, but I finally won. By means of sexological teaching, as well as psychological interpretation and rational analysis, I showed Pamela that while she had obsessive-compulsive *ideas,* she certainly had no true physical compulsions. These ideas, moreover, had both an origin and a day-to-day sustenance; and both their origin and their daily repropagandization could be understood and challenged.

The origin of Pamela's homosexuality (as is often true in so many other instances of pronounced Lesbianism) resided in her strong fears and guilts concerning heterosexual relations —particularly (ironically enough!) her horror of engaging in so-called heterosexual perversions. She had been raised to be so guilty about engaging in fellation, cunnilinctus, and other non-coital sex acts with males that she only permitted herself to have straight "normal" intercourse with her husband and

160

would never under any circumstances engage in oral-genital relations because of their being so "disgusting." Underlyingly, however, she actually craved non-coital even more than coital sex participation; and in her Lesbian relations, of course, such non-coital relations played the major role and she did not find them at all "disgusting."

"Good Lord," Pamela exclaimed in the course of one of our sessions together, "I never would have believed I was so much of a prude if I had not been having these talks with you! I always thought that I was quite liberal sexually and that only the most open-minded girls would do what I had done by having premarital sex relations with my husband with no qualms whatever. But now I see that, during our entire life together, we have never really had any full-ranged sex at all. While with the girls, of course, I am only too eager to go to the very limit, and do things that I don't even enjoy. I have bottled myself up so tightly in one area, the heterosexual, that I go to almost impossible extremes in the other area, the homosexual. Hell (and here she smiled wryly), you might think I was a pervert!"

That was just it: in order to avoid non-coital sex relations with her husband—which she wrongly defined as perversions—she acquired a truly perverted (that is, fixated, fetishistic, and obsessive-compulsive) form of Lesbian sex activity. As Pamela began to understand some of the underlying causes of her compulsive Lesbianism, her homosexual participations began to decline. She still had desires for the girls with whom she worked but they became less frequent and she was able to control them. However, from time to time she would seduce another one of her charges and would come to me to say that she had done so uncontrollably and just could not resist her impulses.

I became more and more skeptical of the uncontrollability of Pamela's Lesbian forays and proposed, when I thought she was ready for it, an experiment. I suggested that for three weeks she resolve to stay away from young girls completely, just so we could determine what effect her abstinence would have on her.

161

She agreed, and she rigorously refrained from touching any girls for the stipulated period.

Much to Pamela's surprise, she found that nothing much happened to her during this time. She did not become unbearably tense, excited, or disturbed. She thought about Lesbian activity and desired it; but she found no real necessity to have it and was easily able to take up the sexual lag by having increased relations with her husband (with whom she was now beginning to enjoy non-coital as well as coital participations). At the end of the three-week trial period, she found that she was automatically considering, every time she thought of having an affair with a girl, whether it was worth it in terms of risk, time wasted, and relatively little sex pleasure gained. Almost always, she decided that it wasn't worth it; and she soon stopped having Lesbian relations entirely, even though from time to time she thought that it would be pleasant to have a homosexual affair.

This patient, in other words, first had a real sexual compulsion. But it was on an ideational rather than the physiological basis she thought she had. As she began to understand herself better, and to see and to combat the Puritanical ideas behind her compulsiveness, her "uncontrollable" urges started to fade. But still preferring some amount of homosexual activity, she was loath to admit that her compulsivity had vanished and she (unconsciously) kept it as an *excuse* for her sex preferences and not because she was any longer helplessly in its throes.

Pamela's final formulations may be summed up by her own statement during our closing session. "I really think," she said, "that I've come a long way, even though I still have occasional homosexual urges and, as you have explained to me, I may well have them for the rest of my life. But now they're only preferences rather than needs; and I can easily do without them —and intend to keep doing without actually giving in to them.

"The real turning point came, I think, not when I first saw that I was much more Puritanical than I had previously thought I was and that I was afraid of oral relations with my husband

and things like that. That was a good revelation and it helped me a lot, but it was only a small part of the thing. What really got me was when you induced me to try that experiment and, in the course of trying it, I saw that all compulsions are really ideas in our heads and are not in our bodies at all, although we strongly think they are. I was trying that experiment mainly because it was a sort of challenge to try it. And just because it was a challenge, and I had something at stake to boost my own ego—although I know, now, that that kind of ego-boosting, too, can be very crappy stuff—I tried like the devil to live up to the challenge and to keep away from the girls at the settlement house.

"And just because I tried, of course, and felt it such an ego-boosting challenge, I had little difficulty in achieving my goal —not merely in refraining from doing anything with the girls, but actually not even wanting them very much, and certainly not needing them at all. That really taught me something. If one idea, I said to myself, the idea I want to do this thing to prove that I can do it, could take such precedence over the other idea, the idea that I always had previously believed, you know, that I just *had* to do it, then—let's see, now, where was I?—oh, well then I just *saw* it. It *was* an idea. The whole obsession was an idea. Any obsession is an idea. And then I saw what you had been trying to tell me all along and that I stubbornly refused to work at seeing, that an idea is nothing but something you keep telling yourself, repeating to yourself over and over until you come to believe it heartily, even though there may be no truth to it at all.

"And the idea that I *must* have those girls was just such an idea that I kept telling myself and convincing myself about. And that idea, for just those three weeks, that I must *not* have the girls and must show how I could accept your challenge, that also was just an idea that I kept telling myself and convincing myself. And if this one idea, I saw, could outweigh the other idea so effectively, then almost any idea one chooses can

163

outweigh almost any other idea one no longer chooses to have. And any obsession, if that is right, and I think it definitely is right, becomes something that you're only creating yourself and that you can stop creating if you have a better idea to substitute for it. Well, when I saw *that,* that was it, and the whole thing became clear, and I saw that my Lesbian obsession was completely self-created and that I could set about, as you again have kept insisting, uncreating it. And, well, that's exactly what I've done in the last several weeks, and now it just doesn't bother me at all."

So vanished Pamela's "uncontrollable" obsession with Lesbianism. Take, now, another patient, whom we shall call Ruth. Ruth considered herself to be a terrible "nymphomaniac" because she was never satisfied with one lover at a time, but required a certain amount of additional relations. When I saw her she was married to a man whom she loved, she said, more than any previous man in her life. She genuinely enjoyed his company, tried to please him in many ways, and wanted to continue living with him indefinitely. But she was, she claimed, relatively little sexually attracted to him if she saw him every day in the week and was much more attracted to her husband when she saw one or two other men during the week and had sex affairs with them.

Ruth, like Pamela, at first insisted that her compulsive promiscuity was completely physical. She was just attracted to many different types of males, she said, and if she did not have them sexually she soon began to gnash her gums and to become so tense that she couldn't think straight. These sex desires had nothing to do with love. She didn't care for most of the men with whom she slept. It was just a physical appetite, like hunger, and it had to be appeased or else. "Or else what?" I asked. Or else she got sick (headaches, pains in her ovaries) and terribly nervous.

I was skeptical from the start but bided my therapeutic time. Gradually, I showed Ruth that it really wasn't sex that was bothering her. Instead of being unusually lustful, as she first implied, she was well within the normal range. She could barely satisfy her husband coitally, since he wanted intercourse practically every night and she wanted it, all affairs included, only two or three times a week. On a given evening, moreover, her husband could easily have two or three orgasms to her one.

When we traced down the basic source of Ruth's compulsive promiscuity, we discovered that what she really was afraid of was becoming too close to any male. She had, in her early life, been very close to her father and then felt that he had seriously rejected her (which he probably had done, because he was beginning to feel guilty about his underlying sex desires toward her). Not wanting to risk being deeply involved and then terribly hurt again, she used her compulsive promiscuity as an excuse to water down her relations with a man and thus avoid the hurt she feared.

Once her neurotic symptom started, moreover, secondary symptoms set in which made matters infinitely worse. Because Ruth loved her husband and feared ultimate rejection by him (particularly since he was more potent than she and because she had always had a low estimation of her own intelligence and appearance), she hedged her bets, as it were, and dated other men as well. But because she felt that her promiscuous behavior was wrong, and keenly sensed (though never accurately verbalized to herself) its self-defeating nature, she severely blamed herself for her actions and through this self-blaming began to consider herself less and less worthy of her husband's affection. The usual vicious neurotic circle was then established: the more insecure about herself she was, the more extramarital affairs she carried on; and the more affairs she had the more guilty and insecure she became. Even though the original source of her feelings of rejection no longer existed (since for the past several years she had got along beautifully with her father and felt no insecurity on his account), her self-rejection was so well established at the time she came for therapy that she was more

165

disturbed than she had ever previously been.

I forthrightly applied a rational therapeutic approach to Ruth's problems and set about convincing her that rejection, by her father in the first place or any other man in the second or third place, was *not* terrible and that only her own definitional ideas about its being so horrendous actually made it so.

"But suppose I *were* rejected by my husband," she asked, "*wouldn't* that be terrible? Suppose he found out about my dates with other men—which he suspects at times but never seems to take too seriously yet—and got very angry about my depriving him of sex satisfaction while I was sleeping with these other men. Wouldn't it be a terrible and well-deserved blow if he found that out and left me?"

"No," I insisted. "It would be a blow; but it wouldn't be terrible—unless you insisted on making it so. Besides, that is really the whole crux of your sickness: you are failing to distinguish between the actual blow of your husband's possibly leaving you—which would certainly be inconvenient, to say the least—and the imagined horror, fantasied terribleness of his rejecting you."

"Aren't they the same thing—being left and being rejected?"

"No, they're actually quite different. Being left by your husband, or by any other individual for whom you care, is a real loss—a loss, for example, of companionship, of sex activity, of financial support, and so on. But being rejected is merely a matter of someone's not liking you, of the wheels turning in a disapproving fashion in *his* head; and that may actually be no loss at all."

"I don't get it. It seems like the same thing to me."

"But it isn't. And that, I again insist, is exactly why you're sick: because you aren't able to distinguish between someone's actually depriving you of something and his merely turning the wheels in his own head so as to *think* that you're not the greatest thing in the world."

"They still seem the same to me."

"I know; but they aren't. Let us take, for instance, your early relationship with your father. At first he accepted you thoroughly; then, later, he withdrew some of this acceptance, probably because, as we have shown, he became afraid of his own sex desires toward you. Is that right?"

"Yes, that would seem to be the story, as far as I now can make out."

"All right. But when he rejected you, and you felt so hurt by his rejection, what did you actually lose? Did you lose anythink by his sexual withdrawal? Of course not, since he had never really approached you sexually in the first place. Did he, because of his rejection of you, give you less money, or less help with your school work, or even less companionship?"

"No, he was just as nice as he had always been. But distant, more distant. He withdrew his *feeling* from me, his *warmth*."

"Exactly. The wheels turned in his head, and consequently in his emotional responsiveness, so that he showed that he did not like you or love you as much as he previously had done. But other than that, actually, his behavior changed very little toward you—isn't that so?"

"Yes, I suppose so. But isn't acceptance, isn't warmth—isn't *that* behavior, too?"

"It certainly is. But, in the last analysis, other people's acceptance and warmth toward you are as much *your* behavior as theirs. They turn the wheels in their heads, all right; but you also turn the wheels in your head to *react* to their wheel-turning; and it is actually your reaction rather than their action which has by far the greatest effect on you."

"So if I didn't react so strongly to my father's rejection and lack of warmth, I wouldn't have felt so badly about it as I did at the time?"

"Right. If you had been able to say to yourself—which admittedly would be most unusual for a twelve-year-old girl to say to herself but which still would have been possible to say —'there goes my poor father withdrawing his affection from me

167

because he is so afraid of his incestuous urges toward me that he feels terribly guilty and impelled to withdraw'; if you had been able to say *this* to yourself, *would* you have reacted so strongly, as you did react, to his rejection?"

"No, I guess I wouldn't have. But how could I say that to myself at that time?"

"You're right; you probably couldn't. A twelve-year-old girl is simply not perceptive or sufficiently well-informed, no matter how bright she is, to be able to say such calm philosophic observations to herself. So, at the time, it was quite appropriate that you became upset, and confused the turning of the wheels in your father's head with a real loss of support from him—which, as you said before, actually did not occur. O. K.: so we very well couldn't expect a twelve-year-old girl to do this sort of thing. But you're not twelve years old any longer! You are, at least chronologically, grown up. You are presumably more perceptive and knowledgeable. You can distinguish between wheels turning in other people's heads and actual deprivations that might occur to you because of such turnings."

"You are referring to the fact, I suppose, that if my husband now rejects me, as my father formerly did, I wouldn't have to exaggerate the real loss—the lack of companionship and that sort of thing—and confuse it with the rejection-loss, which is really only his opinion of me? You mean that I could manage to live with the real loss of my marriage, even though I didn't like it, as long as I weren't telling myself how awful it was to be rejected by him—to have, as you put it, the wheels turning against me in his head?"

"Yes, that's just what I mean. The loss of your marriage would certainly be a hard blow, and one that I think you should try to avoid, since I agree with you that you probably do love your husband and can get along with him well if you iron out this sex nonsense. But even if you were rejected by him, that would not be, as you would now tend to interpret it as, a blow to *your* self-esteem. It would merely be a loss, not a personal catastrophe. Unless you insisted on *making* it so."

"And if I don't take my husband's possible rejection of me too seriously, don't *make* it as you say a catastrophe, then, even if it does occur, I can stand it—is that what you're saying? I can stand it and not think it so terrible, even though I don't like it and don't want it."

"Yes, that's just what I'm saying. A loss of something you want—companionship, sex, money, or whatever it is—is quite different from a horrible feeling of being rejected. The one is real and disagreeable; the other is unreal and falsely catastrophic."

With this kind of continued attack on Ruth's feelings of rejection, she began to change her philosophy. She could now contemplate the possible breakup of her marriage not with equanimity but at least with less of a feeling of dread. The less upset and unworthy she felt in the light of this newer kind of contemplation, the more she was able to ask herself the practical question: "What can I do *not* to destroy my marriage?" And the answer quickly came back: "For one thing, I had better stop this self-defeating extramarital promiscuity."

After several weeks of this newer kind of self-questioning, Ruth's affairs began to decrease. But not to zero. Every fortnight or so she would still manage to sandwich in an extramarital adventure; and she would then revert, at least in part, to her original position that maybe there was something unusual about herself sexually, maybe she just *had* to be non-monogamous. I still wouldn't buy this notion. That she had a desire, and a reasonably normal and legitimate desire, for varietist relations with a number of men other than her husband, I fully acknowledged. But that she was defining that desire into a dire need, making a necessity out of a preference—that I refused to go along with.

After some more very honest soul-searching Ruth finally

169

capitulated. She came to see me one day after she had had, the night before, an affair that had proved to be highly sexually satisfying. "It was damned good," she said, "so good, in fact, that I learned a few tricks that I intend to use with my husband. But even while it was going on, and I was enjoying it immensely, I couldn't help asking myself: 'Would I like to be with this man forever? Would I really like to be married to him, to raise children with him, to share an entire life with him?' And, of course, I answered myself that I would not.

"Then I honestly asked myself: 'Well, who would I like to be married to, to share a life with?' And, as always, the answer was my husband, Robert. As I said, that's nothing new, that answer; and I always feel a sort of little glow when I give it to myself, and pat myself on the back for still having him around and wanting him to stay around. But this time, more honestly, I wasn't in such a back-patting mood. So I said to myself, 'All right, so it's Robert. But do I really *have* Robert? Do I have, with him, the kind of a marriage I'm always thinking about in my mind, the real sharing and the child raising and that sort of thing?' Well, of course, I could only honestly answer: 'No.' I don't have anything of the sort. And the reason I don't have it, as you've been careful to point out to me all these weeks, is that I'm not really committed to having it, but am committed, instead, to having something quite different—one hell of a fine sex life, period.

"So I was quite honest with myself and I saw it. It was great, being in bed with this new fellow—I had picked him up on the train going home, incidentally—and there was no point in telling myself, falsely, that it was not great. It was fine; I liked it; I wanted it. But that's what I then—at long last, as you'll probably say, for it's been a long, hard road to come with you!—finally saw: that I don't *need* everything I like and want and think is fine. I would prefer it; but I don't need it. And I more strongly prefer—and that's what I now have to face and keep

170

facing—not the lovely sex pleasure of the moment, not the additional bang that I can get with other men that I can't always get with Robert, but the full marital relationship, the sharing and the caring together that I *can* get with Robert, but that I'm damned well killing off, and certain to kill once and for all one of these days if I continue this lovely thrill-of-the-moment bed-hopping. So you've finally convinced me—or maybe, better yet, I've convinced myself—a preference is *not* a need, a wanting is *not* a necessity. You're right. I would *like* to have my cake and eat it, but I can't. I'm beginning to see that—no, even better, accept that—after all these years. And it's real good facing up to that kind of reality."

And Ruth did face up to that kind of reality; and still is, to my knowledge, doing so. For the past several years she has been able to be sexually satisfied with her husband without having compulsive urges for extramarital affairs. She does not delude herself that her sex life is now ideal, nor that it wouldn't be more satisfying if she could have some sex variety from time to time; since she still *likes* this kind of variety, even though her *need* for it has gone. But she is able to forego some of her sex likes, just as she foregoes some of her other desires to help her marital relationship. And, all told, she likes herself and her existence.

The third and last illustration of supposed sexual uncontrollability to be outlined in this chapter is that of another female patient, Mrs. Gray, who insisted that she could not control the desire to avoid sex relations with her husband and to have them as seldom as possible. Mrs. Gray said that she had fairly high sex desires and would have liked to have intercourse with her husband several times a week, but that something entered her mind warning her against such relations almost every time she was about to have them; so that she finally ended by having coitus about once a month. She had, in other words, a compulsive fear of intercourse.

171

It was not too difficult to show Mrs. Gray where and how her irrational fear of copulation had originally been instilled. Her mother had continually talked against sex, indicated that she rarely copulated with her husband, and said that intercourse was painful, weakening, and mentally debilitating.

When she had first married, Mrs. Gray and her husband had lived for a while in her mother's home and the mother had done everything possible to interrupt their sex relations. She would walk in on them unannounced late at night or early in the morning, catching them in the act of intercourse on several occasions, and indicating her severe displeasure. She would hide or throw away the contraceptives they used and would talk continually about sexual "excess" and its frightful results.

Mrs. Gray was helped to understand her mother's sexual neurosis and to untie herself from the extremely antisexual attitudes with which she had been raised. Still, she insisted that her compulsion to stay away from relations with her husband persisted. Finally, after months of fruitless sessions, I began to see that I had been sadly bamboozled by my not so innocent patient. Mrs. Gray had actually lost almost all her sex fears and from time to time was having coitus with her husband as often as ten or twelve times a week. But then she would suddenly fall back into her old anxieties and would give up sex relations almost entirely—to resume them again a few weeks later.

All during this time, even when she was having sex relations regularly, Mrs. Gray would minimize the amount she was having and would maximize her fears. "I don't know what happens to me," she would keep saying. "I want to have it and I do have it and I enjoy it immensely. But then a great fear creeps over me and I become afraid that I am doing it too often and that it is weakening me. And I fall back into the old routine and stay away from it. I guess I just can't do it too much. I guess I'll have to give up and go back to the way I was."

"It's not that you *can't*," I would just as regularly reply, "but that you *won't*. You just don't *want* to have regular sex relations with your husband."

"Oh, but I do, I do. I enjoy it immensely."

I was baffled; thought my own words hollow. After all, it's easy enough for a psychotherapist to insist, when the patient doesn't get better, that the patient just doesn't want to improve and that if she did she would. In that way, we can have one hundred per cent successes—and those who don't get well are said to be "resisting" treatment: which, of course, is not *our* fault.

But, I asked myself, was it really so? Was it only the patient's, Mrs. Gray's, resistance to getting better? Or was it that I had slipped up somewhere in getting at the source of her real trouble? Because why shouldn't she get better if, as I suspected, her compulsion was really gone and if she could at times enjoy sex so immensely?

Then, in speaking to Mr. Gray (whom I saw from time to time, as is my wont with the mates of my married patients), I suddenly saw light. I had always known that, because of Mrs. Gray's sex avoidance, rapport between them had never been too good and still wasn't. But, as he gave me details of their marital life which Mrs. Gray had simply avoided speaking about, I could see very clearly that she had been bringing many non-sexual matters into their sexual relations and that the sex issue was not nearly so clear as I had previously thought it was.

As I soon discovered from talking to Mr. Gray, his wife had devised a complex and extensive pattern of cracking down on him sexually whenever (which was rarely) he stood up to her and refused to give her her childish way about things. If he wanted to eat certain kinds of foods which she disliked, or insisted that she was spoiling the children (as she often was), or in almost any other way opposed her, she swiftly brought their sex relations to a virtual standstill. Somehow, getting this idea, he soon was brought back into line, and the sex activity between them would return to normal.

Mrs. Gray, in other words, definitely was resisting; and not merely resisting treatment but steadfastly, doggedly resisting virtually all the assertions of her husband. She would dig up her supposedly compulsive fears of sex, long after these had actually vanished, to employ them as techniques of her resistance. When she had first come to see me there actually had been an irrational, compulsive element in her fear of sex relations. But when we had worked through that fear and overcome her mother-inculcated prudishness, she was loath to surrender her anti-copulatory compulsion because she was able to use it so well in her continual battle of wills with her husband. It was only by showing to her, most concretely, why she had originally become so hostile to her husband and how she kept sustaining her irrational hostility to him that I was able to get at the bottom of her antisexual "compulsiveness" and to break the back of her neurosis.

The cases of the three women considered in this chapter—a Lesbian, a "nymphomaniac," and a prude—seem to offer fairly convincing evidence that a sex compulsion or "uncontrollable" tendency to do or not do a certain sex act may be of two different types: First, it may be a true compulsion, behind which lies some kind of deep-seated neurotic fear. Second, it may be an excuse or rationalization for giving or not giving in to a sexual (or non-sexual) desire or preference. True sex compulsions exist often enough and should be psychologically treated as soon as they are discovered. But pseudo-compulsions of a sexual nature also frequently exist and should be treated by the therapist's becoming fully aware of their nature and not confusing them with other kinds of compulsions.

Can an individual who is in the throes of a supposed sexual compulsion do anything about it himself? Sometimes he can. If he will face the fact that the compulsion may partly or largely stem from the fact that, actually, he has sex preferences rather than needs, and that he may be convincing himself that he is compulsive in order to give in to these preferences, he may be able to get at some of the roots of his "compulsion" and to overcome it. If this does not work—as, in longstanding and complex cases it frequently will not—then he had better go for professional aid. Compulsions and pseudo-compulsions are difficult enough for the professional therapist to unravel and solve; the amateur had better step cautiously in this area.

14

Non-monogamous Desires

The problem of non-monogamous sex desires, as has already been indicated in some of the previous cases discussed in this book, is a recurring one among marriage counseling clients. One of our first counselees, seen many years ago, put the problem this way:

"What is wrong with me, Doctor? I have been going with a man for a year and I love him very much. Just as soon as we get things straightened out financially, we are going to marry. When I am with him and we have sex relations, I am perfectly satisfied. I've had men before, but he's the best of them. Yet, I have to be perfectly honest with you and with myself: I keep getting attracted to other men all the time. I see good-looking males here and there, some of them are light, some are dark, some are strong and some are cute, and I know I want them. What's wrong with me?"

Another client, a twenty-five-year-old male, put the same problem this way: "I know it's wrong, but I can't help it. I get along with my wife fine in bed. Not like it used to be when we were first married, three years ago, but still good enough. But, and maybe it's just after the night I've had her, I go out on the street and see a pretty little piece of ass and goddam it I just look and look and think what a fine thing it would be to have her. I tell myself I'm a bastard, that I shouldn't want that sort of thing. But it's no use: I do want it. And I tell you, honest, Doc, I get along fine in bed with my wife. I just don't understand it."

This is the one side of the problem. Then there's the other side: where non-monogamous sex desires are not only experienced but are actually carried into practice. And the ensuing premarital varietism or post-marital adultery that results is again a source of disturbance to many individuals.

A typical wife, for example, comes to castigate herself bitterly for carrying on an extramarital affair. She thinks that her activities are entirely unforgivable and obviously wants to be lectured severely and ordered to sin no more.

A typical husband, on the other hand, comes to brag about his several adulterous affairs and says that he is not at all disturbed about them. He goes into such lengthy self-justifying statements, however, and tells how frigid his wife is, how she really doesn't love him, how she trapped him into marrying her, and so on, that it is obvious that he is disturbed about his adultery and that he wants to be told that everything is fine and that he should continue to have non-monogamous affairs.

The fact that so many marriage counseling and psychotherapy clients are anxious or guilty about their non-monogamous desires or acts does not prove, of course, that everyone in our culture is equally disturbed in this regard. Literally millions of our people appear to engage in promiscuous or adulterous relations without qualm; and most of them do not end up in a marriage counselor's office. It may still safely be said, however, that at least a sizable minority and perhaps the majority of Americans who have varietist sex urges or relationships are more or less uneasy about their experiences and that many of them are seriously disturbed.

What, then, do we say to those clients who are troubled about their non-monogamous desires or acts? Something similar to what was said to Mrs. Skaluraki, who put her problem as follows:

Mrs. S.: I've told you about my thinking about Mr. Smith, our boarder, so much of the time, and wondering how it would be with him instead of with my husband. Now isn't that crazy of me, thinking of that so much of the time, when my husband does his best to satisfy me and really isn't very bad at all?

Therapist: Let us get one thing perfectly straight, at the very start—and that is that there is absolutely nothing abnormal, unnatural, or perverted about a man or a woman's having varietist desires. Let us forget about the acts to which these desires may lead, for a moment, and consider just the desires themselves.

Mrs. S.: Oh, I haven't *done* anything yet about my feelings for Mr. Smith. I wouldn't think of—

Therapist: Yes, I realize that. You haven't done anything at all. You just think that it might be nice to do something. And that's what you're guilty about—your thought, not any acts, since no acts have taken place as yet.

Mrs. S.: No, nothing at all.

Therapist: O.K.: let's stick to thoughts and desires then, and forget about acts for the moment. As far as we know scientifically, it seems accurate to state that men and women are biologically inclined to be varietist or promiscuous in their sex desires. That is to say, from a biological standpoint, our sex desires are aroused by our sex hormones and these hormones have never been shown to give any particular direction to these drives.

Mrs. S.: We're not born to do one thing or the other sexually?

Therapist: Right: we're not born to be heterosexual, homosexual, or anything else, nor to be desirous of having this or that particular person. When the sex urges are specifically directed toward a given class of objects or toward one special object this direction appears to be largely learned and is not the result of inborn instincts.

Mrs. S.: So I am not attracted to Mr. Smith because he was born to be my soul-mate, or anything like that, but because I have learned to like people who have some of his characteristics?

Therapist: Yes, for the most part. It is possible that some of your inborn tastes—such as a tendency you may have to like the color blue instead of brown—may influence your feelings for Mr. Smith (who may have blue instead of brown eyes); but it is more likely that your preferences for Smith's blue eyes, or broad shoulders, or thick head of hair were learned from your early associations with actual people or storybook figures who also had similar characteristics. Since, however, neither your inborn tastes nor your acquired preferences are likely to apply to just a few individuals—as there are *many* men with blue eyes, broad shoulders, a thick head of hair, etc.—it is most unlikely that you will become prejudiced in favor of *only* Smith, or *only* your husband, or *only* any other single man during your lifetime.

Mrs. S.: In other words, you seem to be saying, we learn to like or love classes of people rather than just individual people, and because many people can more or less fall into the same class, we can easily be rather—uh—promiscuous in our likes and loves. Is that right?

Therapist: Yes. We also learn to love people with several different traits, rather than those who only have a single trait.

179

That is to say, we do not *only* love people with, say, blue eyes; but those who *also* have broad shoulders, a thick head of hair, etc. *Ideally,* we would most strongly be attracted to a person who possessed virtually all the traits that we personally favor. But, statistically speaking, it is difficult for us often to find this ideal person. Therefore, most of us accept second best by being attracted to individuals who have one or more of the several traits we like. Thus, if one person has blue eyes and broad shoulders and another has broad shoulders and a thick head of hair, we may well be highly attracted to both these individuals. Even if we are very much in love with the first of these persons, that will hardly stop us from being quite attracted to the second.

Mrs. S.: In such circumstances, it is a wonder, isn't it, that we ever love in a truly monogamous manner!

Therapist: It certainly is. And, frankly, I doubt whether almost anyone does. There may be a few cases on record where a woman fell in love, let us say, with John Brown when she was sixteen years old and for the entire rest of her life was sexually and amatively attracted to and obsessed with only him and no other man. Such cases may exist; but in my long experience as a human being and my fairly long practice as a therapist and marriage counselor, I have never yet found one. If and when I do, I shall wonder about the pathology involved in this utterly monogamous individual.

Mrs.: You're beginning to make me wonder, too!

Therapist: That's what I'm trying to do: to make you wonder about how "normal" or "natural" truly monogamous—which means once-in-a-lifetime—sex-love attachments are. Anyway, in addition to our being born with distinctly plurisexual, varietist tendencies, we actually learn, even in this Puritanical society in which we live, to be super-anti-monogamous. Theoretically, of course, our culture holds that we should have sex urges toward only one member of the other sex at a time; but our whole upbringing conditions us in the opposite direction. This

180

is particularly true of males in our culture. We literally teach these males that *any* pretty girl is a desirable sex object and we accentuate their desires for *any* good-looking female by flaunting before their eyes endless series of cover-girls, etc.—all of whom are distinctly designed to attract him, to stimulate his senses.

Mrs. S: And we do much the same for females, too, don't we?

Therapist: Yes. With our females, too, though for somewhat different reasons, we do the same thing. We do not specifically encourage the female to look for one male lover after another, but we definitely try to motivate her toward marriage and child-raising; and to get her interested in marriage, we stress romance—which means, largely, the physical and emotional attractiveness of the romantically inclined male. Consequently, the female in our society who is not, by the time she reaches late adolescence, physically and psychologically attracted to literally dozens of movie stars, orchestra leaders, television Romeos, and plain boys on the street is not only a rarity but is probably mentally or emotionally retarded.

Mrs. S.: Now that you mention it, I can certainly remember my own teens, when I had a crush on some matinee idol or popular singer every other month or so.

Therapist: You and twenty million other American girls of your age! You see, now, that even though we theoretically train our youngsters to marry and lead a perfectly monogamous life, we actually train them to be highly promiscuous in their sex-love attractions. The very first thing we must acknowledge, then, if we are to take an intelligent view of this area, is that non-monogamous desires are thoroughly normal—biologically, culturally, and statistically. They are as perfectly natural and expectable as, say, the desires that millions of people have for new foods, new sights, new adventures. Those of us who do *not* have distinctly varietist sex urges are the ones who may be suspected of being "abnormal" or peculiar.

181

Mrs. S.: That all sounds very well; and I am sure you are describing conditions accurately. But what about what most of the religions say? What about the Bible? The Bible not only declares that adultery is wrong but also emphasizes that he who even thinks about it, or lusts in his mind's eye after a member of the other sex, is wicked. Do you mean to say that the Bible is wrong about that?

Therapist: In a word, yes. If the Judeo-Christian Bible, or any other tract which contains a code of sex morality, wishes to inveigh against actual fornication or adultery, it is certainly privileged to do so—as are non-conformists free to inveigh against Biblical interdictions. Whether codes that ban premarital sex relations and adultery are beneficial for individual human beings or the community as a whole is still a debatable question, with much that may be said on both sides. Modern scientific and clinical evidence, however, would seem to point clearly to the fact that there is no debate about the beneficence of codes that ban even the mere thinking about, or desiring, of premarital or adulterous affairs. Such codes would seem to be indubitably impractical, impossible, and emotionally harmful.

Mrs. S.: You mean that, if the Bible or any other moral code wants to ban fornication and adultery; that may be within reason; but that if it bans *thinking about* these same kind of acts, it is highly unreasonable?

Therapist: That's it, precisely. The only possible way for human beings to stop thinking about varietist sex relations, especially when they are raised in a culture like our own, is for them to become rigid, repressive, withdrawn, or otherwise seriously emotionally disturbed. Stop a man or woman from being fornicative or adulterous and you have a problem, but not necessarily an insoluble problem, on your hands. Stop this same man or woman from thinking, imagining, or fantasizing about non-marital relations, when this individual is still young and healthy enough to have efficiently working hormones, and you have a neurotic or a psychotic on your hands. Perhaps the

182

quickest and best way to assure the existence of a terribly disturbed, and almost schizophrenic, population is to hold that population to the strictest letter of the Biblical commandments regarding sex thoughts and desires.

Mrs. S.: Well, perhaps you are right about the normality of promiscuous or adulterous sex desires, but what about actions? Is it right for me actually to have an affair with Mr. Smith, even though I may not be a beast for *thinking about* such an affair?

Therapist: Actions may be in a quite different category from thoughts or desires. Granting that it is perfectly natural for you to have non-monogamous desires, it may by no means be sane and logical for you to give in to them on all occasions. Take, for example, premarital relations. Suppose that you are going with a male, before marriage, are in love with him, and perhaps expect to marry him before long. At the same time, however, you desire to have intercourse with other males. You might very logically decide to be strictly monogamous in this event, because you would not want to arouse your lover's jealousy, or because you could not devote as much time to him if you had varied relations, or because you were afraid that, if you went off with another male, he might go off with another female, and might even wind up by marrying her.

Or suppose that, being a member in good standing of some religious, political, or other group that opposes premarital sex relations, you believe that such relations are wrong and do not wish to have them. If you really feel that the advantages of subscribing to your particular creed and its code of sex morals outweighs the disadvantages of giving up non-marital relations, you should naturally give up the latter for the former. Under these conditions, you will almost surely suffer some amount of sex discomfort; but you will also, presumably, have certain moral or religious gains for feeling this discomfort, and your physical and emotional well-being may not be seriously affected.

If, on the other hand, you do not actually believe in the code of a group to which you formally belong, and are merely blindly and unthinkingly refraining from sex relations because this group says that you should, that seems more than a bit silly, and will soon lead you into irreconcilable self-contradictions and emotional upset.

Mrs. S.: I can understand that all right. But how about me and Mr. Smith. That's more to the point in my case right now!

Therapist: Forgive my wandering off into theory. Back to you and Mr. Smith! In general, the matter of adultery is not unlike that of premarital affairs. If you desire to achieve a certain kind of this-above-all relationship with your spouse; if you want to keep your husband secure and happy; if you believe that the general advantages of your marriage outweigh the possible disadvantages of foregoing adulterous pleasures—then by all means remain monogamous. Every married individual has to make various important sacrifices to achieve a good, sound relationship. One sacrifice, in our society, usually is the giving up of extramarital affairs; and it will hurt the average husband and wife relatively little to make this sacrifice, while they may gain significantly from it.

Mrs. S.: Which means, if I apply this to my own case, that if I want to have a better-than-average relationship with my husband and not jeopardize it in any serious way, I had better forget about Mr. Smith—at least as far as actions are concerned.

Therapist: Exactly, as far as actions are concerned. If you want to keep thinking about Mr. Smith, fine—provided that you do not think of him too often or too intensely, in an obsessive-compulsive manner. But if you want to *do* anything about your thoughts, then you take the risk of destroying your entire marital relationship. If, because of other factors, your marriage doesn't mean much to you, and you would just as soon as not see it end, then of course you would not be jeopardizing very much by having an affair with Mr. Smith or any other man. But if you really think that you have or could work toward having quite a good marriage, you would certainly be foolish to

184

risk sabotaging that marriage for a few rolls in the hay with your boarder.

Mrs. S.: The way you put it—well—. That is, I think you seem to be saying that the question of whether one should or should not give in to one's non-monogamous desires is very similar to the question of whether one should jeopardize one's marriage in many kinds of non-sexual ways.

Therapist: You've hit it quite rightly. One of the greatest mistakes we consistently make about sex activity and morality, in our society, is to separate them arbitrarily from non-sexual activity and morality. If we would put them closer together, most of our sex problems would fairly easily be solved. Thus, instead of asking ourselves whether or not we should have extra-marital relations, if we asked ourselves whether we should do some non-sexual act which we distinctly desired to do but which might lead to serious difficulties with ourselves or our mates, we might get a quick and decisive answer to our question.

Mrs. S.: If I thought of my having or not having an affair with Mr. Smith in the same category as some other risky and possibly marriage-breaking thing I might do, some other thing of a non-sexual nature, then you think I could easily answer my own question?

Therapist: Yes. If, instead of thinking about Mr. Smith and the risks involved in having an affair with him, you thought of the risks to your marriage of purchasing some very expensive gowns that your husband might be incensed about, or moving to another city that he hates, or taking a job that might keep you out nights, then you would put your decision in better perspective. If you do not value your marriage highly enough to give up buying expensive gowns, or moving to another city, or taking a night job, then it is quite probable that you do not value it highly enough to refrain from adultery with Mr. Smith or some other prospect.

Sex is surely an important, biologically based human urge;

185

but it is hardly the only or necessarily the most important urge. It, like your strong desire for almost anything else, definitely can be, to a large extent, sacrificed for other goals and ideals. But—mark this well!—it should be honestly, unhypocritically sacrificed. And it is the sex *act*—the possible adultery with Mr. Smith—that should be sacrificed, if you think your marriage is worth making such a sacrifice for. Sex thoughts and desires are in quite a different category from sex acts and cannot easily be equally well squelched or suppressed.

Mrs. S.: You seem to be saying that conscious suppression of sex acts is quite possible, and not necessarily deleterious to a marriage or to the suppressing person. But hypocritical or unconscious repression of a sex desire or thought is only likely to lead to trouble.

Therapist: Precisely. To live successfully in society, we must consciously suppress many acts we would like to perform —such as, walking naked in the streets when it is very warm, or killing our boss when he unjustifiably gives us a hard time. But to deny that we have the *wish* to walk naked in the streets or the *desire* to kill our boss at times—that is unconsciously, shamefully to repress our thoughts. And that, as Sigmund Freud pointed out many years ago, is one of the main roots of neurosis.

Mrs. S.: Well, even though I may not like it, I can see the answer to my problem about me and Mr. Smith.

Therapist: You mean—?

Mrs. S: I mean that Mr. Smith has got to go. Not as a thought, as you point out, or a wish. But as a real possibility of a lover. Too bad; but I really do love my husband and think that we can continue to have a good marriage. And if I must give up this additional dessert, in order to be able to keep eating the main course, that's the way it is. If I must, I must.

Therapist: It's your decision. And probably a wise one. Desserts are fine in their place—but the main course, as you say, is more important. And as long as you're going to remain faithful to your husband because you honestly think that would be the better, less self-defeating plan (and not because you think that adultery is wicked or horrible in itself), you should come out fine. The honest monogamist is one who soundly thinks through the problem and truly convinces herself that, in her own particular case, monogamy is the better part of valor: that it better befits her own goals, ideals, and preferences.

Thus, with certain variations, do we often counsel patients. Most of them listen carefully and give the matter careful consideration. Some of them do not.

In the latter category fall some seriously disturbed individuals. In one case, by way of illustration, a husband came for counseling because he was quite upset by his wife's adulterous desires for another man, which he accidentally discovered by overhearing a phone conversation. He was so angry and bitter that he completely refused to listen when he was told that most married individuals have desires of a non-monogamous nature and that, in themselves, they are not necessarily evil.

"What do you mean?" he shouted. "*I* have no such desires. I never even look at another woman than my wife. The Lord said that it was evil to have such thoughts and I never have them. I can't see why my wife has them, even if she has never acted on them yet. She's just abnormal and you can't tell me any different!"

He was right: he couldn't be told any different. But it soon became clear, from his unusual disturbance and some of the hints he dropped about never looking at the pretty young girls in his office, that he did have quite a few non-monogamous thoughts. After much beating about the bush, he finally admitted that he was having frequent sex fantasies about his secretary; then he withdrew this admission; and then he bolted out an agonizingly painful confession, in the course of which he cursed and damned himself in the direst terms. It was only with the greatest difficulty that he was calmed down and prevented from going out and harming himself.

187

It took many months of intensive psychotherapy before this husband was fully able to accept his own non-monogamous desires, to see that they were harmless and normal, and to be able to understand his wife's sex leanings. At the same time, he worked through the problem of his own semi-impotence (which had been one of the factors in his wife's desiring sex relations with other men), and was able to achieve and maintain a far more harmonious marital relationship than he had ever achieved before.

When, in other words, people are at odds with themselves they usually also become at odds with their spouses. When they do not acknowledge and face up to their own non-monogamous desires, they generally become prey to enormous inner conflicts. In some instances, ironically enough, these very conflicts lead to compulsive acts of a non-monogamous nature.

A married woman of thirty-three, for example, kept having adulterous affairs without having any sex satisfaction and was not able to give a good explanation of why she continued having these affairs. When, in the course of several months of intensive psychotherapy, the basic reasons for her peculiar behavior came to light, it was discovered that she had always had non-monogamous desires, had literally ripped these desires out of her conscious awareness because of her severe guilt about them, and then had to resort, compulsively, to unsatisfying affairs in order to keep her desires from rising to consciousness.

This patient was made fully aware of her desires, as she underwent a rational therapeutic analysis. She was induced to accept the normality of these desires and, especially, to stop blaming herself severely for having them. As soon as she started to question and challenge her self-blaming tendencies—to ask herself: "*Why* am I a louse for having these desires? Why should I *not,* even though I am married, keep having them?"— she lost her feelings of guilt, stopped being obsessed with the question of adultery, and was able to stop her compulsive affairs. Her compelling need for these affairs returned to a mere state of preference for them; and since she preferred, even more strongly, a solidly knit relationship with her husband and child, she was able to curb her adulterous desires and remain strictly monogamous.

Summing up: Non-monogamous desires are perfectly normal, natural, and expectable, and should freely be faced and acknowledged. Non-monogamous actions may or may not be satisfactory, depending on the general goals and ideals of the individual who wishes to engage in them. Suppressing, consciously, non-marital sex urges may be perfectly compatible with emotional health and happiness, particularly if the suppressing individual is obtaining at least a moderate amount of sex satisfaction in his or her marriage. *Re*pressing, unconsciously, non-monogamous desires and one's feelings of shame about having such desires usually leads to serious emotional difficulty. To be or not to be monogamous—rather than to think or not to think monogamously—is the real issue, and one which can be effectively answered if one is ruthlessly self-honest.

15

Communication in Marriage

As we stated earlier, most couples who enter marriage today have two main expectations: that they will achieve regular sex satisfaction and the enjoyments of intimate and secure companionship. Although we have just been giving a large portion of our attention to the sex area (which, in our Puritanical society, is often the source of great confusion and neurosis), sex and companionship cannot be separated in a successfully functioning marriage. In full marital love the two are inextricably blended. Adequate communication is necessary for the achievement and maintenance of such a fusion of sex and companionship.

"At least I never lost my temper and said things I'd be sorry for," said Mrs. Dee. Her tone of voice was self-righteous and her manner that of suffering nobility.

"That's most unfortunate," I answered, "and not a virtue to be proud of. Too bad you didn't let yourself go sometimes and give your husband an inkling of what you were thinking. If you had communicated better, even about your dissatisfactions, instead of proudly holding them within yourself, your marriage would probably be in a lot better shape now."

Mr. Dee had been in to see me prior to my conference with his wife. He told me that during the two months of their marriage all his efforts to get her to talk about mutual concerns had dismally failed. He had tried humor, cajoling, threatening, exploding. Nothing worked. He did not have the slightest idea what his wife thought or felt about anything other than the trivial, emotionally meaningless aspects of their life together. He could get her to hold forth briefly on strictly impersonal matters, but not on anything that had personal and emotional significance. While he had noticed this tendency in his wife before marriage, he had shrugged it off then as an indication of premarital shyness about intimate and personal matters.

Somewhere along the road of life, at some early milestone, Mrs. Dee had picked up the concept that silence is golden. She failed to understand her husband's complaints, in order that she might keep picturing herself as a kind and loving wife. When Mr. Dee became argumentative, she became silent. Why wasn't this virtuous? she now wanted to know. Why wasn't he, not she, to blame for their difficulties?

Whatever the old adages may tell us, I explained to Mrs. Dee, silence is appropriate treatment, perhaps, for your enemies but not for your loved ones. Gandhi and other leaders of passive resistance used silent non-cooperation as the Indian means to independence. It is also the means to independence—that is, divorce—in marriage. Like the British in India, a husband or wife who is faced year after year with silent non-cooperation comes to see that there is no other solution than the granting

191

of independence to the non-cooperator.

Mrs. Dee was a real expert in achieving independence. I soon discovered that she had silently suffered her way through to three prior divorces. Husband number four, Mr. Dee, had fortunately sought help early in this marriage; and Mrs. Dee's three previous failures made her a little less sure of her virtue, a little more amenable to psychotherapy. At first, however, all she could do in the therapy sessions was to show how awfully sorry for herself she felt. She thought that she had been misused and abused since childhood. She felt that her first three husbands, and now her present one, were following the pattern set by her parents and her brothers and sisters. They all mistreated her and she could not understand why. She returned their unkindness with kindness, their mean words with silence.

Mrs. Dee was essentially right regarding the facts of her familial and marital relationships. But what she had to be helped to see was that her own actions elicited mistreatment, that unconsciously she was *asking for* abuse. In some ways, she resembled Mrs. Kay (the "shrike" of our earlier chapter). Like Mrs. Kay, Mrs. Dee lacked basic self-esteem and self-love. She was sure underneath that she would not be loved or respected by others. Her childhood relationships with her parents and her brothers and sisters had been the source of her low self-esteem and the early confirmation of the belief that others did not care for her. Like all humans, Mrs. Dee developed her self-image from these early reactions of others to her. As a defense against her severe feelings of worthlessness, she adopted the martyr role—the method of silently turning the other cheek for the blows from her associates that she was constantly (and almost paranoiacally) expecting.

Martyrs like Mrs. Dee feel that they are unworthy characters; and in some instances they also (unconsciously) feel that they deserve to be punished because of their unworthiness. Since many of the people with whom these martyrs come in contact have hostile attitudes resulting from their own life frustrations and their view that the world has treated them oh! so unfairly, there is no likelihood that there will be a shortage of punitive responses dealt by them to the Mrs. Dees they encountered. It is almost as though people like Mrs. Dee wear signs which read "kick me." Since such "kicking" serves as a temporary release of tension for many hostile people, the Mrs. Dees have no trouble finding "kickers" and are thus constantly vindicated in their martyrdom.

This had been the case with Mrs. Dee and her husbands —all four of them. Being frustrated in their efforts to work out a satisfactory relationship with her, and not themselves being sane enough to tell themselves that frustrations are a pain in the neck but that they are not necessarily horrible or annihilating, her first three husbands eventually got around to kicking her—out.

Her dramatic silence signaled a martyr's "strength" to Mrs. Dee; but to her husbands it signaled her unwillingness or inability to cope with her problems—and consequent frustration for them. Their efforts to talk over difficulties, work out solutions, only brought forth more "golden silence" from Mrs. Dee.

After her first three husbands had finally given up the futile battle and had awarded her the independence she seemed to want, husband number four, being more secure in his own right, had shown an unusual willingness to stop kicking and to hang around for Mrs. Dee's long, hard pull away from silent suffering to outspoken self-respect. And self-respect, and the ability to risk speaking up for her own fundamental wants and preferences even though others might disagree with her and temporarily withdraw their support,—these were the goals which I, as therapist, and Mrs. Dee, as patient, worked on for quite a while and finally were able to achieve. Her "golden silence" turned to straightforward expression of her views and her gripes; and her marriage with Mr. Dee, which to my knowledge is still solidly continuing, took an immense turn for the better.

Is Mrs. Dee a very unusual case? Extreme non-communication; four marriages; a severe self-martyring pattern of neurosis. Yes, somewhat extreme in her degree of difficulties. But Mrs. Dee is hardly alone; and a use of silence as a self- and/or mate-punishing mechanism is quite common in more moderate form in many other marriages. A case like Mrs. Dee's simply brings out the underlying problems with more dramatic emphasis than a milder form of non-communication might do.

Non-communication almost invariably involves a sense of frustration and futility on the part of both marital partners and seriously augments the difficulties of handling the problem about which the silent treatment hangs. The more the communicative mate talks, the deeper the non-communicative one tends to withdraw into hostile silence. The talker feels more and more silly, useless, hurt. He may try shouting or even using physical violence. He wants to drive his mate from the retreat of silence and to hurt her for her attempt to punish him by non-communication. This is, of course, irrational behavior on the part of the talking partner (for he is blaming his non-communicative mate for being disturbed, and thereby helping make her more disturbed and the situation worse); but it is a very common response to the silent treatment.

Somewhat like the problem drinker, the habitual non-communicator fools himself into believing that he is handling his problems.

His flight from reality is not too dissimilar in some respects to that of the alcoholic, since he has buried his sense of responsibility and run away from his problems as effectively, almost, as if he had numbed his senses with alcohol. Such a person as Mrs. Dee is even likely to feel that she has nobly avoided a squabble. But in the long run the non-communicating flight from reality can be almost as cruel an illusion as flight by hard liquor. Problems go unsolved and pile on top of each other, and every escape makes more difficult the eventual facing of these problems.

Fortunately, many marriage partners have not sunk so deeply into their habits of non-communication that they cannot be helped. Some need considerable sympathetic support from their husbands or wives. They need experience in facing and working through everyday difficulties. Provided their marriages have not reached too deep a state of deterioration, the psychotherapist can get the more communicative mates to cooperate by encouraging and accepting even the most awkward and inappropriate expressions of resentment, anger, and outright hate from their formerly silent partners. Negative feelings that habitually silent individuals have sat on for years are likely to be the first to emerge in explosive and childish form in the early phases of therapy.

It will also help for the habitually non-communicative person to practice at first talking over some of the smaller and less emotion-charged matters with his or her mate. Mrs. Dee, for example, was induced to practice the art of discussion in areas where her resentments were more likely to be mild. She learned to talk over with her husband such annoyances as spilled cigarette ashes and clothes-draped chairs before she was able to deal with greater and more complicated emotional matters. Although she was sometimes awkward, childish, and anything but calm in dealing with these relatively trivial matters, her husband and she were better able to tolerate the practicing of communication arts in these areas of less vital significance for the marriage. After Mr. and Mrs. Dee developed skills in facing, discussing, and understanding relatively inconsequential matters, they found that these same methods were applicable to major marital problems.

Silence is by no means the only block to adequate communication between husbands and wives. There may be an ample two-way flow of words, but they may be just words: that is, words without conviction and without validating action. Mr. Que, for example, always *said* the right thing. He told Mrs. Que and he told other people that he loved his wife. He said he

195

admired and trusted her and he spoke highly of her homemaking abilities and many other qualities and skills.

But Mr. Que's actions communicated other thoughts and feelings. All bank accounts, for instance, were not joint, but were in his name only. This spoke loudly to Mrs. Que of his lack of trust for her, even though Mr. Que had many high-sounding rationalizations to utter about why it was necessary to have the accounts in his name alone. Mr. Que also did all the purchasing of groceries, of clothes for each member of the family, and of the household items. He said it was to save his wife the trouble, but the meaning she caught from his *actions* was that he considered her too stupid and unreliable to do the shopping. He alone drove the family car, too. He *said* it was because it saved wear and tear on Mrs. Que's nerves, but Mrs. Que had not asked to have her nerves thus spared.

Mr. Que had to be helped to realize that a basic lack of confidence in and respect for women in general and his wife in particular underlay his interactions with Mrs. Que. Although he had learned the proper words for an intimate, democratic relationship of equals in marriage, his deep feelings (as expressed in his inner conversations with himself and his outward actions toward his wife) were patriarchal. Stated more forcefully, he was a male-centered fascist. Although he verbalized sex equality and democracy, he felt and acted as if his wife were a second-class citizen at best and an untrustworthy slave at worst.

There are many male-centered fascists hiding in the word-clothes of marital democrats. The difficulties are not all from the side of the patriarchal male, however. The Mrs. Ques are often not prepared, themselves, to assume the full responsibilities of marital equality. The woman in this case, for instance, communicated a desire to be treated as a beautiful, delicate, and not too bright child in certain special circumstances, and then bitterly resented such treatment in other situations, such as those we have cited.

The more a woman matures emotionally, however, the more she is likely to reach out for opportunities for freedom, growth, and responsibility equal to, but not necessarily identical with, those of her husband. Limitations that may not have seemed important early in the marriage often begin to trouble the more mature woman.

Patriarchy may work for a few couples who still go along with remnants of our authoritarian past, but most modern wives, as well as husbands, find patriarchal attitudes real roadblocks to learning to live happily together. Under patriarchal circumstances, communication often increasingly deteriorates, as in the case of the Ques. In these instances, therapy for both husband and wife includes democratic reeducation of the basic thoughts and emotions of the individuals concerned. It means the learning of some of the skills of action (not just words) which are meaningful for real marital equality.

Perhaps nothing helps more than a sense of humor to establish or reestablish effective communication in marriage. It is easier, of course, to see humor in other people's marriage troubles than in one's own. It is also easier to find something funny about one's mate's predicaments than about one's own. For humor to facilitate marital communication, it must be *shared* by husband and wife.

Such sharing of humor can be learned. I have yet to meet a totally humorless man or woman. I have met people who did skillful jobs of concealing humor from themselves and others, and I've seen many husbands and wives whose senses of humor were working at cross purposes. I've also, alas, encountered people who felt there was no proper place for humor in the dreadfully serious matters of marriage.

Take Mr. Williams, by way of illustration. The heart of his communication difficulties with his wife seemed to be his refusal to be relaxed, casual, or good-humored about dealing with any of the problems he and Mrs. Williams met in marriage. I made direct efforts, in my sessions with him, and indirect ones

197

in my sessions with his wife, to get him to relax a little, to lighten his load of anxiety, to take a more casual attitude toward his marital problems. Such attempts were steadfastly rejected—a very serious matter, this marriage, he insisted, and he was going to have no part in any inappropriate clowning about it. In fact, he told me, his main objective with his wife was to get her to stop being so casual and to be more earnest, sincere, grave, and dignified.

An unscheduled telephone call when we were in the midst of his fifth session helped to indicate to Mr. Williams the desirability of a lighter approach to life and to marriage. Mr. Williams could tell from my end of the conversation that the phone call brought very sad personal news. It was about something fully finished, however—some completely spilled milk. So I turned away from the phone and back to Mr. Williams with something of a shrug and a smile.

"Well," I said, "we can chalk that up as another of life's little tragedies. Now let's get back to your problems."

As is often the case, where words had failed, example turned the tide. Mr. Williams seemed flabbergasted that a basically serious person like myself could deal so undisturbedly with a life situation about which he (Williams) would have moaned, groaned, and stewed. My talking about his needing to learn to deal less grimly with his marriage had meant little or nothing. But my treating my own problems with casual rationality and good humor hit home. At that point, some of my verbal recommendations began to make sense to him and his communication with his wife began to improve steadily. In fact, Mr. Williams became something of a devoted student of the let's-not-be-grim-about-our-problems school of marriage. He often liked to refer thereafter to a difficulty he and his wife were having as "another of life's little tragedies." And when he said that, he smiled.

Does this mean that married couples who want to learn to live happily together need to become rather nitwittish about serious difficulties? Does it take a third-rate comedian to succeed in modern marriage? No, it takes acceptance (if not immediate resolution) of differences. Since, however, anxiety is an omnipresent block to understanding and accepting and dealing rationally with differences between two intimate associates, and since humor is one of the best methods of reducing anxious blockings, *shared* humor in marriage is one of the better communicative techniques.

Mr. and Mrs. Williams are now doing no injustice to the serious and significant sides of their marriage because they can share some laughs about their problems and themselves. In fact, injustice comes from over-seriousness and over-grimness, which prevent humor from dissolving some of the anxiety blocks in the lines of communication between husband and wife.

While a therapist's working with one partner in a marriage can sometimes result in considerable improvement in the communication between the spouses, it is generally desirable to get cooperation from the other partner, too. Whatever skills and knowledges are demanded for success in marriage (and by this time it should be clear that the authors of this book feel that such requisite knowledges and skills are manifold), a minimum need is for the two partners to communicate adequately with each other.

When one mate is reluctant to cooperate in a marriage counseling process designed to improve a relationship, pose of pride, or ego-defensiveness, is usually at the root of this reluctance. The therapist and the willing partner must then devise some effective method of breaking through the unwilling partner's defensiveness.

One method which we employ in this connection is to instruct the cooperative partner to say to the less cooperating one: "I know, dear, that you think that there is no good reason why you should talk to my therapist. But he says that he can probably help me better overcome my own difficulties, which are helping create problems in our marriage, if you will see him and give him your impressions of me. After all, I may be omitting

199

significant details, particularly in relation to my own shortcomings, in my session with him. And if you will go and fill in some of these details, that might well be most helpful." When the cooperative partner speaks to his or her mate in this fashion, it is surprising how many of these reluctant mates who will not admit that *they* need help or that *they* have serious problems will go to talk to a marriage counselor.

In our own practices, we find that some of the people who come to see us because of such an initial strategic maneuver by their mates merely take advantage of an opportunity to air their grievances but never buckle down to anything more constructive. Others come in a more generous spirit of wanting to help us to help their spouses; and, once they are in the office, we are usually able to get them gradually to face their own responsibilities and problems in regard to their marriages (and, for that matter, in regard to non-marital aspects of their lives).

Another way to get some reluctant spouses to seek therapeutic aid is to ignore them for awhile and to go ahead with the willing partner. When the attitudes and actions of the help-seeking individual alter with psychotherapy, the help-resisting mate sometimes decides that he had better go to see the therapist either (a) in self-defense, because he can no longer cope with his stronger and less upsettable mate; or (b) because he sees how much progress his mate has made in therapy and wants to make similar progress himself.

A more drastic method of getting a resistive spouse to consult a therapist is to have the cooperative partner issue an ultimatum. This is only infrequently used, as a last resort after other methods have dismally failed and where further progress depends upon the cooperation of the reluctant mate. The nature of the ultimatum to be issued varies, of course, with the particular people and circumstances.

For a spouse who refuses to see the therapist, but who claims that he or she wants the marriage to work, the counseled partner may say something like: "I've tried in every way I know to improve our relationship. You say you are similarly trying. You should then be willing to go at least once to my therapist to tell him how you feel. If you don't show such willingness, I'll just have to assume that we've reached an unbreakable stalemate. If this is so, and you won't try through therapy to break the stalemate, I think we should separate."

Then, of course, the person who issues such an ultimatum has to be prepared to carry through. He or she should not play bluffing games. We never approve of such ultimatums unless the husband or wife who has been seeing us has reached a point of real desperation where separation is preferable to continuation of the existing marital holocaust.

Sometimes a quite different type of ultimatum seems appropriate where the mate who is resisting consultation with the therapist states that he or she wants a divorce. Then the other mate may say: "I won't even consider divorce until you have seen the counselor." Since divorce is much more readily obtained with the cooperation of both parties to a marriage, such a statement will usually bring the reluctant partner in.

Not only are ultimatums to be regarded as last resorts in getting spouses to seek therapeutic help, but it is only fair to note that frequently thus-forced clients are unresponsive to counseling. Resistance and resentment are likely to be too high. Shotgun marriage counseling, like shotgun marriage, is at best a far from felicitous business. Sometimes, however, it works surprisingly well.

The person who is reluctant to see a marriage counselor or psychotherapist is more often the husband than the wife. Men are more strongly prejudiced, in our culture, in favor of the proposition that they *should* be able to handle their own problems. Otherwise, they think, they are not "manly." They are therefore usually more inclined than women to think of counseling as unnecessary, silly, a waste of time, the work of a quack, and a racket which feeds on suckers.

Although women are more rarely reluctant to see a counselor,

201

those who are set against the idea are quite likely to remain so. They are most difficult to lure to the counselor's office and tend to remain distinctly uncooperative if and when they finally come. This may be because their opposition to therapy is less likely to be based on vanity, ignorance, and hearsay prejudice and more likely to be grounded in personal disturbances.

When a person's refusal to see a counselor is based on his or her determination to separate or divorce, refusal can still at times be changed to acquiescence by convincing the reluctant spouse that the therapist's role is to help in solving or easing their problems and not necessarily to save the marriage. Some of the best therapeutic work is needed in helping people to prepare themselves for the problems of separation and divorce, as against keeping them married against their wills.

It has been our experience that in the majority of cases where the man takes the more active role in consulting a therapist, the marriage has reached a very serious state of breakdown or near-breakdown. Because most women view marriage as a central value of life, many are willing to undertake all kinds of difficult corrective programs, including psychotherapy, early in the game. For many men, however, marriage is one of a number of values in life and consequently the relationship has to be terribly bad before they will consider taking the initiative in consulting a counselor.

Fortunately, however, there are many instances where both parties to the marriage are fairly willing to cooperate with the therapist and where the relationship itself has not yet reached an extreme point of deterioration. In such instances, what are some of the things the therapist tries to do?

In the first place, he gathers information and, even while gathering it, suggests tentative plans for improving the relationship. Largely, he tries to improve communication between the mates—to enable them truly to understand themselves and each other and to convey, mutually, their understandings to each other.

Sometimes help in improved marital communication comes almost automatically once counseling gets under way. Psychotherapy is itself a new shared experience for the married partners and the husband and wife again have a sense of something positive in common, once they undertake it. This attitude of shared new experience tends to develop whether the mates are having joint or separate interviews with the therapist.

Not only does the couple share therapy, but also the same therapist. Husband and wife exchange opinions about their therapist, what he said, how he acted, what he meant, what strange kind of animal he seems to be. Already, by sharing the new experience of therapy and their new-found intimate associate, the therapist, some husbands and wives begin to experience an improvement in intercommunication.

Along with this sense of sharing of therapy, some couples experience a feeling of satisfaction from trying to do something constructive about their problems. They have taken action. They have a beginning sense of accomplishment which, at least momentarily, often helps each mate to view the other with slightly more sympathy and understanding.

The therapist cannot, of course, allow the mates to rest very long on such vague feelings of good will. Concrete steps toward more lasting improvement of communication must be undertaken from the first interview onward. The exact nature of the steps to be taken in helping this process is different for each marital situation; but certain common elements to be corrected are found in most impaired marital communication systems.

Most troubled husbands and wives have long established habits of *assuming* that they understand what their mates mean by certain actions, or feel in certain situations, or intend by various words or gestures or tone of voice. Their negative assumptions about their mates' motives frequently produce the very kind of behavior that they have already assumed existed.

203

One highly recommended change for improving communication between a husband and wife, then, is for them to stop assuming. Early in therapy, we emphasize the importance of the *art of asking* in marriage. Each partner is instructed to ask his or her mate about what is meant, felt, thought, or intended concerning some of even the most elementary aspects of their marriage. Then, after he or she explains his or her meanings, feelings, thoughts, or intentions, the spouse is instructed that he or she should still not assume complete understanding.

Thus a husband is asked to give his wife *his* version of what *he* thinks she means by one of her statements. Then if she says: "Yes, that's right; that's what I actually meant, felt, thought, or intended," then, and only then, is the other partner legitimately to feel that he is on the right track.

Even with this somewhat tedious (though frequently highly illuminating) practice, many persons continue to make false assumptions about their mates. After they have tracked down specific feelings, meanings, thoughts and intentions held by their spouses, they want to generalize.

"If my husband has such and such a point of view (as he has clearly said he has) about the discipline of children, then he *should* believe thus and so about nursery schools."

She is assuming again. She is generalizing from one specific husbandly attitude about one phase of child development to some psychological principle in which she believes and she is then applying this generalization to what she thinks her husband should believe about nursery schools. As her counselor, I urge her to *ask* her husband how he feels about nursery schools and other questions and she begins to get answers, some of them gratifying and some not, which never could have been predicted from her own assumptions.

A closely related element in the breakdown of marital communication systems is the *false principle of logical consistency*. If the wife insists on an orderly living room, it should logically follow, says this false principle, that she should not strew bobby pins, hair curlers, facial cream jars, nylon stockings, half-squeezed lemons, and clippings from last week's Sunday supplement in the bathroom. Perhaps it logically follows. But logic has little, if anything, to do with some of the habits that people develop. Many communication difficulties in marriage can be removed or reduced by helping people to stop looking for logic as the basis for the life-long habits of themselves and their mates.

As any course in philosophic analysis will quickly make you aware, it is not logical to use a dollar's worth of gasoline to buy a bargain which saves you thirty cents, to squeeze the toothpaste tube in the middle instead of at the bottom, to check the lock on your door five times instead of once, to chat lengthily with your mother by long distance phone the evening before you are going to visit her, and so on. It is not logical, but sane people do such things.

One of the most important things that married couples can understand—with or without the psychotherapist's help—is that highly irrational beliefs and feelings (as well as some clearly rational ones) are the motives of many human actions.

"Don't ask yourself or your mate if his (or her) actions are logical," we often say to marriage counseling clients. "Chances are that they are not. Ask yourself (and sometimes, but not always, your mate) what motives are being fulfilled by these actions. What notions (sane or insane) about love, joy, sorrow, or aspiration may be served by this particular illogical mode of behavior of your spouse? What fear, anxiety, or insecurity may be temporarily assuaged by this silly habit? Try to understand your mate's action and the (good or bad) reasons behind it instead of cavalierly condemning it as illogical."

This does not mean that we, as psychotherapists, become the staunch ally of irrationality. Quite the contrary. After helping the husband and wife to accept each other with many irrational and illogical motivations, we then go on to try to help each of them to function with much greater rationality. It is very sane in one's interpersonal relations to realize that many of one's own and other people's actions are nonrationally motivated. But it is idiotic and ineffective to attempt to cram one's own conception of logic and rationality down the throat of one's mate. Calmly and unemotionally accepting the *existence* of irrational behavior does not mean that one has to help perpetuate it or do nothing to combat it. On the contrary, the calmer and less emotional one's initial acceptance of its existence is, the much better is the chance that one will effectively be able to fight it.

Mr. Morford, for example, clearly saw that his wife was "crazy in the head" when she tried to get everyone, including himself, to pay attention to her every minute of the day and night; and he frankly, violently, and condemningly told her so. He assumed, of course, that this kind of outright condemnation of his wife's irrationality would drive her to do something. He was right. It drove her to be more irrational, to insist that he did not love her at all, and to attempt, more than ever, to win his continual attention.

At my behest, Mr. Morford calmed down and temporarily began accepting his wife's severe disturbance and her dire need for attention and approval. After he stopped telling himself and her what a dunce she was for having this need, he was for the first time able to ask himself, "What can I possibly do to reduce her insecurity and her irrationality?" He soon figured out an answer to this question. By, on the one hand, giving her more attention for a period of a few months, and at the same time steadily encouraging her and showing her that she *could* get along very well without his or others' approval, he was able to help her to become distinctly more secure. Eventually, she became in much less need of his attendance and approbation.

Another principle which I endeavored, and with a good deal of success, to get Mr. Morford to apply to his relations with his wife, was the basic principle of *respect for another's individuality and personality.* For love and companionship to

206

develop and flourish in marriage, as I showed him, intercommunications between husband and wife must be rooted in both self-respect and respect for the spouse. Each mate must learn to proceed on the fundamental conviction that nothing is so important as to warrant the violation of his own and his mate's integrity.

Spouses, in other words, must try to communicate with each other with the conviction that all of us matter *as people* and not merely as mates, parents, bread-winners, housekeepers, or what you will. It is, moreover, not our *words* that matter nor the *principle* of this or that thing, nor what *others think* of us, nor even what the psychotherapist says. The one and paramount thing which really matters is the *person*-ality of the mates themselves—their individual likes and dislikes, preferences and distastes, ideas and attitudes. If each partner in the marriage learns to deal respectfully and lovingly with the you, me, and us of their relationship, meanings will come to be adequately communicated. And marriage will be enjoyable much of the time.

Thus, in Mr. Morford's case, when he stopped looking at his wife as (a) a spouse who just *had* to follow certain "good" marital rules; as (b) a woman who just *had* to think logically and rationally; and (c) a pain in the neck who just *had* to stop bothering him with her silly ways;—when, instead of having this kind of picture of his wife, Mr. Morford started looking upon her as a unique, distinct individual in her own right, who very well could, and did, act "badly" or "illogically" because of her own peculiar perceptions of the world around her, he began to understand her previously "meaningless" words and actions. Then he actually began to communicate (rather than just to talk emptily) to her.

Solid marital communication is, at bottom, based on reducing one's own grandiosity, accepting temporarily whatever outlandish words and deeds one's mate may seem to be spewing out, and then calmly seeking a way to help this mate understand himself or herself. This is just another way of saying what has been said several previous times in this book: that good marital relations are concomitants of self-respect and respect for the individuality of another.

16

Children

One of the commonest assumptions among married people is that they *should* have children. The next most common assumption seems to be that children increase the happiness of a given marriage. Although you can find hordes of individuals who consciously believe these two assertions, there is very little objective evidence to support them.

Our own observations of thousands of marriages (not only of clients but of friends, relatives, and associates as well) have led to the following convictions about children and marriage:

1. The only time when reproduction is truly desirable for the children, for the married couple, and for society as a whole is when (a) the marriage is a distinctly good and happy one,

(b) the husband and wife are more mature emotionally than the average man and woman in their social group; and (c) *both* mates not only want children in a sentimental sense, but are eager to make parenthood a major enterprise for the next quarter of a century and realize that this means considerable hard study and hard work and sacrifice of many other satisfactions.

2. The relatively few couples who meet the foregoing criteria are likely to have their happy marriages made happier by having children. In fact, for this minority, the joyful labors of parenthood probably bring as deep a sense of creative achievement as is available in life. This does not mean that these people must have offspring in order to be happy, nor that they could not find vital interests (in people, things, and/or ideas) if, somehow, they could not have children. But it does mean that by inclination and ability they are able to have enormous child-raising satisfactions.

3. There is no appropriate "should" about having children, at least under contemporary social circumstances. "Be fruitful and multiply" is very poor advice in the face of world overpopulation and accompanying socio-economic problems. A modern married couple is no more to be considered a social enemy for not raising a family than for not playing bridge or not caring to join the neighborhood bowling league. Such a couple may, in fact, be sparing the community a number of needless social and psychological problems which could emerge if it had duty-produced offspring.

4. Happy couples who do not prepare themselves seriously for the hard work and real sacrifices of parenthood are often in grave danger of having their marriages undermined by the children and the accompanying increase in life's stresses.

5. Couples who were relatively unhappy before having children are likely to find that the additional burdens of parenthood bring added misery and may lead to complete bankruptcy of their marriages. Unhappy marriages are most rarely rendered

happy by producing offspring.

6. People who stay married "just for the sake of the children" do great disservice to themselves and their offspring in most instances. Although children do not like their parents to separate, they also resent a home atmosphere where their parents are belligerently sticking together. As adolescents and adults, these children of unhappy homes frequently express the wish that their parents had had the courage and wisdom to separate. Moreover, the poor marital models which the parents of such homes set for their children frequently result in these children's later being jaundiced against marriage or being poor marital partners themselves.

7. Many of the people who urge married couples to have children and try to make them feel guilty if they do not are resentful of the freedom and enjoyment of life shown by some childless couples. "I'm tied down with a life I dislike because of my having a family; why shouldn't you be likewise?" is what is unconsciously being thought by some of the people who are overtly saying: "Nothing like kids to make life worthwhile; you shouldn't be without them." Such propagandizers for reproduction are malefactors, not benefactors, of the couples they propagandize, the children they help foist on these couples, and mankind in general.

Such observations as those just outlined may be judged evil and antisocial by many individuals; but any less severe approach to the responsibilities of parenthood seems to us truly anti-human. Whenever parenthood is an involuntary function and/or one for which the individual is grossly unsuited, ill effects are most likely to ensue for all parties concerned.

Both the matter of desire and competence for parenthood are, however, relative. No parent is *wholeheartedly* happy about his role as a child-raiser and certainly no one is *perfectly* equipped for the responsibilities of parenthood. But surely people who function as mothers and fathers, predominantly contrary to their wishes and skills, do injustice to themselves, their offspring, and their society.

Let us take a closer look, now, at some of the attitudes and competencies needed for parenthood. An essential prerequisite, we have said, for effective child-raising is a happy marriage. This does not mean that every happy couple is automatically qualified to be parents; but it does mean that without marital happiness, virtually none is fully qualified. Why do we make this flat assertion? Because research studies undertaken from widely differing psychiatric, psychological, sociological, and other aspects point with unanimity to the great significance of the home environment and of the parental influence on the development of the personality of the child.

Of the two parents, the one with the most significant influence, both in quality and quantity, is usually the mother. The home atmosphere and the maternal attitudes are to a considerable degree a reflection of the state of the marital relationship. This is because one of the main interests of the mother is her marriage, out of which her child or her children have emerged. Normally, her own attitudes are predominantly optimistic and happy or pessimistic and depressed as a result of the felicitous nature of her relationship with her husband—or how she looks at this relationship.

In addition to the direct bearing which the mother's sense of happiness or unhappiness has on that of her children, we also have the important influences of the home atmosphere and the tenor of the family life. These, too, are chiefly set by the husband-wife interactions. The children are inevitably directly and indirectly affected by these interactions.

Generally speaking, then, unhappy marital relations and unhappy mothers turn out tense, miserable, maladjusted children. Some such children, true enough, are helped to become happier and better adjusted by their associations with others in school, social, neighborhood, and other groups, but many more go through life with obvious marks of their early home and parental crippling influences. We have more than enough tense and depressed people by any count, without encouraging unhappy husbands and wives to bear and rear us further fruit of this kind.

Some brief notions of the nature of emotional maturity and its importance in marriage were brought out in the early chapters of this book. But even more exacting than the demands of a marital relationship on personal adjustment are the burdens of having children! Many couples who have been barely able to achieve reasonably good personal and marital adjustment are simply not equipped for the additional stresses of parenthood. Yet it is common practice to make married couples feel that they are abnormal, selfish, and in other ways unworthy for not having offspring.

Mr. and Mrs. Esteban came for counseling because they said that they wanted to have children and the physicians they consulted about their problem of sterility thought that they were perhaps too tense about various things, including bearing children, and that therefore Mrs. Esteban was not conceiving. In the course of several counseling sessions, it became clear that they were much too tense, all right. And that one of the main things that they were tense about was the fact that neither of them, and particular Mrs. Esteban, was sure that they really wanted children in the first place.

This couple was getting along fairly well as far as its marital relationship was concerned—but only because both partners were working very hard at pleasing each other and sacrificing many of his and her own interests. Thus, Mr. Esteban really wanted much more outdoor activity of the fishing and hunting type than his wife could stomach; but he quietly surrendered most of his desires in this respect and cultivated bridge and cocktail acquaintances with his wife as a definitely second-best choice. On her part, Mrs. Esteban would have really liked to be on the go and out socializing virtually every evening of the week; but she held herself down to two or three social affairs per week mainly because she knew that her husband could not too easily take more than this number.

If Mr. and Mrs. Esteban, who kept up their marginal but still adequate marital adjustment by working so hard and earnestly at it, had actually had children, things would have almost certainly got worse rather than better. Mr. Esteban would have really only enjoyed sons, and if he had them would have been always going on outdoor-type jaunts with them—which would have taken him farther away from the social life his wife enjoyed. Mrs. Esteban would probably not have enjoyed having sons at all and would have only got along well with daughters, if she had them, when they were old enough to socialize with her.

But because virtually all the friends and relatives of this couple kept making jokes, asking questions, making accusations about their not having children, they talked themselves into believing that they really wanted children—until, in the course of therapy, they were able squarely to face this issue of child-raising and see that it was simply not their *own* personal choice.

It is surely important for a considerable number of happy, well-adjusted, intelligent world citizens to dedicate themselves to reproducing the human race, just as it is important for a sufficient number of capable individuals to dedicate themselves to other activities closely related to human welfare, such as science, medicine, engineering, law, and education. But while there are a number of reasons to fear race extinction a low birth rate is not currently among them. Indeed, some of the people who are now over-reproducing do not meet many of the best standards for parenthood, and we might well prefer that some of the people who are under-reproducing increase their output. Qualitative population improvements, however, are not likely to be achieved by any method of forcing unwilling or unqualified persons to increase their reproduction.

Let us make no mistake in underestimating the additional stresses that parenthood in contemporary society places on a couple and in overestimating the number of persons who are capable of successfully handling these stresses. It is customary

214

to speak of the "joys" of parenthood, as if these were sure-fire characteristics of child-raising. It would be somewhat comparable to characterize the life of a soldier during wartime as idyllic because, on occasion, he was given all the chicken and ice cream he could eat.

There sometimes exists, as an accompaniment of brain injury or other serious disease, a condition which is called anosognosia, which means the denial of illness. A patient with anosognosia may be paralyzed in his right arm, for example, and yet stoutly deny the existence of his paralysis. He apparently so reorganizes his perceptions that he is able to "remove" the paralyzed limb from his field of reality. Being afraid to face the grim reality of being paralyzed, he blithely denies it.

The denial of the difficulties, burdens, and displeasures of parenthood, it would seem, involves much the same psychological process. Many of us are afraid to face the unhappy realities of parenthood and feel more comfortable denying that they exist. We prefer to believe, instead, the myth that having children is a sure route to bliss.

Careful observation reveals that travail is frequently ushered into the life of the average couple by the arrival and continuing presence of an infant. This "bundle of joy" thoroughly disrupts most of the patterns of satisfaction that the couple had previously worked out. The demands of time, energy, insight, and devotion on both parents are severe. Just to minister to the child's gross physical needs, not to mention the more subtle psychological ones, takes an unholy amount of concern, responsibility, understanding, and care.

It is true, of course, that often the mother and occasionally the father find sufficient compensation for efforts made during the child's infancy. Babies for a period of time are beautifully dependent, cuddly creatures. Even for a mother who is not too mature, loving, or dedicated to the disciplines of parenthood, there are many narcissistic satisfactions to be derived from this small, pliable, helpless extension of her ego. For the first year or so of the child's life, the mother (and to some extent the father) can enjoy the satisfactions of a life created and a love unquestioningly accepted: a life and a love totally dominated and possessed.

Infants do stop being infants, however. They take ideological and activity pathways far different from those of their parents. Even by the beginning of the second year, they often undertake behavior that demonstrates a strong will of their own. The narcissistic satisfactions of absolute power, of total domination and possession, are more and more lost by the parent.

Here the denial of the difficulties of parenthood tends to become increasingly absurd. The healthy child should grow toward independent functioning as a separate human being. The healthy parent should desire and assist this growing separation of the child. But to fulfill this responsibility, to help a child to become gradually an adult, to provide the wise and happy guidance needed by the youngster—this, besides being one of the most important, is also one of the most difficult of human tasks. It takes an exceptionally capable, loving, and integrated person adequately to fulfill this job.

Parenthood, in other words, is not a task that the average person can just muddle through and hope to be successful at. It is not something to be lightly undertaken. It is, rather, a creative *and* an arduous responsibility. There is no use shouting at those people who incautiously launch into totally unprepared ventures into fatherhood and motherhood; but perhaps we can at least convince a few of them to stop denying the reality of their difficulties.

It is generally agreed by most students of human behavior that what the infant primarily needs is unconditioned love, warmth, and acceptance. During the first year of its life, parents are not only wasting their time and energy, but possibly doing the child some damage if they try to push any kind of learning or discipline or training. This goes for most of the rules on how or when to eat, to sleep, to defecate, to urinate, to vocalize, etc. There is no more ludicrous, and yet pathetic, sight than the stern-looking parent who is trying endlessly to force a baby to swallow a spit-up chunk of oatmeal or to empty his bowels at a specified time in a specified container. All the parent usually achieves is discomfort for both herself and the baby. The wished-for lesson that "it's about time he learned that he can't always have his own way" is almost completely lost on infants. And worse: for at least the duration of the stern disciplining period, and perhaps permanently, the child tends to experience a security-shaking, anxiety-producing sense of severe frustration and rejection.

As the child grows, he requires not only the unconditional love of infancy. He also comes to need the setting of definite limits, in terms of his own welfare, as his actions take him into increasingly wide areas of living. But—and here is the difficult and delicate paradox of parenthood—almost as soon as the parent begins to set limits for the child, he needs to begin to remove them. That is, as the parent tells the child, "This you must do and that you must not do," he also has to encourage the youngster himself to take over the enforcement of his own do's and don't's. The good parent shows the way and then, as the child matures, increasingly withdraws authoritarian enforcement—even if the child rejects the parental way and chooses another.

Let us cite an example. One of our recent clients was a professor in a large university. He had an only child, a son, and had great hopes that this son would choose some scientific or scholarly career. The professor set an excellent example (and example is probably the most significant and effective teaching instrument a parent can use with a child) of earnest pursuit of intellectual matters. He also did everything he could to encourage his son to develop in the desired direction.

The son's interests, however, tended more and more toward mechanics, sports cars, and auto races. In consequence, father-son relations had reached a point of crisis just prior to the pro-

217

fessor's coming for help. The son was graduating from high school and expressed no interest in attending college. The father foolishly issued an ultimatum to the effect that the boy would either go to college or he (the father) would write his draft board and demand his son's immediate conscription.

It is not clear whether or not the son realized the emptiness of this threat. Fortunately, draft boards are not normally given to basing their procedures on the positive or negative wishes of fathers. In any case, the son quickly indicated his unwillingness to be bullied and showed his independence by action: he enlisted in the Navy. Whereupon the father began bemoaning the physical and psychological separation from his son. If only, he wailed to himself and others, he had been able to accept his son's right to make his own decisions as an independent individual; but now it was too late, and his son merely hated him.

This professor affords us a good illustration of the common tendency of parents to use their children as an extension of their own ambitions and, even more tragically, as a compensation for their own failures. The client was not a failure in his chosen intellectual lines. But it soon became clear in discussions with him that his achievements had been much more modest than his original ambitions. In the potential successes of his son he had long fantasized a furthering of his own goal-seeking, a more impressive culmination of his intellectual dreams, a more clear-cut realization of his idealized self-image.

But when his son refused to play the role of Einstein-like genius, the professor was thrown back on his own disappointment. He was forced perilously close to facing the fact that he had long tried to keep from awareness—that he himself was simply a competent, but not very original, academician. When his son balked at taking even the first step toward the intellectual life, the professor became exaggeratedly bitter over his own disappointment in himself.

A parent's projecting his own problems onto his children may be considerably more subtle and damaging than that of the professor with his son. Whatever special forms such projections take, they consist primarily of the parent's feeling that he has not been able to drink fully of his own life cup, so to speak, and his consequent determination to drink vicariously through the vessel of his child. Such misguided parental efforts are almost invariably doomed to failure, for three fundamental reasons.

First of all, each individual must live life directly, not vicariously, in order to gain sound and lasting satisfaction. Even in the rare instances where a child fulfills the specific dream-goals of his parent, the realization of these goals tends to leave the parent with an empty, flat, second-hand taste from the "draught of life."

Secondly, many children (like the professor's son) develop wills of their own and simply refuse to bother about their parents' dream-goals. Even children who are so pliable and docile as to comply with the parent's wishes in every detail turn out to be disappointments as persons in most instances. This is because, by giving up selfhood to fulfill a role that is outwardly foisted on them, they become shallow, passive puppets, and hollow in their own right.

Finally, failure is assured the parent who tries to live vicariously through his child or children; because any individual who cannot guide his own life productively, is highly unlikely to be able to guide his child's life to productive fulfillment. The same qualities that led to the parent's failure as a human being and a creator will, in one way or another, probably be inculcated in the child and lead to similar failure in the second generation.

We do not endeavor, as a counselors, to make parents, such as the professor, guilty about their failures in their relationships with their children. It is impossible, we feel, to be a parent, without at times failing—without exercising incorrect judgment and undertaking mistaken courses of action. So be it.

At the same time, we cannot, as conscientious counselors, go to the other extreme and encourage parents to feel that their mistakes with their children do not matter at all and that they are doing just fine when they get into difficulties such as the professorial client did. It has unfortunately become the fashion in some parent education circles to approach this kind of white-washing extreme. Parents who are ill-prepared for child-rearing are reassured despite their ignorances, stupidities, and gross errors. These incompetent parents are told by "child experts" that they are really doing marvelous jobs with their children just by being themselves. The influence of parental education on children has been exaggerated, anyhow, they are told; so they should feel no anxiety about their execrable performances.

If one is forced to walk a tightrope under perilous circumstances, one can take two main courses of anxiety-reducing action. One, is to develop all the knowledge and skill one can amass about tightrope walking and thereby increase the safety of the venture. Two, is to hide from oneself the true nature of the activity and thus set up defenses against possible anxiety.

Parenthood is something like tightrope walking and in some ways worse, because parents not only may endanger their own lives but those of their children. The obvious moral is: As a parent, one had better not bury one's head in the sand, but instead learn all possible relevant information about effective child-raising.

There are few specific rules of thumb to follow in being an effective parent. In addition to giving the child as unconditional a love as possible (especially in its early years), the parent must set limits, give a strong guiding hand toward positive goals, specifically teach the child that it should *not* be over-concerned about gaining the approval of others, and (as noted previously) more or less simultaneously help the child to feel less and less need for the externally set limits and the guiding hand. *No* parent perfectly walks this tightrope. All any parent can do is to try his relatively unanxious best to walk the line between over- and under-guidance.

The parents who come closest to doing an adequate job of child-rearing are generally those who are also doing well with their individual lives and their marriages. There is no magic involved here. Parents with a history of adequacy in life in general and in the emotional intricacies of marriage are much more likely, consciously and unconsciously, to create an emotional and social atmosphere in which children can grow into adequate individuals themselves.

Such parents not only present their children with relatively mature and integrated models of individuality but they are also (out of their own sense of self-esteem and life satisfaction) able to perform the specific tasks of parenthood with minimum anxiety and maximum intelligence. Because such parents have tasted life enjoyments from other sources, they are less likely to blanket their children with a grim and desperate over-watchfulness or Puritanical inhibitions. Just as anxiety can easily spread from parent to child, so can self-confidence and happiness be effectively communicated.

Few, if any, of the people who come with marital and family difficulties to the counselor's office have maliciously or deliberately fouled up their marriages. Similarly, most of the horrors of child-rearing are committed by parents who are in no way criminals with forethought. Instead, they are rather nice, respectable, well-intentioned persons with significant confusions and incompetencies. While, as counselors, we lament the confusion and ineptitude thus transmitted from parent to offspring, we have great compassion for the parents and can sometimes help them to function in less confused and inept ways. Sometimes when this cannot be done, progress can be made with the children instead.

Thus, in the case of the Korinskys, I had the full cooperation of Mrs. Korinsky, who was willing to admit that both she and her husband had been very wrong in being so critical of their fifteen-year-old son and always urging him to do better than he had done, even though some of his achievements were

221

rather remarkable. But Mr. Korinsky flatly told me that, whether I was right or wrong, he had no intention of lying to his son, pretending that the boy was right when he was wrong, and being lenient when he made serious mistakes. That was stuff and nonsense, said Mr. Korinsky, and only resulted in lack of moral fiber in children.

Having little other choice, I saw the Korinskys' son, and had little difficulty, since he was an intelligent and serious lad, in showing him that his father had perfectionistic standards, that this was the father's problem, and that he, the son, would just have to accept the fact that his father did have a problem in this area, and would have to stop taking the father's criticism seriously. Said the boy, after I had seen him three times:

"I'm certainly glad that you agree with me about father. I always felt that he was too strict and that there was something bothering him to make him so critical. But since he seemed to be so efficient and intelligent in other respects, I began to doubt my own notions and to think that maybe I, and not he, was wrong. Now that you're telling me those things about him and other people who tend to be so critical, I can see right away what you mean, and I know that I was not wrong, and I intend to stick by my guns—at least in my own mind. Don't worry: I won't fight with him, just as you warned me about. But as long as I can explain to myself why he is being so nasty to me, I am sure that his words won't hurt me any more."

And, surprisingly enough, they didn't. Almost from that time on, the Korinsky boy stopped getting disturbed about his father's carping; and therapy which had been quite ineffective when the attempt was made to work through the parent became amazingly productive of good results when applied directly to the boy himself.

The handiwork of grossly inadequate parents is, alas, easily observable wherever children gather. The term "underachieving child" is currently employed in many schools, clinics, and camps to describe the child who obviously has more capability than he is manifesting in his interpersonal relations or in his other activities. This term is actually not too different in its basic meaning from the older and more pathological-sounding phrase, "neurotic child." Since many individuals are more likely to be frightened by the term "neurotic," there is merit to using "underachieving."

A neurotic or underachieving person—whether he is an adult or a child—is essentially a non-stupid individual who characteristically behaves in a stupid way. He falls short of his own capabilities, acts below his own par. All children and adults sometimes fall short of their own abilities and are hence at times "underachieving" or "neurotic." But these terms are properly applied to those individuals who *consistently* behave more stupidly than is appropriate to their evident intellectual potential.

Tony is a fairly typical example of an underachieving child. He is a product of continual interactions with parents too confused (neurotic) to comprehend and execute important responsibilities in their own lives and therefore in no position to serve as good models to Tony. His mother, Louise, has had three marriages and divorces and is busily seeking a fourth husband, with whom her pattern of marital failure is quite likely to be repeated.

Louise and Tony (who is a product of her first marriage) currently live with Louise's mother. This is a regular between-marriage pattern of Louise: six of Tony's nine years have been spent in Grandma's home. Grandma has let Louise know all her life that she considered her an ineffectual human being and she has had a similarly hostile and disdainful attitude toward Tony. Louise has fought her mother's criticism with the one tension-reducing method she ever learned: temper-ridden rebellion. Many of her rebellions, most notably her three marriages, have tended to "prove" to her and her mother that the label of ineffectual was a "correct" one. After each failure, she has crept back into a dependency relationship with her mother.

With her extreme lack of self-esteem and self-confidence, Louise has been ill-prepared for the job of being Tony's mother. Tony thus has not only had the disadvantages of having his mother's three marriages crash about his ears and of having a parent who herself feels and acts inadequately, but he has also been infected by the original source of his mother's neurosis, Grandma, who has had a direct, depreciating influence on his own life for two-thirds of his years.

Tony started school prior to the age of six (his birthday is in January). He is now repeating the third grade, has not learned to read or write, and has difficulty with all classroom activities because of an extremely low attention span and a tendency to act the fool and distract other children. His Stanford-Binet I.Q., however, is 134, and he shows considerable ingenuity in getting attention. In play activities, he also demonstrates a low attention span and moves quickly from activity to activity. Whenever the slightest difficulty arises, whether in work or play, Tony moves away from his current problem on to something else. He obviously sees himself as thoroughly incompetent, even though his intellectual capacity far exceeds the demands made upon it by the problems with which he has to cope.

Both Louise and Grandma have indelibly indoctrinated Tony with the notion that he is stupid and unlovable and that the best he can hope for in life is attention rather than love or acceptance. He has therefore used his intelligence to devise clever ways of grabbing the center of attention, holding it for a brief but glorious moment, and then retreating to his solitary sense of inadequacy and unlovableness.

Tony's behavior is analogous to that of an undersized boy who watches his large and brawny associates play a game of football. Suddenly he sees the ball lying loose on the field between plays. He jumps out on the field, grabs the ball, and runs with it. He knows that he is not really a player in the game, that he is violating the rules, and that he will be scorned and perhaps punished for his ball-stealing action. But for a brief and wonderful moment he is the center of all players' and spectators' eyes.

Tony is underachieving in regard to the demands made upon him at home and at school because he has been made to feel afraid and hopeless in relation to these demands. He has been told, in effect, that he has already lost in the game of love and approval, that he lacks the ability to be a good player. He therefore feels that all he can hope for are brief moments of glory in little attention-getting games of his own.

What hope is there of this underachieving child's becoming a more achieving one? Some, probably, for the school has persuaded Louise to place Tony in the hands of a psychologist and she herself has begun to go for psychotherapy. Louise's treatment is probably much more important in this instance than Tony's. Since, no matter how Tony is psychologically helped, if he must always return to the same home environment, with Louise and Grandma acting the same as ever, it is doubtful if he can withstand the continual negative indoctrinations of his mother and grandmother.

Nonetheless, Tony is being helped by seeing the psychologist —whose main efforts are directed at counteracting his depreciating image of himself and helping him feel that he is capable, lovable, and worthwhile. Not that these three things are exactly the same—as too many psychological writers, unfortunately, tend to assume. One can be both lovable and worthwhile even though one is not capable. Even a mentally deficient individual is, just because he is human, essentially worthwhile and lovable. Tony, in the last analysis, must be taught just that: that *every* human being no matter how little or how great his accomplishments, is intrinsically valuable; and that even if his mother, his grandmother, and most other people do not happen to like or approve of him, or think he is sufficiently achieving, he is *still* a most worthwhile, valuable person.

Tony, however, *is* potentially capable, and there is no reason why he should not be enabled to fulfill many or most of his potentialities. This is what the psychologist is trying to help him do: (a) to feel worthy, whether or not he achieves anything in life; and (b) to fulfill his potentialities for achievement, once he has begun to feel worthy, not because such achievement will make him "more worthy" or "better" but simply because he will invariably enjoy himself more if he does in life what he potentially can do and actually wants to do.

The psychologist, then, is teaching Tony that it is safe to try the things he would like to do; for the simple reason that it does not really matter if he fails to do them, nor if people criticize him for such failure. The main thing *is* the trying, not the succeeding. Success is nice; but it is just the icing on the cake, not the cake itself.

Like Tony, virtually all underachieving children are afraid to try. They are blocked from using their intellectual and other capacities for fear of failure—because they believe, have been indoctrinated to think (most falsely!) that it is horrible, it is awful to fail, to make mistakes, to do the wrong thing. Once they believe this nonsense, that it is dreadful to fail and to be criticized or rejected because of such failure, they resort to many different kinds of neurotic symptoms.

Thus, the underachieving child may retreat from the school environment and become a withdrawing, inattentive, daydreaming individual. Or he may openly attack those who do not love him when he fails or makes mistakes and may become an aggressive, rebellious troublemaker. Or he may, like Tony, express defiance a little less directly by being an attention-grabber, playing the clown, being a little trickster. Or, finally, he may express his fear more subtly by overanxious compliance and may become zealously cooperative but still unable to achieve his potential because his fear-induced tensions block him and divert him away from solving the real problems of his life.

There is another type of underachieving child whom we should briefly discuss. This is the child who has capacities

226

frozen not by fear but by boredom. The bored child may behave similarly to the fearful child. In fact, boredom may be his disguise for fear. Sometimes, though, a child's boredom seems to be a direct response to an insufficiently stimulating environment. A youngster may retreat into boredom simply because he sees no interesting reason to do otherwise when faced with an excessively traditionalized, routinized teaching program.

In general, where we find an underachieving child it would be wise to look for an underachieving parent. Adults, it should be remembered, are usually more skillful than children in hiding their feelings of inadequacy, their anxieties, and their hostilities. Sometimes even well-trained professionals are taken in by what outwardly seem to be exceptionally nice, highly interested, exceedingly cooperative parents. But underneath their sweet exteriors, these parents may be most self-depreciating and hostile and may teach, directly and indirectly, their own kind of behavior to their children.

Are we, then, in this chapter trying to discourage all present parents from having more children and prospective fathers and mothers from having any? Not exactly. But we are trying, and quite forcefully, to induce husbands and wives to learn more about the responsibilities of parenthood and then, if they still feel qualified for this difficult task, to proceed bravely and cautiously. We can only repeat that children tend to be greater loads of responsibility than bundles of joy. This, whether we like it or not, is the down-to-earth reality of parenthood. The realization and acceptance of this view seem our surest and best guide to improved happiness in today's and tomorrow's marriage and family living.

17

In-laws

It may seem a shame to spoil a fine, forward-looking book on marriage, such as this one, with the unsavory topic of in-law relations; but many a marriage will hardly be fine or forward-looking if this topic is neglected. Of the many couples whom the authors see every year for marriage counseling, it is surprising what a high percentage are in more or less difficulty partly or mainly because of serious in-law problems.

Nor, in almost all instances, is there any good reason for this. Not that in-laws cannot be highly difficult, dunce-like and even dangerous persons. They can be. Nor that wives and husbands cannot be childishly and expasperatingly bound to their parents. They, too, can be. Nonetheless, according to the

228

basic principles of rational psychotherapy, *all* human intense and prolonged unhappiness that is not specifically caused by physical pain or deprivation is completely illegitimate and unethical. And that goes for unhappiness over in-laws.

Take, by way of illustration, the case of the Mastersons. Mr. and Mrs. Masterson, when they first came for psychotherapy, both insisted that they had just about the worst in-law problem in the world and they were most seriously considering getting divorced in order to "solve" this problem. Mr. Masterson alleged that his wife was completely devoted to her mother and that the mother hated him bitterly and did everything possible to break up their marriage. She feigned all kinds of illnesses, he said, in order to keep her daughter continually attendant upon her; and, far from ever trying to get along with Mr. Masterson, the mother-in-law frankly said that his presence made her sick and that she never wanted to see him, if possible. Also, he claimed, she tried to alienate his thirteen-year-old daughter from him by telling the child what a terrible person he was.

Mrs. Masterson, when I heard her side of the story, did not claim that her husband was overly attached to his parents; in fact, she said that he really didn't seem to care for them at all. But, because he had been roundly indoctrinated by them with a sense of family obligation, he insisted on visiting his parents (who lived quite a distance away) at least once a week. In addition he never wanted to miss a single affair in which his very large family was involved. Again, complained Mrs. Masterson, it would have been different if he really liked his family members and wanted to be with them on birthdays, anniversaries, and other occasions; but he just went, she contended, because he felt that he had to, and not because he really wanted to do so. Such craven obeisance to family protocol, said Mrs. Masterson, was positively disgusting, and she didn't see why she had to suffer by being dragged along to so many of her husband's family gatherings just because he was such a moral coward.

I first got to work on Mr. Masterson. During the first few

weeks I saw him, his wife was so busy taking care of her mother, who had just had her third so-called heart attack (and Mr. Masterson insisted, entirely pseudo-attack) that year, that she had no time to come to see me. As is usual in these cases, I began by assuming that his story about his wife and her mother was absolute gospel, and that he was not significantly exaggerating the facts involved. I was sure that Mrs. Masterson, when I saw her, would tell a quite different story; but I deliberately assumed that the husband's story of his in-law difficulties was correct.

"Let us suppose," I said to Mr. Masterson, "that you are describing the situation with your mother-in-law quite accurately, and that she actually is the kind of a woman you say she is. Why are you upset about the situation?"

"What do you mean why am I upset!" he fairly screamed at me. "Wouldn't you be, wouldn't anyone be upset if this sort of thing were going on in their home, and going on for the last fifteen years, mind you! Isn't that good reason for me to be upset?"

"No," I calmly replied, looking him squarely in the eyes. "It isn't."

"It isn't! Then what is, then; what *is* good reason to get upset?"

"Nothing," I just as calmly replied. "I never heard a good reason for anyone getting upset about anything."

"Oh, piddle! You don't really mean that. You're just saying that to—well, I don't know why you're saying it, but you just are."

"No, I'm deadly serious. I never heard of a good reason for anyone getting upset about anything. Even about physical pain—which is the only legitimate excuse for unhappiness that I can think of, really—I see no reason to get upset. If you have a toothache, I certainly don't expect you to like it or be deliriously happy about it. But getting upset will hardly cure it or make it better. What's the point, then, in getting upset?"

"But how can—how can you help it, damn it? How can you help getting upset?"

"Very simply: by stopping telling yourself the absolute drivel which you are telling yourself, and definitely must be telling yourself, in order to create your upsetness!"

"Drivel? What drivel?"

"You know. Drivel such as: 'Oh, my God, how can she do this to me?' And: 'That lousy bitchy mother-in-law of mine, I hope she drops dead!' And: 'I just can't stand going on like this, with my wife acting in that perfectly idiotic and vicious manner!' And so on, and so forth."

"I can't see anything drivel-ish about that," sulked Mr. Masterson. "She *is* a lousy bitch, my mother-in-law; and I hope she *does* drop dead. No, I can't see anything drivel-ish at all in that."

"Obviously, you can't; or you wouldn't keep repeating that nonsense to yourself. But when I convince you, as I intend to do, that it is utter bosh, utter balderdash to keep infecting yourself with this upset-creating stuff, then you will stop doing so. And, lo and behold! your upsetness will then completely vanish."

"Quite a trick—if you can do it!"

"Yes. But it's trickier than you think. For, actually, I intend to persuade *you* to do it—to get *you* to change your thinking and stop telling yourself this drivel. For I can't, of course, do it for you. I can convince you, perhaps, that it is nonsense that you're telling yourself. But unless, finally, I get *you* to desist from feeding yourself this pap and get you, instead, to tell yourself good sense, all my sessions with you will go to waste."

"I still say: quite a trick—if you can do it!"

"Quite. But let's get back to the problem. You're upset, I insist, not because of the way your mother-in-law is—and I am taking your word, mind you, that she is that way—but because of the nonsense you're telling yourself *about* the way she is. Instead of calmly telling yourself the truth, namely: 'That's

231

the way the old gal is; too bad; but there's nothing I can do to change her at her age, in all probability; so I'll just have to accept the way she is, and stop exciting myself about it,' you're quite falsely telling yourself: 'How can she be the way she is? She *ought* not be the way she is. It's *unfair* that she's the way she is,' and similar drivel."

"I still can't see why it's drivel."

"It's really very simple, if you look at it (which you're not really doing). To ask how a woman can be the way she is when, quite patently, she *is* that way is the worst nonsense under the sun. And to say that an old woman like your mother-in-law, who has been raised to be the way she is, *ought* not be that way is equivalent to saying that it *ought* not rain when it is raining. Also: to say that it's unfair that she is the way she is, is like saying that it's unfair that the sky is blue when you'd rather it were red, or that people are ignorant when you'd prefer them to be well-informed. It isn't unfair at all; even though, from *your* standpoint, it may be quite *unfortunate* that these things are the way they are, rather than the way you'd like them to be."

"So you think that I should just accept my mother-in-law the way she is, whatever the hell harm she inflicts on my wife, my child, and myself, and just let it go at that?"

"No, I don't think anything of the sort. I think that you should *first* accept her the way she is—by which I mean stop senselessly *blaming* the poor woman for being as disturbed as she is. And then, after you first manage to accept her in the sense of not blaming her, you should, of course, try to change her—or, more practically, perhaps change your wife's attitude toward your mother-in-law, so that it doesn't matter how your mother-in-law behaves.

"The way you're doing things now—getting terribly upset about your mother-in-law and the way she unfortunately is— you haven't a hoot in hell of a chance of changing her (except for the worse); and, what is perhaps more important, you are ceaselessly antagonizing your own wife, and haven't any chance of changing her attitude toward her mother, either—except, again, for the worse. Now how is all *that* kind of behavior on your part doing you any good?"

"Doesn't look like it is doing me much good at all, does it?" Mr. Masterson rather sheepishly admitted.

"No, it certainly doesn't. So I don't care if you ever get to love the old gal, or care for her at all in any way. But just as long as you waste your time and energy, as you have been doing for fifteen years, hating her, you're bound to make matters much worse. Moreover and perhaps more importantly, you're also bound to keep yourself decidedly upset. And what's the percentage in that?"

"Very little, I have to say."

"Darn right, very little. So I still insist: it's not, no it's positively never, what your mother-in-law or your wife is doing that's upsetting you; it's only your silly, childish, unrealistic attitude toward what they're doing that is bothering you. And if you can take an honest and full look at your own attitude— which you can—and then question and challenge it and give it a good kick in the teeth—which you definitely can, since *you* are the one who originally adopted it and have ever since been maintaining it—then nothing in the world that your mother-in-law and your wife can or will do will seriously upset you. You won't *like,* naturally, many of the things they do; but you definitely will not upset yourself, needlessly and gratuitously, by telling yourself—falsely, falsely, I still insist!—that what you don't like is terrible, horrible, awful."

Naturally I didn't quite convince Mr. Masterson, in the course of this session, that all his hostility and gut-gnashing about his mother-in-law and wife were entirely pointless; that he was completely upsetting himself in this connection; and that he could and should stop this nonsense. But after several more sessions of the same kind of forceful depropagandization, reason and I began to win out, and one day Mr. Masterson came in and said:

"You know, these sessions seem to be doing me some good. The other day—I would hardly have believed it a few weeks ago—my mother-in-law pulled one of her very worst tantrums. She not only got my wife to run to her side again, as usual, but started her rumpus at four in the morning, when we were soundly sleeping. Said she was having another of those so-called heart attacks again. Of course, as usual, my wife fell for the whole thing, and insisted on running off to see her and getting me up, no less, to drive her there, even though she knew I had a cold myself and felt like going out at that time, in the middle of the night, like I felt like—well, committing suicide. Ordinarily, I would have been fit to be tied, and probably would have had a battle royal with her, and ended up by seething about it for days.

"But, almost to my own surprise, I said, this time, I said to myself, that is, and *not* to my wife. 'Well, there it goes again. Just as I knew it would, and was predicting to myself just last night. The old bat's at it, as usual, and of course my wife, poor misguided soul that she is, can't resist the old biddy yet. Well, no help for it right now. Too bad; but no help for it. Since I have to go, anyway, I might as well do so with as good grace as possible, as my therapist would say, and at least not give *myself* a hard time in the process.'

"And, believe it or not, I *didn't* give myself a hard time; and though I certainly didn't *enjoy* driving Martha to see her mother, I wasn't particularly unhappy about it either. And even the old bat, when she saw what kind of a mood I was in, seemed to take things better for a change and wasn't so negative against me. You know, you're quite right: it *can* be done. You can think yourself out of anger just as, as you keep telling me, you think yourself into it. The other night was quite an eye-opener to me!"

And thereafter for the next few weeks of psychotherapy, Mr. Masterson continued to work on himself and to improve significantly in his attitudes toward his wife and his mother-in-

234

law. So significant, in fact, was the change he began to effect in himself that even his mother-in-law noticed it; and, for the first time in fifteen years, she began to look upon him differently, accept him as a son-in-law, and stop carping about him to his wife. Coincidentally enough, her attacks of serious sickness also began to abate.

Meanwhile, as Mr. Masterson was improving, I began to see his wife regularly. I had a fairly easy time of it with her, since she was most grateful, from the start, about what I had done to help her husband accept her and her mother. She admitted that her mother was most difficult and that she herself was often put out by the old woman's tantrums. But she felt that she just had to keep catering to most of her mother's whims and she was now very happy that her husband had begun, at least partly, to see things her way in this respect.

As for Mr. Masterson's over-allegiance to his own family, she still stuck to her guns on that point. And again, as I usually do with my marriage counseling clients, I assumed that she was entirely right about his conventional adherence to his family's social functions (even though I already knew, from talking to Mr. Masterson, that he was not exactly that conventional, but partly kept up good social ties with his family because of business dealings which he also had with them and because he wanted to ensure the possibility of acquiring a sizable inheritance from some of the wealthier family members). As with her husband, I showed Mrs. Masterson that however wrong Mr. Masterson might be in his dealings with his family, that was essentially *his* problem, and there was no point in her getting over-excited or upset about it.

"But doesn't his problem also involve me?" she objected. "Don't I have to go to these damned social affairs with him?"

"Certainly," I admitted, "his problem involves you to some extent. But not as much as you think it does. In the first place, you do *not* have to go to all the family affairs that he attends, but can frankly set, with him, a maximum number that you will attend a year, and stick to that maximum. That will make it all the more his problem if he insists on going to more than your maximum. Secondly, if you calm down and stop upsetting yourself *because* your husband presumably has a problem in this family area, you will almost certainly be able, two intelligent people like you, to work things out so as to minimize the effect of his problem on you. But if you continue to rant and rave, as you have been doing, instead of sitting down to a series of calm discussions about what to *do* about his problem, things will only get worse and worse—as they have been doing."

"That's for sure!"

"Right. So I'm not promising you any perfect solution to the problem, if you calm down and look at it *as* a problem. But at least, under those conditions there's a good chance that the two of you will come up with some kind of compromise solution. This way, we get no solution at all; and only a continual worsening of the situation."

"But isn't it unfair that I have to be bothered by the fact that he has this problem and that I have to discuss it with him and make all kinds of compromises, when, really, he should just face the problem himself and get over it?"

"Let's suppose, for the sake of discussion, that it *is* unfair (although, actually, he could say to me that it's unfair that *you* do not see things his way and that *he* has to go to the trouble of compromising, etc.). Let's suppose that it's one hundred per cent unfair to you that this kind of situation exists. O.K.: so it's unfair. The world is full of all kinds of unfair things—of crooked politics, people starving to death while others live in luxury, and so on. And merely to cry about and carp about its being that unfair is hardly going to help change things, is it? So if your husband is unfair in having this problem—which seems a little silly to say, doesn't it? since he hardly raised *himself* to have it—that's tough. As I said before: so it's 'unfair.'

"But the thing for *you* to do, when faced with an unfair situation is (a) try to change it or (b) temporarily accept it as long as it can't for the moment be changed. And your crying and whining about how unfair the situation is, certainly is not going to help you do either (a) or (b). Is it?"

"No, I guess it isn't."

"All right," I said, "then when are you going to stop the nonsense—the nonsense, that is, that you keep feeding yourself? Granted that your husband may, as you say, have serious problems in regard to his family, your problem is that you take his problem too seriously. Instead of understanding him and trying to help him *not* be so over-attached to his conventionalism, you are castigating him for his attachment—beating him over the head, as it were, for being neurotic. Will that help him be *less* neurotic? Or will it not, since neurotics become disturbed in the first place because of being severely criticized by others and taking this criticism to heart, will it not help him become, if anything, *more* disturbed?"

"I see what you mean. What, specifically, then, should I do?"

"The same thing anyone can specifically do in a case like this, where an intimate associate is acting badly because of his own fears or hostilities. First, you must stop telling *yourself* how horrible his activities are. Second, you must accept him and his behavior, for the time being, just because it exists, because this is the way he is. Thirdly, when you are calmly accepting your husband's acts as undesirable but still not horrible, you can then ask yourself what you can do to increase his own security, so that he does not have to be so fearful or hostile; and, as we said before, you can arrange various compromises, so that *you* do not have to be too badly affected even if, for the time being, he continues to act in much the same manner. In other words: the calmer you are and the more you stop giving yourself a hard time about your husband's behavior, the more chance you have of helping him change that behavior and of protecting yourself from the worst effects if he continues to behave in much the same way. Does that give you a more specific idea of what you can do to try to help the present situa-

237

tion?"

"Yes, I think it does."

And, like her husband, Mrs. Masterson did do some tall talking to herself. She did get much less disturbed about her husband's participation in family affairs, and was able to show him understanding and help instead of carping and negativism. In consequence, even though he still felt that it was desirable to keep seeing his family on many occasions for economic reasons, he was able to compromise by seeing them less often and by frequently arranging to see them when his wife was not present. This former area of severe disagreement between Mr. and Mrs. Masterson soon became no issue and they were able to spend much more of their time planning and talking about more enjoyable aspects of life.

Can, in a similar manner, in-law problems be met in all other instances? To a great extent: yes. Almost always when there are serious in-law differences, one of the mates is highly disturbed because either his in-laws are not behaving in the way he thinks they *should* behave or his spouse is not acting toward his in-laws in the manner he thinks that she *should* act. Once the highly upset mate begins to question and challenge his own *shoulds*—rather than the behavior of his mate or in-laws—he almost immediately, in most instances, will begin to feel much better, much less angry. And the better and less angry he feels, the greater, almost always, are his chances of doing something to ameliorate the situation he dislikes.

This is not to say that any husband or wife is not entitled to dislike the thoughts or actions of his or her spouse or in-laws. Dislike, yes; that is very often legitimate. But when dislike turns to severe irritation, hatred, and continual backbiting— then, illegitimately added to the sentence, 'I wish this kind of behavior did not exist,' is the irrational sentence, 'Because I wish this kind of behavior did not exist, it *should* not exist, it is wholly *unfair* that it exists.' And this second sentence is nonsense. Tackling that nonsense—rather than tackling the mate or one's in-laws—is the real solution to this kind of problem.

In general, then, the line of attack to be taken on almost any serious dissension that exists because of in-law difficulties may be as follows:

1. Accept your in-laws' shortcomings and/or your mate's illogical attitudes toward your in-laws as an undesirable but, for the time being, an unchangeable problem or annoyance.

2. Expect your in-laws and your spouse to act just the way they do, to be for the present just the way they are; and stop telling yourself that it is awful, terrible, and frightful that they are this way.

3. Do not personalize your in-laws' behavior toward you. Even if they are vicious, unfair, and thoroughly unreasonable, that is *their* problem, and has nothing intrinsically to do with you. If they hate you, that does not make *you* a hateful person. If they are obstreperous or interfering, that does not make *you* weak. Cultivate your own garden, and take care of your own thoughts and feelings, and there is very little that they can actually do to you.

4. By all means, if you can, do not keep too close physical contact between you and your wife, on the one hand, and your in-laws on the other hand. See them relatively seldom; do not live in the same apartment house, or even neighborhood with them if you can help it. But if you must, for some reason, see them relatively often, do not think that proximity with them, in, of, and by itself need be harmful. The worst they can do normally, is act nastily toward you or call you names. So what? What difference does it make? What can they really *do* to you?

5. Once you understand your in-laws and their problems, by all means try to change them for the better, if you will. But don't *expect* them to change because you want them to. And try to change them by honestly trying to see their point of view, being on their side, helping them for their own sake as well as your own. Don't try to change them by criticism, carping, grim

239

silence, or persecution. Try to *help* them change, not blackmail or force them into changing.

6. Don't allow yourself to be exploited, physically or emotionally, by your in-laws just because you *are* related to them. You owe them (a) normal human politeness and (b) acknowledgment of the fact that they are the parents of your spouse, and that for his or her sake you will try to be as pleasant as possible to them. But you do not owe them complete allegiance, self-sacrifice, or extreme going against your own grain. If you cannot get along well with them you can, without being downright unpleasant, calmly but firmly emotionally divorce yourself from them—and thus even, perhaps, set a good example for your spouse. But if he or she still wants to be very closely tied to your in-laws, then you should again calmly accept these ties, for the nonce, while intelligently and lovingly trying to do something about undoing some of them.

7. If your in-laws, in spite of everything you can do, insist on remaining a thorn in your side and are truly obnoxious, and if you cannot possibly get sufficiently far from them or keep them from unduly influencing your spouse, then you had better philosophically accept the fact that conditions in this respect are bad—but that, again, they are not necessarily frightful and awful. Perhaps you cannot reduce your annoyance at your in-laws' behavior but you can at least stop yourself from needlessly augmenting it.

8. There is no law against your liking your in-laws and actually getting along very well with them. Particularly if you do not take them too seriously, if you realistically accept their limitations, and if you do not expect them to be perfect or act exceptionally well to you, you may very well find that they are quite decent, helpful, nice enough people with whom you have some things in common and can get along very pleasantly in many ways. They did, after all, bear and rear your spouse, who presumably has some nice as well as unfavorable qualities; and it is most unlikely that they are complete ogres. The better

you accept yourself, the less you personalize their views of you, and the more philosophic you are about many of life's irritations and annoyances, the more are you likely to find excellent points in your in-laws and to be able to enjoy them in important respects.

Again, as ever, we must insist on one thing in this book: that almost all your problems are your *own*; that *you* have the ability to disturb or not disturb yourself; and that, therefore, whatever problems your in-laws and their relationship with your spouse may seem to create, your attitude toward these troubles, rather than the difficulties in themselves, will determine whether you are completely miserable or pretty well satisfied with your marriage and your life.

18

Marital Incompatibility Versus Neurosis

I had rarely seen so unhappy a husband. What was worse, as he freely admitted, he actually had nothing about which to be unhappy.

Three months before, he had come to me with a long tale of woe. His wife, he said, didn't show him any affection, didn't satisfy him sexually, was a pathological liar, and was a poor housewife and mother. As a result of his story I had seen the wife, had concluded that she was distinctly neurotic, and had recommended psychotherapy. She was receptive to this notion and I had been seeing her regularly since that time on a once-weekly basis.

The wife's main problems had been surprisingly easy to

solve. She had been fairly attached to her mother, who had died when she was fifteen, and had been deeply resentful of her older sister, who was favored by her father. After her mother's death, her father had neglected her sadly and she had begun to hate him bitterly—and to be unconsciously guilty about this hatred.

At the first opportunity, at the age of seventeen, she had left home and gone to live by herself. To compensate for her father's indifference, she had desperately tried to marry as well and as quickly as possible, in order that she might raise a large, fine family of her own, to prove to her father how wrong he had been in depreciating her.

Being so greatly in need of compensating for her own feelings of inadequacy, this wife, whom we shall call Mrs. Gee, had never grown up and kept resorting to fantastic and unbelievable lies to aggrandize herself. She would fabricate to her husband—and others—that she had written poems or made leathercraft. She would have a ready—and obviously poor—excuse every time she was late for an appointment. She would even boast about her own pregnancies that had not yet occurred.

At the same time, Mrs. Gee thought only about herself; badly neglected her husband and children; and would make no effort to satisfy herself or her husband sexually. She knew, for example, that Mr. Gee liked her to wear flimsy, sexy underclothes and negligees; but instead, she would go to the other extreme and wear thick nightdresses and the plainest slips and bras. During three months of psychotherapeutic sessions with Mrs. Gee it was not too difficult to show her why she was behaving in such a self-defeating manner and how she was taking out on her husband all the pent-up hostility that she had felt for many years toward her father. Once I induced her to tackle her underlying irrational philosophies of life—especially the silly notions that her father (and others) *should* love her and that it was terrible if she did not accomplish all the things in life that others accomplished—Mrs. Gee began to change significantly. She understood why she had been lying in such a needless, unintelligent way; and she not only stopped doing so but became intent on developing the ability to face unpleasant facts and to work through them instead of lying to herself about them.

"What's the point of my lying any longer?" she remarked during her eleventh session. "Even if I can fool others, I certainly am not fooling myself. And why should I *have* to waste my good time and energy fooling others? If they can't accept me pretty much the way I am, to hell with them! Lying won't actually make me any better than they are. And that, especially, is what I've been seeing recently, since I've been talking to you: that being better than other people, or trying to pretend that you are, is itself ridiculous. Why should I have to compare myself to *anyone*? I'm me, and what I do is my business and what they do is their business. If they're better or worse than me at being a mother, or writing a book or anything else, it really doesn't affect me, doesn't affect *my* life. I'm still the same as I was. And I intend, from now on, to be happy the way I am, with my own likes and dislikes, instead of always trying to live the way other people think I should—or the way I think they think I should."

With her new-found philosophy of standing on her own feet and not being overly concerned with what others thought of her, Mrs. Gee began to lose her worried preoccupation with herself and consequently to become a better wife and mother. She lost her hostility toward her husband (and toward other men as well) and was quite willing to satisfy his desire for sexy underclothes and nighttime attire. In fact, she began to take pleasure herself in this kind of clothing and to become more sexually aroused through helping to arouse her husband.

All this, Mr. Gee now admitted to me, was fine; in fact, it was almost miraculous. But he really couldn't see that he was very happy about his marriage yet, and was quite troubled about this. He wanted to discover, now that his wife had changed, why he was still unhappy and what could be done about his lack of marital satisfaction.

I knew something about Mr. Gee's background, as a result of his previous visit, but now I questioned him more closely and soon brought to light some important facts. In the first place, he had had a premarital affair, before he met his wife, and seemed to be still guilty about this affair. Secondly, he felt that his wife was beautiful enough, especially when she was undressed and they were having sex relations; but he also thought that her long, hooked nose was ungainly and, because of it, he was sometimes ashamed to be seen with her in public. Thirdly, he felt that he could no longer be close to his parents, as he had been before his marriage, because they didn't approve of his wife and didn't think that she was good enough for him.

Because of these reasons, Mr. Gee, in spite of the almost unbelievable change that had been taking place in his wife as a result of her psychotherapy, was most unhappy. Before speaking to me, he had not realized exactly why he was unhappy and vaguely blamed his feelings on his wife and her lacks. He kept telling himself that he still was basically "incompatible" with her, in spite of her improvement; and he obviously wanted me to tell him that this was true and that the only sensible thing to do was to pick a wife with whom he would be more "compatible." This I refused to do.

"You remember," I asked Mr. Gee, "what we spoke about when you first came to see me three months ago?"

"Yes, I remember."

"And you remember how I explained to you, at that time, that there are two basic causes for marital disagreement?"

Mr. Gee seemed puzzled and obviously remembered only partly, if at all, what I had previously said. "Let me refresh your mind," I continued. "We may roughly divide the reasons for unhappy marriages into two main causes: one, real incompatibility between the spouses; or two, neurotic disturbances on the part of either or both the husband and wife which make

245

them think and act in such a manner that there appear to be fundamental incompatibilities between them."

"Oh, yes; I remember your going into that," said Mr. Gee. But he clearly was still very vague in his remembrance; so I continued:

"By incompatibility I mean truly irreconcilable differences in the basic attitudes, ideas, and interests of the marital partners. Thus, the wife may mainly be interested in raising a family, reading, and spending quiet evenings at home and the husband may mainly be interested in socializing, having a gay time, and working for a political cause much of the time. Both the husband and the wife in such circumstances, may be reasonably well-adjusted individuals who would be happily married to someone else with similar interests but who are rather unhappy married to each other. This may be called true incompatibility and is the result, usually, of making a poor marital choice. The main remedies consist of striving for mutual interests. This, often, is quite difficult and results in conscious or unconscious hostility on both sides. The alternative is divorce. Then both parties marry other mates who, this time, are more intelligently selected."

"But that's just the point," said Mr. Gee. "I wonder if Marilyn and I have intelligently selected each other. We just don't seem to think the same way or like many of the same things. That is why I think we may truly be incompatible."

"I know you think that way. But so do most mates who are not getting along well—and whose troubles may be the result of something quite different from basic incompatibility of interests."

"And what's that?"

"That is common garden variety neurosis. Take, for example, the husband I just used illustratively, who is hell-bent on social gatherings and political causes. Perhaps he just likes such pastimes. But perhaps, too, he is driven toward them because of his own serious disturbances, because of his need to

246

show other people what a great guy he is. If so, and if we rid him of his disturbances, he may lose his need for considerable socializing and may be very content to stay home more often with his wife. In such an instance, his so-called 'basic incompatibility' with his wife, which was really a function of his neurosis, vanishes."

"Perhaps so," said Mr. Gee. "But what about my own case? Do you think that *my* so-called incompatibilities with my wife are a result of *my* neurosis?"

"Very frankly," I answered, "I do. Although, when your wife first came to see me, it was clear that her neurotic reactions were the source of much of your marital difficulty, that is not true today. But now, from what you have just told me and what I already have learned from her, it would appear that you are using her supposed failings as a smoke-screen for your own deep-seated feelings of guilt and inadequacy and that your main problem is not with her but with yourself."

"Can you be more specific?"

"Certainly. Take, for example, what you have been telling me about your wife's nose. Actually, as you have said, you like her looks and find her quite satisfactory in bed. But because when you go out with her, *other people,* including your own parents, may be critical of her looks, and because you neurotically cannot face the negative views of these others, you are practically set to throw her out of your life. Isn't *that* a little odd—that you let the views of others mean so much to you?"

"Well—I suppose—well—"

"And what about the business with your parents? Why *must* you still be so close to them, as you once were, when you now have a perfectly nice family of your own, and could well spend more of your time getting closer to *them*? Your parents, you must realize, are pretty old, and are probably not long for this world. But your wife and children are likely to live for quite a long time. How come that you do not feel the need to be so close to *them*?"

"Well—I—I must admit you've probably got a point there."

"Yes, I probably have. And then this nonsense about your having a premarital affair. So what were you supposed to do— stay entirely abstinent until the age of twenty-seven, when you married? Aren't you really telling yourself, underneath, some bosh, such as: 'If people, including my Puritanical-minded parents, knew that I had this premarital affair, they wouldn't approve of me, wouldn't love me. And since I am such a despicable person, and so unlovable, I have to have a wife who is perfect, physically and otherwise, so that people will approve of her and raise their esteem of me through liking her. And since Marilyn is not perfect, they may think even worse of me; and this would be terrible!' Isn't that, or something along those lines, what you keep telling yourself?"

"Uh—you know, I wouldn't be surprised if you were right. I think I really am telling myself something like that, and finding fault with Marilyn because I don't like myself enough, underneath as you say, and don't feel that she can make up for my own underneath feeling of worthlessness. Yes, you could very well be right!"

"Think it over some more and I believe that you will see that I am. For, from what I have seen of you and your wife, I doubt very much whether incompatibility, in itself, is the real issue. You both seem to have fairly similar goals and ideals of marriage and of life. And when you are by yourself without any outside interference or influence, you seem to get along quite well. But when outside thoughts intrude—or, rather, your own internalized thoughts which you originally learned from outside influences but have now unfortunately neurotically made your own—then you quickly look for and find 'incompatibilities' between the two of you. But the main incompatibility, right now, frankly seems to be that your wife is doing an excellent job of overcoming *her* neurosis—and you are not."

Mr. Gee was an intelligent individual who saw that what I said was fairly incontrovertible and he therefore agreed to get down to a series of intensive psychotherapy sessions himself, to get to the bottom of his neurotic trends. I should like to be able to write a completely happy ending to this story, but I must in all honesty admit that it fell far short of that. Mr. Gee, partly because of the concerted opposition of his parents, who were most threatened by his coming for therapy, only attended his sessions sporadically, and after a short while said that he was much improved and quit entirely. Although he ceased being as unhappy as he had been, and stopped talking about leaving his wife and made a better marital adjustment, Mr. and Mrs. Gee's relations remained only fair to moderately good and probably could have been considerably improved, if he had worked harder at therapy and really solidly undermined his neurosis.

Is psychotherapy, then, the only means to happy marriage? Of course not. As previously noted in this book, an even better answer is good, sane selection of one's marital partner in the first place. And when a less than ideal selection of a mate is made, one may still, if one has a rational philosophy of life, have a reasonably good, and sometimes a very good, marriage. It is when one does *not* have such a rational value system that psychotherapy is called for.

19

Divorce

The divorce situation in the United States may be briefly stated as follows: We indoctrinate most people from a very early age—in their home, school, church, and various other settings—to feel that any person who has to get a divorce is a horrible personal failure and a dreadful sinner. We then force the individual who, in spite of this negative conditioning, actually contemplates divorce, to go through a jungle of legal technicalities and socio-economic difficulties which are unusually discouraging. Nonetheless they do not prevent approximately half a million American couples from seeking divorce each year.

When, as a result of the anti-divorce indoctrinations and

difficulties which society imposes on unhappily married individuals, some of these persons do get divorced and are anxious, confused, and otherwise disturbed about their legal separations, moralists frequently point to their symptoms as "proof" of the thesis that divorce is a terrible thing. This is somewhat comparable to administering electric shock to sheep every time they attempt to cross a line into a pasture and then stating that the sheep tremble, jump, and bleat because of the intrinsically evil nature of the pasture.

The social aspects of divorce may be divided into the legal and the nonlegal. It is sometimes sociologically convenient to think of law as the outgrowth of the moral customs and attitudes of "the people." If so, our divorce laws certainly bear strong testimony to the overwhelming moral confusion of the American populace. No two states in the Union have the same laws. Our founding fathers tried to prevent chaos from arising by declaring, in the full faith and credit clauses of the Constitution, that court rulings made by each state in the interpretation of its own laws must be accepted by all other states. Nonetheless, the *jurisdiction* of the divorce-granting state may be challenged by another state, which may thus be able effectively to prevent the recognition of the first state's decree.

Why, then, should not one obtain a divorce in one's state and be safe from all legal challenge? For the simple reason that many states have quite complex and punitive divorce laws which make it impractical and almost impossible for their residents to break their legal marital ties. In the most populous state of the Union, for example, New York, the legal grounds for divorce are insanity, complete disappearance of one of the mates for many years, and adultery. If you and your spouse entirely agree on divorce, but are of sound mind, prefer to remain in New York rather than "disappear," and do not wish to commit adultery in public, you can do one of two things if you insist on sticking strictly to the New York laws: you can remain miserably together or you can perjure yourselves. Most of your fel-

251

low New Yorkers (and, through the years, millions of other Americans) in such a situation as this decide to take up perjury. The rest throw in the sponge in New York and go out of the state or out of the country to obtain their divorces.

Willful lying under oath is, then, one of the most usual products of our "moral" laws concerning divorce. The most common procedure in New York, of course, is to set up a phoney adultery situation, with hired witnesses to testify to the sexual iniquity of one of the spouses. Or, if the New York couple prefers a more fastidious form of perjury, an out-of-state divorce can be obtained by one partner's swearing that he is now and intends to remain a permanent resident of a state such as Nevada.

Divorce perjury, it must be pointed out, is hardly a monopoly of New Yorkers. In one way or another the laws of most states make perjury practically inescapable. For example, the vast majority of divorces in the United States are uncontested. This means that in one way or another the husbands and wives involved have *agreed* to divorce, however reluctant and tacit the agreement may be in some instances.

These husbands and wives cannot honestly go into court and say: "We've decided to dissolve this marriage." If they do, the divorce must be denied by the court, for the couple is guilty of collusion. In every United States jurisdiction, divorce is granted only where there is a "guilty" party and an "innocent" one. At least one of the spouses (usually played by the husband, because of our lingering concept of knightly courtesy) is the dastardly wrongdoer; the other is a sweet, guileless, guiltless citizen who has been grievously wronged.

Not only will collusion prevent divorce in any American jurisdiction; so, too, will two-sided culpability. Divorce is legally recognized only as the reward of innocence. Mrs. Miller had been engaging in flagrant adultery for a long time, and her husband had tried many ways to save the marriage—even going to the extent of trying to discover, in the course of psychotherapeutic consultation, whether he was somehow the cause of his wife's sexual wanderings.

Mrs. Miller refused to discuss matters with her husband or to get professional help. She also refused to agree to get a divorce, because she liked the social and financial status provided by her marriage. Why did not Mr. Miller get a divorce without his wife's cooperation? Because on one occasion, feeling lonely and sorry for himself and having been deserted for the evening by his wife, he was foolish enough to get himself in a situation with another woman where there was sufficient circumstantial evidence to point to his infidelity. He claimed that he actually had not committed adultery; but there was no question that he had had the opportunity to do so and he could not prove that he had not made the most of this opportunity.

Because of his indiscretion, divorce was now a legal impossibility for Mr. Miller. If he went to court with his proof of his wife's adultery, she would bring "proof" of his. This, his lawyer assured him, would be enough to have the divorce denied. Mr. Miller would come into court with "unclean hands" and hence he was not deserving of the reward of divorce.

Several years ago a committee of the judiciary estimated that perhaps four million Americans were exposed to potential legal danger because of the peculiar nature of their divorces—since they had been obtained in out-of-state or out-of-country jurisdictions, and often under conditions where the plaintiff did not have bona fide residence in these jurisdictions. Such dangers are for the most part hypothetical; since there is little likelihood of several million divorces suddenly being invalidated by legislative action. Nonetheless, if one wants to obtain a perfectly safe out-of-state divorce one normally must make sure that both partners are legally represented (if only nominally, by having their lawyers appear) at the divorce proceeding. This amounts, for all practical purposes, to divorce by agreement. But so long as such an agreement is not openly referred to in court, both parties legally pretend that it does not exist.

253

Without the actual cooperation of one's spouse divorce is difficult in most states. If Mr. Miller had not committed his own indiscretion, or at least had not been caught at it, he could have readily obtained a divorce on the grounds of his wife's well-established adultery. Usually, however, mates who refuse divorce do not leave the kind of trail Mrs. Miller left. The divorcing mate, therefore, has to resort to detective snooping—a sickening and expensive business. Moreover, where neither mate has committed adultery even though one may be an exceptionally nagging, petty, frigid, unkempt, and emotionally disturbed person, the discontented partner will just have to go on living with the obnoxious one, in most of our jurisdictions.

Is there no recourse open to a man or woman who wants a divorce from an unwilling mate in a state where grounds are strict? Often, there is only one thoroughly legal, safe way out: for the discontented partner to move permanently to a state with more lenient grounds and sue for divorce there. If, for example, a person were to move to Nevada, get a divorce, and then stay in Nevada, the legal challenges of the disgruntled mate who was still residing, say, in South Carolina, would be in vain. But if the mate obtaining the divorce got homesick for little old South Carolina, he might have a rough time of revisiting his former state; for if he has, in the meantime, remarried he may be subject to prosecution for bigamy.

Such is the confused legal picture regarding divorce in the United States. In regard to the personal and social confusion engendered by divorce, the situation is often even more confusing, largely because of our punitive moral attitudes toward divorce, as well as because divorce brings major changes in modes of living.

Any important change in life circumstances, even without legal entanglements or moral censure, is likely to bring temporary anxiety and adjustment difficulties—especially to basically insecure individuals. Witness, for instance, the concern of the unoriented college freshman, the poorly instructed newcomer on a job, the bewildered army inductee, and the awkward novitiate at any sport. We might well expect, therefore, that even if full social approval existed for divorce, the newly disentangled individual would show some anxiety and confusion regarding his social role and self-conception. Such anxiety can scarcely be cited as "proof" that divorce is intrinsically undesirable—especially since people's staying together against their will invariably results in much more insecurity and unhappiness.

Our experience in working with many hundreds of people who were in various stages of divorce and post-divorce adjustment has led to the conviction that there is no such thing as a "divorce problem" in itself. Divorce, rationally viewed, is an essential component of democracy. Just as there should be no major abridgments in freedom of speech, assembly, worship (including freedom *not* to worship); just as there should be no prevention of a person's responsibly taking and quitting a job; so there should be no interference with a person's responsibly entering or leaving a marriage.

All human rights are subject to misuse, and divorce is no exception. In the hands of immature, seriously disturbed individuals divorce can be cruel, indecent, exploitative, tragic. But so, too, in the same hands, can any human relationship, especially including marriage, be pernicious. In the hands of mature and self-respecting individuals, on the other hand, divorce (and other relationships and disagreements) can be humane, kind, intelligent, spirit-freeing. No one wishes to abolish automobiles because they can lead to tragedy when driven by irresponsible persons. To abolish divorce because neurotic and psychotic individuals sometimes turn it into a hellish affair would be equally idiotic.

Mrs. Buchanan, for example, was a woman whom her husband (and others) fairly accurately described as "a stinking bitch of the first water." Although she obviously cared not a jot for Mr. Buchanan and had plenty of independent financial resources in her own right (since she came from a very wealthy family), she gave her husband a most difficult time during their divorce proceedings, and made him pay through the nose in terms of a cash settlement and alimony. She also considerably limited his visitation rights to the children (who cared for their father much more than for their mother) and she tried to show the children that the divorce was entirely their father's fault (quite forgetting that her own marital behavior, which included both adultery and sad neglect of her children, was the prime cause of the separation).

The divorce proceedings of Mr. and Mrs. Buchanan, from start to finish, were brutal. No one, particularly the children of the marriage, gained by them; and even Mrs. Buchanan herself got terribly upset in the course of negotiations, and had to run off to Florida for several weeks to "rest her nerves." When, shortly after her return, she was driven to get psychotherapeutic aid (in order to get sufficient "strength" to finish the divorce proceedings), Mrs. Buchanan was quite surprised to find that the psychiatrist she saw by no means entirely sided with her, but thought that perhaps she might herself be making the divorce proceedings much more difficult than they had to be. When she saw what this psychiatrist's attitude was, Mrs. Buchanan immediately left him and looked for help elsewhere. After trying several other psychotherapists, she finally wound up in my office, thinking that, as one who specialized in marriage counseling, I would be solidly on her side.

I wasn't. But apparently I was tactful enough to keep Mrs. Buchanan seeing me for a longer period than she had seen any of the other therapists. And I was able to show her (as they had all apparently tried to) that there might well be something in her own attitudes and thinking which had led her husband to be the "beast" she thought he was and which was now leading her to demand an eye for an eye and a tooth for a tooth in regard to the serious wrongdoings which she believed he had wreaked on her.

Mrs. Buchanan's main illogical belief, which she had learned largely from being raised to be a terribly "spoiled brat" by her parents, was that the world owed her a living, and that she herself had to fulfill no responsibilities or obligations to obtain this living. She thought that her husband's main, and almost only, role in life was to satisfy all her wants—including her desires to be physically caressed for hours at a time without having intercourse or orgasm—and that her role was to do just about what she pleased—which was, after being caressed by her mate for a long period of time, to curl up and go to sleep like a baby, without making any attempt whatever to satisfy him sexually. When, after years of this kind of one-sided sex activity, Mr. Buchanan finally rebelled, and insisted that he, too, had sex desires which asked for satisfaction, his wife said he was selfish and beastly and became angry and upset.

When I gently but firmly questioned Mrs. Buchanan's philosophy of life, and showed her that requiring her own pleasure in marriage was certainly legitimate—as long as she concomitantly gave her husband something as well—she finally began to see herself clearly, to question her basic assumptions, and to become a more cooperative individual. She changed so radically that, if her husband hadn't been already thoroughly fed up with her and involved with another woman, they well might have effected a reconciliation instead of a divorce. At least, however, she took quite a different attitude toward the divorce, was much more reasonable in her financial demands on her husband, and cooperated fully in giving him full visitation rights with the children. Mr. and Mrs. Buchanan are now, though divorced, on better terms than they ever were while married and they and their children have suffered minimally by the breakup of their marriage.

One of the frequent factors present in marriages where one or both parties want a divorce is the "triangle"—that is, the involvement of one of the spouses with another man or woman. Although such involvements frequently occur, they are not so often the true *causes* of divorce; rather, they tend to be precipitating factors. Failure to distinguish between basic causes and precipitating factors of separation can add significantly to the suffering of both parties to a marriage before, during, and following the divorce process.

The third party in a triangle is by no means always a woman but for convenience in our discussion let us assume that she is. When a wife, such as Caryl Bates, learns of her husband's involvement with another woman, she typically goes through several stages of over-reaction. Caryl first felt shock and disbelief and a little self-pity; followed by anger (after the self-pity became full-blown and deeply entrenched); and finally, self-righteous martyrdom (self-pity, still, covered by a hard exterior of defensive "superiority"). These were the attitudes that society, directly or indirectly, had taught her to have. And such attitudes not only encourage a wife to function ineffectively in doing anything constructive about her marriage; they often insure that her husband will divorce her and marry the other woman.

This is because the husband—Mr. Bates in this case—is simultaneously undergoing his own stereotyped reactions. Typically, he felt quite guilty about his extramarital activity (as our society had practically made certain that he would). While his guilt feelings were not strong enough to keep him from getting extramaritally involved, they were sufficiently intense to keep him from wholeheartedly enjoying his adulterous affair. And because he felt guilty, he (as many men do) felt impelled to tell his wife about his involvement—or at least to leave telltale clues that she could hardly miss, so that he had no actual need to tell her.

Once Mr. Bates had let Caryl know about his affair, he felt considerably relieved. But then, naturally, her shock and disbelief reinforced his original feelings of being a "real heel," and he began to think of the horrible things he had done to this wonderful girl. If Caryl's reactions had stopped at the first stage of shock and disbelief her husband, out of deep guilt, would probably have dropped his extramarital involvement and gone back a little sheepishly to his marriage.

But, as noted above, this is what did not occur. Mrs. Bates quickly went into stage 2—anger. Faced by a rage-filled Caryl and unequivocally told how much of a stinker he was (in regard to his affair and a variety of other real or imaginary ways), Mr. Bates' own defense reactions were aroused. He began to justify his extramarital relationship in two ways: (a) after all, let's face it, life was terrible with Caryl—as a single look at this angry shrew now conclusively proved; and (b) life would doubtlessly be wonderful with his mistress because she really loved him (she said) and, of course, he must really love her.

Thus, what started as a mere dalliance on the part of Mr. Bates—for he actually was not that discontented with his marriage but was flattered by the attentions of the other woman—began to transform itself into great hostility against Caryl, true love for his mistress, divorce, and remarriage. Here again, society's teachings proved to be most important; because the only justification our mores provide for marital departure is the idea that true love just overwhelms people and cannot be stopped ("it was bigger than all of us").

The concluding episode in regard to Mr. Bates' extramarital affair arrived when Caryl moved into stage 3 of her reactions to discovering her husband's affair—the stage of self-righteous martyrdom. If her husband up to this time had any doubts about divorcing her, his doubts were beautifuly drowned (as they usually are) by stage 3. Few self-respecting men long find it possible to live with a self-righteous martyr; and Mr. Bates was no exception to the rule.

As in so many other cases of this kind, Mr. and Mrs. Bates' neurotic friends, drawn like sharks to a sinking ship, helped along their movement toward divorce. They reinforced Caryl's feelings of self-pity and self-righteousness; practically made it impossible for her to undertake a rational examination of her marital situation and her own failures and maladaptations that had been contributing to her husband's having an affair; and they also reinforced Mr. Bates' guilt feelings by treating him as if he were a horrible criminal. In these and various other ways, they blocked the Bateses' feeble efforts to communicate rationally with one another—as good friends in our culture frequently do ("Leave her alone, you beast! Can't you see that she's hysterical? Haven't you hurt her enough already?").

This was just about the final straw. Having some degree of spirit, Mr. Bates, like many other husbands in a similar position, felt further pushed away from his marriage with Caryl and further impelled toward his new love. The other woman became not only the wonderful romantic dream which his self-justifying tendencies had begun to make her, but the only person who treated him as if he were deserving of anything other than a lynching. The result was inevitable; and a bitter divorce soon ensued.

Can a therapist, when brought into a triangular marital situation even at a late stage in the game, be of any real help? Sometimes. Even though emotions, by the time he sees the participants, are at fever pitch, he may be able to help bring some degree of rationality into one or another stage of the proceedings. Thus he may be able to induce the marital partners to separate their evaluation of their marriage from their evaluation of the current emotional involvement with the third party, to distinguish between the desirability of divorce and the desirability of marrying the other woman, and to see the difference between the facts of the triangular situation and the social myths (leading to feelings of guilt and recrimination) about these facts. All of which is, of course, easier to outline than to accomplish.

The application of rationality, even when successful, does not necessarily mean that a husband will go back to a marriage or even that he will decide not to marry his paramour. People sometimes achieve desirable and rational ends by undesirable and irrational means. This is true despite another social myth —that "bad" means always lead to "bad" ends.

Let me illustrate this point by two analogies. Suppose I believe in ghosts and become convinced that my house is haunted. In panic, I move out and place my house in the hands of a realtor. He sells the house at a nice profit. A few months later, I learn that the city has bought land and made plans to build a prison on nearby acres which had provided a rural environment for my former home. The value of the property, esthetically and economically, has consequently taken a decided dip. For an idiotic reason, then, I have done what turns out to be a desirable act. I have been lucky.

Let's take another analogy. Because your employer refuses to let you come to work in Bermuda shorts and loud-colored, open-necked sports shirt, which happens to be your favorite attire summer and winter, you quit your job in a huff. As you leave the office, still blindly angry, you bump into and knock down an old man. You apologetically pick him up and recognize him as a very famous architect. You have long sought an interview with him to show him your creative efforts in architecture. In the bruised and dazed condition produced by his encounter with you, he agrees to look at your drawings. He likes them. You are made. Is this proof that you were smart to leave your job in a state of childish anger? No, of course not. You, again, are just plain lucky.

Now people who go around leaving houses and jobs in such irrational fashion as shown by our analogies usually are not so fortunate. One stupidity generally leads to another, and such people generally get into deeper and deeper trouble. The same is true of many of the people who irrationally leave marriages. They *may* live to be very happy about their decisions; but they also may not.

At the same time, someone who leaves his marriage for a poor reason which he can adequately articulate may actually have a much better and quite unarticulated reason behind this poor one. Thus, a man who leaves his wife because, he says, she will not dance the rhumba with him, or because their marriage lacks magic and romance, or because he has finally found his one true love, may be speaking utter nonsense. But this does not mean that he may not have a good reason, too, for his divorce. He may sense, for example, that his wife hinders his and her growth and development by her tyrannical possessiveness. Or he may vaguely feel other qualities about his marriage, of which he is only semi-conscious, that actually constitute excellent reasons for his leaving it.

Particularly in cases where one mate leaves the other for a third party there may be good half-understood motives for doing so. Either the person who wanders may be too immature to continue a satisfactory relationship with the spouse; or the one who stays may actually be an unloving, seriously disturbed individual who is quite unsatisfactory as a mate.

Love of another woman, whether it exists in fact or not, is not necessarily the most important or most relevant factor in a triangular situation. Just because two people love one another does not mean (a) that they should or must get married or (b) that they would necessarily be well-mated if they did. Furthermore, it does not prove (c) that a man does not love his present wife just because he loves (or believes he loves) another woman. The notion that people can only truly love once, or even one person of the other sex at a time, is an irrational myth born of medieval romance.

Earlier in this book we dealt briefly with the sentimental notion that two people can live compatibly together for a lifetime once it is simply established that they love one another. Let us consider this question briefly again in the context of our present discussion of divorce.

Love, as noted earlier, certainly assists compatibility in marriage, makes it more likely to rise and grow; but it obviously does not guarantee it. But so firmly fixed, in our society, is the idea that true love must bring marital happiness that couples who once professed undying love and who are now getting divorces frequently maintain that they must not have loved each other in the first place, or else their marriage would have succeeded. This is something like asserting that mammals cannot fly. And then, when you discover that bats fly well, you are most reluctant to accept the fact that they could be (as they are) mammals. By the same token, if you show the average person an instance where two people love each other and yet are not maritally compatible, he is inclined to say that they cannot *really* love because love brings lasting marital compatibility.

This, we insist, is nonsense. Love, as we have noted throughout this book, helps compatibility in marriage; but it does not necessarily create it. And many couples—millions perhaps— are quite compatibly married even though their emotional attachments for each other are quite unintense and unromantic. Compatibility can be measured in terms of such questions as: Does a couple get along well together most of the time? Do they interest rather than bore each other in non-sexual and non-romantic situations? Do they help each other grow in interests and active participation in various life activities? Couples who largely obtain negative answers to such questions as these are, at least for the nonce, reasonably incompatible; and, however much they may love, should avoid marrying. Or, if married, and if nothing (including psychotherapeutic counseling) can improve their compatibility, they should seriously think of separation or divorce.

As we have noted, the reasons why people get divorced are often inaccurate and irrelevant. The reasons they give themselves and others for *not* separating are also, in many instances, just as inaccurate and irrelevant. A very commonly given reason for giving up the idea of divorce is "for the sake of the children." While this is undoubtedly a genuine concern on the part of many parents who are considering divorce, it may also be a disguise for some quite different concern—such as the fear of adverse public opinion if one gets a divorce when children are involved. Quite frequently, in marriage counseling, we find that, whatever reasons people give for not divorcing their mates, the real reason is that they feel unable to stand the negative judgments of friends, relatives, and associates.

In cases where children are a serious consideration, no general answer to the question of whether the parents should stay together for these children's sake can be given. What is good for the children of a marriage depends, usually, on whether the marriage itself can be good for its participants. Such relevant questions as these may be asked in this regard: Apart from the children, does this particular marriage have a constructive future? If so, how can the partners proceed to realize this constructive potential? If not, is it not foolish to suppose that the maintenance of an admittedly destructive marriage will have anything other than a destructive effect on the children?

Another myth that keeps coming up in connection with suggested divorce is the belief that because two people once enjoyed life together there *must* be a basis for reconciliation. Such a possibility is surely worthy of exploration in each instance; but to feel that people who were once happy together can inevitably, with sufficient effort, reestablish marital bliss is often unrealistic. Interests, attitudes, activities, and goals of people change. And to assume that every boy and girl who married in a happy flush of young love at, say, age nineteen will find life delightful and interesting together at age thirty-five is to believe in fairy tales and magic. Some wise and/or fortunate people find themselves changing toward even greater marital compatibility. But other people find their marriages have become dull, flat, uninteresting. Some, but not all, of these less fortunate people can be helped to rediscover happiness in marriage.

To insist that marriages which remain dead, despite all efforts at resurrection, should nevertheless remain intact is to cloak sadism in the mask of morality. The following of such a creed amounts to lifetime punishment to the spouses for having made an initial mistake or for having diverged in their life interests and values.

When, then, is a divorce desirable? Whenever, we would say, it is desired over a considerable period of time by one or both partners and when, in spite of serious efforts at reconciliation that are made by the mates, preferably with psychotherapeutic aid, it is still desired. As marriage counselors, we can sympathize with legal provisions in some communities which make it mandatory for a husband and wife to go for counseling before the court will grant them a divorce. But we nevertheless feel that in a democracy people should be allowed to separate legally even if they do not accept counseling. To *encourage* them to seek professional aid before divorce is fine; but to *force* them to do so smacks of fascist-like dictates that are more dangerous than beneficial.

At most, we feel that divorce should be barred to individuals for a short cooling-off period of time (say, a few months). Other than that, we are solidly in favor of its being granted by mutual consent or at the request of even a single party to the marriage. Would this suggestion, if adopted, constitute a radical revision in our present-day divorce practices? Actually not: since, in effect, though by perjury and subterfuge, tens of thousands of divorces a year are granted to United States citizens by mutual consent or at the request of one of the married individuals. All that our suggestion would do, actually, is to legalize what is now extra-legally already taking place.

It must be recognized, in this connection, that almost everyone—including religious authorities and outraged and vindictive spouses—recognizes in practice that you cannot make a consistently unwilling husband or wife *function* in marriage. By punitive legal, financial, religious, or other rules, you may keep an unwilling spouse under the same roof or keep a separated spouse from remarrying, but you cannot force a person who consistently desires divorce to be a real husband or wife in a

265

"maintained marriage."

However desirable divorce by personal request or mutual consent may be, the American people show no signs, at the present writing, of putting this type of legal separation into legislative action. Most of our myths about marriage and divorce still show vigorous strength and appear likely to resist early change.

Will not divorce be roundly abused if we freely allow it, because some people irresponsibly leave marriage, get a divorce, then remarry, then get another divorce, and so on? Indeed, such "abuse" will sometimes occur—just as, when divorce is not freely allowed, some people irresponsibly marry the first time and then just as irresponsibly desert their mates without benefit of legal decree. But shall we, because *some* people are irresponsible, prevent *all* people from marrying— or from freely getting a divorce? Or shall we not, rather, help people to be more responsible, more mature, and more rational, so that they can be more constructive about both their marriages and their divorces? Would this latter procedure not be in greater harmony with the democratic principles to which our nation is presumably dedicated?

It is, of course, sometimes financially difficult and in some instances virtually impossible for a couple who wish a divorce to meet the burdens of two separate households. This is especially true where the care of young children or some other factor keeps the divorced wife from working. Even if divorce were more freely granted, therefore, not all spouses who would like to avail themselves of it could, from a practical standpoint, afford to do so.

The question may therefore legitimately be raised: Would it not be desirable for society to provide some help in family situations where divorce is strongly indicated but where lack of finances prevents its accomplishment just as it has come to assume social obligation in many other types of family emergency? It is highly unlikely that, in the near future, this

266

question will be answered in the affirmative and then implemented by many of our communities. Yet the question deserves asking.

To summarize: Divorce, especially when children are involved in a marriage, is not a particularly good thing and often presents many difficulties and disturbances. But enforcedly maintained marriage, where one or both partners definitely would like to separate, is also undesirable in many or most instances and presents serious problems. Perhaps the sanest answer to this troubling issue is to make marriage somewhat less easy to enter and easier to leave. Our own feeling is that it would be distinctly wise if virtually no couple married until they had maintained a sex-love-domestic relationship—that is a living together in every true sense of the word—for a period of at least a year before the legal bonds were officially tied. Once marriage had legally taken place (and, usually, children were borne and reared), divorce should be freely granted by mutual consent or the firm request of one of the marital partners, provided that (a) some cooling-off period was passed, (b) the estranged mates were encouraged rather than forced to go for marriage counseling, and (c) suitable agreements were reached between the partners concerning financial settlements, alimony, visitation rights, etc.

As noted above, it is unlikely that society will in the near future adopt this kind of liberalized attitude toward marrying and divorcing. But that is no reason why the more enlightened among us cannot keep working toward its adoption.

20

Succeeding in Marriage

We have tried, in the preceding chapters of this book, to help you with your marriage, present or future. In our effort we have stayed as close as possible to true-to-life ways of handling marital problems. Our illustrations have been as down-to-earth as we could make them—and have come right out of the lives of actual persons we have counseled and helped.

Reality, in and out of marriage, is often less glamorous and dramatic than fiction. Most of us have been suckled on a great deal of fiction about mating. From early childhood onward, we have heard and seen enactments of high-flown romantic dreams. On our radio and TV sets, in our story books, in our magazines and newspapers, and on our movie screens we are subtly and brazenly propagandized with many strange and magical notions about the nature of male-female relationships. But outside these dream worlds, such relations are usually radically different. Not inferior, nor less interesting; but lacking the wondrous enchantment of all problems being solved by "a love most true, dropped from the blue."

Life, including married life, is not like that. The individual indeed "makes his own bed," psychologically speaking. It is no "bed of roses," no matter how much he may wish it to be. But, if he works with consistency and persistence in a rational way, he can make his life and his marriage a solid, comfortable, interesting, and pleasurable "bed of reality." It is toward the construction of such a way of life that the reader is guided in this book.

Have we, at times, strayed into somewhat over-theoretical pathways? Perhaps. But our theories have been tested and proved workable in the lives of real people: our patients and counselees. Although material derived from close and intimate clinical work is not alone productive of good marital theory (since academic and statistical investigations, such as those done by the Kinsey researchers, Ernest Burgess, Lewis Terman, G. V. Hamilton, and others are very valuable too), we feel that individualized, clinically derived material is still much needed.

Some of our suggestions may seem difficult for the reader to follow, not only because they lack the familiar ring of Hollywood make-believe or the voice of wisdom from the halls of ivy, but also because they are designed to make him pause and rethink some of his *own* ideas, rework some of his *own* attitudes. Such invitations to change of outlook cannot be effectively issued by material that confines itself to simple rules of thumb or a series of cavalier recipes. We have therefore tried to stimulate the reader to develop his own broad principles by which he can aim or direct his own general and marital life. To this end, we have included some more fundamental ideas than a list of do's and don't's about sex, companionship, children, and in-laws.

In our treatment of the topics of children and divorce, for example, we have tried to present some unconventional views that will induce the reader to examine critically some assumptions that he, along with most members of his society, has probably never stopped to question. Such examination may well strengthen some of his existing convictions, on the one hand, and help catalyze new points of view, on the other. Out of the critical questioning process itself, we hope and believe, a more rational over-all pattern of individual beliefs and actions is apt to emerge.

We are convinced that a certain amount of individualism and nonconformity regarding marriage and other aspects of life is virtually mandatory for a person to function rationally and happily in contemporary society. As Erich Fromm, the renowned psychologist and unorthodox analyst, has recently made clear: present-day society is *not* sane, does *not* provide consistent patterns of behavior which, if followed, will lead to individual self-fulfillment and happiness. If he and many other enlightened social thinkers are correct, any self-help marriage book which is designed to be worthy of its name must offer the reader some assistance in developing his own individual, rational, critically questioning, somewhat nonconforming pattern of living. A careful reading of all the material in this book—the specific practical suggestions, the broader principles of social challenge, and the concrete counselor-guided case studies—will, we think, open the way for the sincere and hard-working reader to develop or extend his own realistic approach to happy marital living.

Let us review, in broad perspective, some of the ground we have tried to cover in this book. In our opening chapter, "Modern Marriage: Hotbed of Neurosis," the very title warns the reader that we have no "sweetness and light" illusions to offer. We lay straight on the line the fact that sex satisfaction and loving companionship are intimately interrelated in marriage and that both are closely tied to general personality patterns and life expectations of the marital partners. Individual irrationalities, we point out, interact with and compound marital difficulties—so that only by acquiring a detailed view of some of the how's and why's of emotional disturbance is one likely to be well prepared for felicitous mating.

We then go on to delineate and expand upon some of the how's and why's of disturbance and trace them to some of the main irrational ideas to which one or both partners may be addicted and with which they may keep reindoctrinating themselves. Such unrealistic philosophies can be boiled down to several major categories—such as (a) a dire need to be loved; (b) perfectionism in trying for achievement; (c) a philosophy of blame and punishment; (d) needless catastrophizing about life's frustrations; and (e) the groundless belief that destructive emotion is uncontrollable.

We next consider some of the main causes of marital disturbances—including background differences of various kinds, interest incompatibilities, physiological and psychological sex differences, and ignorance about various aspects of marriage. Some methods of preventing marriage failure are surveyed—including focusing on things to do constructively (instead of on worry and fear of failure); fully accepting differences of action and reaction between mates; working at and modifying those temperamental and preferential differences which can to some degree be changed; limiting, by careful planning and mutual consent, the negative effects of unchangeable differences; and de-emphasizing over-romantic notions of supercompatibility.

Concrete aspects of handling marital problems are then delineated. It is shown that couples have to admit the existence of a particular problem, be willing to talk about it, and determinedly seek for its sources. Instead of impeding problem-solving by blaming themselves and their partners, mates should accept responsibility for their own errors and imperfections, forgive their spouses' failings, and persist in working at difficulties instead of easily giving up.

Mistaken conceptions of love and infatuation are considered and the cases for and against marrying in modern society are carefully weighed. This leads to a discussion of sexual preparation for marriage and to a detailed presentation of some of the important aspects of and possible solutions for male impotence and female frigidity. Problems of deep-seated sexual neurosis and of non-monogamous desires versus actions are also assessed.

Non-sexual difficulties of marriage, particularly lack of adequate communication between spouses, are examined; and specific issues relating to children, divorce, and in-law relations are presented and analyzed. So we start this book with a view of marriage as a hotbed of neurosis and end it, nineteen chapters later, with a view of divorce as being often desirable and perhaps even necessary. Do we, then, take a negative, tragic, helpless, cynical view of marriage?

Quite the contrary. We firmly believe as we have stated and demonstrated throughout this book, in facing the full realities—however black they may seem—about life in general and marriage and family life in particular. But we are equally convinced that no aspect of reality is so difficult or so negative that it cannot be somewhat (and often greatly) improved. Such improvement, as we have frequently reiterated, can usually be effected by a change in the individual's own attitudes. And such changes can often be brought about by his own intelligently directed actions.

One final illustrative case. Six months before the writing of these words there came for counseling a thirty-five-year-old husband who was separated from his wife and three children and who wanted psychotherapeutic help. His concern was not for his marriage, which he considered to be a total loss, but in relation to his affair with a twenty-three-year-old divorcee who was giving him "one hell of a hard time" and bringing him "within an inch of a nervous breakdown." The counselor took him at his word, and without even referring at first to his "hopelessly crazy" wife, went to work on the problem of how he could get along better with his mistress.

It quickly transpired (as it usually does in cases like this one) that Mr. T.'s problem was neither his mistress nor his wife nor anyone else, but only himself. He had spent twenty-four years, before his marriage, allowing himself to be thoroughly dominated by his widowed mother, who still lived (at his suggestion and expense) a few blocks away and still purchased most of his clothes and other personal things for him. Not only did he, after his marriage and after leaving his wife, remain seriously under his mother's sway; but, as might be expected, he had selected both wife and mistress largely because they were dominating women who told him exactly how to comport himself and who got very upset whenever he contradicted them in any major way.

Although Mr. T. said, at the beginning of therapy, that he mainly wanted to learn how to get along with his mistress, most of the sessions were devoted to discussing how he could get along with his mother—whom he actually feared more than loved and would have liked, but could never bring himself, to tell off in no uncertain language. As soon as he did stand up to her in any way, he became inordinately guilty; and he felt much more comfortable quickly giving in to her again than carrying around his terrible burden of guilt.

In a highly directive manner, and brooking no excuses or shilly-shallying from Mr. T., the therapist forthrightly attempted to show him that (a) his mother, wife, and mistress all had remarkable resemblances to a certain Herr Adolf Hitler; (b) Mr. T.'s reactions to the three important women of his life were nauseatingly pusillanimous; (c) there was no good reason whatever why he *owed* obedience or servitude to his mother

just because she was his mother; (d) it would never be catastrophic if he chose his own clothes and made his own decisions,
even though he might fail miserably at some of his choices; and
(e) he had no chance whatever of solving his love and domestic
problems until and unless he solved the basic problem of his
own cowardice and guilt.

Mr. T. did not capitulate very quickly or easily. But the
therapist, a hard man in his own way, persisted. Mr. T. begged
for mercy. The therapist still persisted.

"Look," said Mr. T. "I realize that this stuff about my
mother is important, and I know that I brought it up myself.
Sure I still have trouble with her. Sure I'm still afraid of her.
Sure I'm guilty when she wants me to do some plumb stupid
thing her way and I know that that's not the way it should be
done. But I've been this way with her for thirty-five years now,
how do you expect me to change?"

"Bosh," said the therapist. "So you've hit yourself over the
head with a hammer every day for thirty-five years, you say.
Does that mean that you have to *keep* doing it? When are you
going to stop?"

"I know it sounds crazy, but what can I do? Do you expect
me to change, after thirty-five years—just like *that?*"

"No, not just like *that.* Like this: with continual practice,
with hard work, with telling yourself what nonsense you've been
telling yourself for those last thirty-five years."

"All right. All right. You're right. I know it better than you.
But how *can* I change? How *can* I?"

"You mean: how *can't* you?"

"I don't get it. What do you mean 'how *can't* I'?"

"Exactly that. How can you afford *not* to change, seeing the
results of the last thirty-five years?"

"Oh—that. Yes. Yes: how *can't* I?"

"Yes!"

"So, you mean, I—I just got to. There's no other way. I
just can't get this thing with my girl over with, can't really

solve it, until I solve this other thing, this mother-thing, this all-my-life-goddam-mother-thing. That's it, eh?"

"Do I have to answer that question?"

"No. That's it. This all-my-life-goddam-mother-thing. It's got to go, doesn't it?"

"Doesn't it?"

"Yeah. You're right. It's got to GO!"

And it did go. By the very next session Mr. T. was telling how he had, for the first time in his life, purchased his own new shirts, taken his clothes to the cleaners, and even tidied up the apartment in which he was living. And within a few weeks more even though his mother was protesting loudly and long about cruelly being put out of his life, he was doing scores of other things for himself, and guiltlessly paying her no mind. Within a couple of months, he was definitely breaking up with his mistress, whom he saw as being basically the same kind of person as his mother; and he began talking to his wife (who was amazed at the changes that were taking place in him) about the advisability of her coming for therapy, too. At the present writing, six months after Mr. T. was first seen, he is living harmoniously with his wife (who, if anything, has benefited even more than he from her therapy). He is for the first time a truly responsible and loving father to his children and has broken away from his exploitative boss to set up in business for himself. As he remarked just the other day:

"My God! Who would have believed that coming to see you about getting along better with my girl friend would have resulted in all this? If I had suspected anything of the sort when I first came, you couldn't have got me in that door with a tractor! It only goes to show!"

It does go to show—that even the most difficult and impossible of marriages may be radically altered for the better—if the spouse's thinking and acting are altered. We can only say, then, in closing: we have drawn upon our personal and clinical experiences in this book to provide some help toward the reader's achieving clearer and more rational direction of his marital and non-marital behavior. We hope that our message has in large part come through. To each of our readers—the best of luck! By which we mean: the best of rational understanding and hard work.

Selected Readings

Books which deal with such topics as marriage and the family and neurosis and psychotherapy should be read with skepticism. That goes for the present volume, too.

The broad and complex science of human behavior is still in its early phase of development; and fallacies are abundantly interwoven with facts. Because, however, one may stumble along or wander from the road to truth does not mean that there is no value in trying to keep to it. Much progress may be made in understanding oneself and others if one intensively and extensively reads even the existing imperfect products of behavioral science.

Any selected list of readings is necessarily biased by the views of the selectors. We have tried not to load the following list with books which entirely support our own prejudices and we do not pretend that it includes all the best or most basic books in the field of human relations. The list does include, we think, an interesting and helpful group of books for readers who may be stimulated to move forward in their understanding of themselves and others.

277

Adler, Alfred. *Understanding Human Nature*. New York: Greenberg, 1927.

Aldrich, C. A., and Aldrich, Mary M. *Babies Are Human Beings*. New York: Macmillan, 1954.

Alexander, Franz, and French, Thomas M. *Psychoanalytic Therapy*. New York: Ronald, 1946.

Anderson, Camilla M. *Saints, Sinners and Psychiatry*. Philadelphia: Lippincott, 1950.

Ansbacher, Heinz, and Ansbacher, Rowena. *The Individual Psychology of Alfred Adler*. New York: Basic Books, 1956.

Bach, George. *Intensive Group Psychotherapy*. New York: Ronald, 1954.

Baruch, Dorothy. *How to Live with Your Teen-Ager*. New York: McGraw-Hill, 1953.

————. *New Ways in Discipline*. New York: McGraw-Hill, 1949.

Beigel, Hugo. *Encyclopedia of Sex Education*. New York: Stephen Daye Press, 1952.

Brenner, Charles. *An Elementary Textbook of Psychoanalysis*. New York: Doubleday, 1957.

Brown, M. Bevan. *The Sources of Love and Fear*. New York: Vanguard, 1950.

Cameron, Norman, and Margaret, Ann. *Behavior Pathology*. Boston: Houghton Mifflin, 1951.

Comfort, Alex. *Sexual Behavior in Society*. London: Duckworth, 1950.

Cory, Donald Webster. *The Homosexual in America*. New York: Castle Books, 1960.

Cuber, John F. *Marriage Counseling Practice*. New York: Appleton, 1948.

————, Harper, Robert A., and Kenkel, William F. *Problems of American Society: Values in conflict*. New York: Holt, 1956.

Devereux, George. *Therapeutic Education*. New York: Harper, 1956.

Dollard, John, and Miller, Neal E. *Personality and Psychotherapy*. New York: McGraw-Hill, 1950.

Eastman, Nicholson J. *Expectant Motherhood*. Boston: Little, Brown, 1957.

Ellis, Albert. *The Folklore of Sex*. New York: Charles Boni, 1951; New York: Grove Press, 1960.

————. *The American Sexual Tragedy*. New York: Twayne, 1954; Lyle Stuart, 1959.

————. *How to Live with a Neurotic*. New York: Crown, 1957.

278

————. *Sex Without Guilt.* New York: Lyle Stuart, 1958.

————. *The Art and Science of Love.* New York: Lyle Stuart, 1960.

————, and Abarbanel, Albert. (Eds.). *Encyclopedia of Sexual Behavior.* New York: Hawthorn Books, 1961.

————, and Harper, Robert A. *A Guide to Rational Living.* Englewood Cliffs, N. J.: Prentice-Hall, 1961.

Erikson, Erik. *Childhood and Society.* New York: Norton, 1950.

Fenichel, Otto. *Psychoanalytic Theory of Neurosis.* New York: Norton, 1945.

Fishbein, Morris, and Kennedy, Ruby J. R. *Modern Marriage and Family Living.* New York: Oxford University Press, 1957.

Folsom, Joseph. *The Family and Democratic Society.* New York: Wiley, 1943.

Ford, Clellan S., and Beach, Frank A. *Patterns of Sexual Behavior.* New York: Harper, 1951.

Freeman, Lucy. *Fight Against Fears.* New York: Crown, 1951.

Freud, Sigmund. *Basic Writings.* New York: Modern Library, 1938.

————. *Collected Papers.* New York: Basic Books, 1959.

————. *An Outline of Psychoanalysis.* New York: Norton, 1949.

Fromm, Erich. *Escape from Freedom.* New York: Rinehart, 1941.

————. *Man for Himself.* New York: Rinehart, 1947.

————. *The Sane Society.* New York: Rinehart, 1955.

Fromm-Reichmann, Frieda. *Principles of Intensive Psychotherapy.* Chicago: University of Chicago Press, 1950.

Garfield, Sol L. *Introductory Clinical Psychology.* New York: Macmillan, 1957.

Grant, Vernon. *Psychology of Sexual Emotion.* New York: Longmans, Green, 1957.

Guyon, Rene. *The Ethics of Sexual Acts.* New York: Knopf, 1934.

————. *Sexual Freedom.* New York: Knopf, 1950.

Hall, Calvin S. *A Primer of Freudian Psychology.* Cleveland: World, 1954.

Harper, Robert A. *Marriage.* New York: Appleton, 1949.

————. *Psychoanalysis and Psychotherapy: 36 Systems.* Englewood Cliffs, N. J.: Prentice-Hall, 1959.

Horney, Karen. *The Neurotic Personality of Our Time.* New York: Norton, 1937.

————. *New Ways in Psychoanalysis.* New York: Norton, 1939.

Jones, Ernest. *The Life and Work of Sigmund Freud.* 3 vols. New York: Basic Books, 1955-1957.

Joseph, Harry, and Zern, Gordon. *The Emotional Problems of Children.* New York: Crown, 1954.

Jung, C. G. *The Practice of Psychotherapy*. New York: Pantheon, 1954.

Kelly, George A. *The Psychology of Personal Constructs*. 2 vols. New York: Norton, 1955.

Kelly, G. Lombard. *Sex Manual*. Georgia: Southern Medical Supply Co., 1943.

Kinsey, Alfred C., Pomeroy, Wardell B., and Martin, Clyde E. *Sexual Behavior in the Human Male*. Philadelphia: Saunders, 1948.

————, and Gebhard, Paul H. *Sexual Behavior in the Human Female*. Philadelphia: Saunders, 1953.

Kirkpatrick, Clifford. *The Family*. New York: Ronald, 1955.

Knight, John. *The Story of My Psychoanalysis*. New York: Pocket Books, 1952.

Kraines, S. H., and Thetford, E. S. *Managing Your Mind*. New York: Macmillan, 1947.

Maslow, A. H. *Motivation and Personality*. New York: Harper, 1954.

May, Rollo. *Man's Search for Himself*. New York: Norton, 1953.

————, Angel, Ernest, and Ellenberger, Henri F. (Eds.). *Existence: A New Dimension in Psychiatry and Psychology*. New York: Basic Books, 1958.

McCary, James L., and Sheer, Daniel E. (Eds.). *Six Approaches to Psychotherapy*. New York: Dryden, 1955.

Mullahy, Patrick. *Oedipus: Myth and Complex*. New York: Hermitage, 1948.

Munroe, Ruth L. *Schools of Psychoanalytic Thought*. New York: Dryden, 1955.

Oliven, John F. *Sexual Hygiene and Pathology*. Philadelphia: Lippincott, 1955.

Pennington, L. A., and Berg, Irwin A. (Eds.). *An Introduction to Clinical Psychology*. New York: Ronald, 1954.

Pillay, A. P., and Ellis, Albert (Eds.). *Sex, Society and the Individual*. Bombay: International Journal of Sexology, 1953.

Ribble, Margaret A. *The Personality of the Young Child*. New York: Columbia University Press, 1955.

Riesman, David, and others. *The Lonely Crowd*. New York: Doubleday Anchor Books, 1953.

Rogers, Carl R. *Client-Centered Therapy*. Boston: Houghton Mifflin, 1951.

Sappenfield, Bert R. *Personality Dynamics*. New York: Knopf, 1954.

Silverberg, William V. *Childhood Experience and Personal Destiny*. New York: Springer, 1952.

Spock, Benjamin. *The Pocket Book of Baby and Child Care.* New York: Pocket Books, 1957.

Stern, Catherine, and Gould, Toni S. *The Early Years of Childhood.* New York: Harper, 1955.

Stokes, Walter R. *Modern Pattern for Marriage.* New York: Rinehart, 1948.

Stone, L. J., and Church, Joseph. *Childhood and Adolescence.* New York: Random House, 1957.

Sullivan, Harry Stack. *The Interpersonal Theory of Psychiatry.* New York: Norton, 1953.

Terman, Lewis M. *Psychological Factors in Marital Happiness.* New York: McGraw-Hill, 1938.

Thompson, Clara. *Psychoanalysis: Evolution and Development.* New York: Hermitage, 1950.

Thorne, Frederick C. *Principles of Personality Counseling.* Brandon, Vermont: Journal of Clinical Psychology, 1950.

Vincent, Clark E. *Readings in Marriage Counseling.* New York: Crowell, 1957.

Westermarck, Edward. *The History of Human Marriage.* New York: Macmillan, 1922.

Wolberg, Lewis R. *The Technique of Psychotherapy.* New York: Grune & Stratton, 1954.

281

Directory of Marriage Counseling Services

In most instances, the most detailed and reliable information about counseling and psychotherapy services can be obtained from individuals or agencies in or near the reader's own community. Ministers and church offices, physicians and medical societies and bureaus, lawyers and legal aid societies, social workers and social agencies, psychologists and psychological or mental health associations, universities, colleges, clinics, boards of education, and county health departments usually offer valuable local help in these matters. If the agency or individual you contact cannot give you the information you seek, you will probably be directed to the place or places where you can be more specifically assisted.

Sometimes, however, individuals prefer not to make direct local contacts or are at a loss as to how they may proceed locally to acquire the knowledge or assistance that they want. Under these circumstances, a letter to one of the following national organizations may bring a helpful lead. The reader should be forewarned, however, that all of these groups operate on very limited budgets. For that reason, a response to your request for help may be long delayed (or perhaps never be forthcoming). If your question is not answered in a reasonable period of time, it is suggested that you try writing another organization. But, if you are in a hurry, you had better explore your own community!

1. American Academy of Psychotherapists, 30 Fifth Avenue, New York 11, N.Y.
2. American Association of Marriage Counselors, 27 Woodcliff Drive, Madison, N.J.
3. American Board for Psychological Services, 10 East Sharon Avenue, Glendale, Ohio.

282

4. American Eugenics Society, 230 Park Avenue, New York, N.Y.

5. American Group Psychotherapy Association, 1790 Broadway, New York 19, N.Y.

6. American Institute of Family Relations, 5287 Sunset Boulevard, Los Angeles 27, Calif.

7. American Personnel and Guidance Association, 1605 New Hampshire, N.W., Washington, D.C.

8. American Psychiatric Association, 1700 18th St., N.W., Washington, D.C.

9. American Psychological Association, 1333 16th St., N.W., Washington, D.C.

10. American Social Health Association, 1790 Broadway, New York, N.Y.

11. Association for Family Living, 1360 Lake Shore Drive, Chicago 10, Ill.

12. Central Conference of American Rabbis, 1124 Prince Avenue, Athens, Ga.

13. Commission on Marriage and the Home, National Council of the Churches of Christ in America, 297 Fourth Avenue, New York 10, N.Y.

14. Family Life Bureau, National Catholic Welfare Conference, 1312 Massachusetts Avenue, N.W., Washington, D.C.

15. Family Service Association of America, 215 Park Avenue South, New York 3, N.Y.

16. Marriage Council of Philadelphia, 3828 Locust Street, Philadelphia 4, Penna.

17. Menninger Foundation, Topeka, Kansas.

18. Merrill-Palmer Institute of Human Development and Family Life, 71 East Ferry Avenue, Detroit 2, Mich.

19. National Association for Mental Health, 10 Columbus Circle, New York 19, N.Y.

20. National Council on Family Relations, 1219 University Avenue, S. E., Minneapolis 14, Minn.

21. Planned Parenthood Federation of America, 501 Madison Avenue, New York, N.Y.

22. Rabbinical Assembly of America, 3080 Broadway, New York 27, N.Y.

23. Society for the Scientific Study of Sex, 1 East 42nd Street, New York 17, N.Y.

INDEX

284